Architectural Design
January/February 2009

Theoretical Meltdown

Guest-edited by Luigi Prestinenza Puglisi

IN THIS ISSUE
Main Section

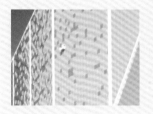

DECONSTRUCTING THE PRESENT
Michele Costanzo talks to Bernard Tschumi about the enduring pertinence of his earlier theoretical contributions and the current shifts in his strategical thinking. P 24

LIZ DILLER ON 'THE THEORETICAL LULL'
Olympia Kazi interviews Liz Diller of Diller + Scofidio on art and architecture, the 'death of theory' and the continuing relevance of cultural production. P 56

FREEDOM FIGHTERS
Emiliano Gandolfi reports on a generation of architects who are liberating themselves from formal concerns and are tackling pressing environmental and social issues worldwide. P 78

WORK IN THE MEATPACKING DISTRICT
Jayne Merkel profiles WORKac's elegant studio for fashion designer Diane von Furstenberg in the west side of Manhattan. P 104+

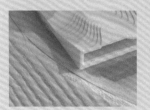

ROCKING THE BAROQUE
Andrew Saunders of Rensselaer reinterprets the Baroque through the parametric, revealing afresh the complexity of 17th-century trigonometry. P 132+

WILEY
wiley.com

Architectural Design

Vol 79 No 1

Jan/Feb 2009

ISBN 978-0470 99779 6

Editorial Offices
John Wiley & Sons
International House
Ealing Broadway Centre
London W5 5DB

T: +44 (0)20 8326 3800

Editor
Helen Castle

Regular columnists: Valentina Croci, David Littlefield, Jayne Merkel, Will McLean, Neil Spiller, Michael Weinstock and Ken Yeang

Freelance Managing Editor
Caroline Ellerby

Production Editor
Elizabeth Gongde

Design and Prepress
Artmedia Press, London

Printed in Italy by Conti Tipocolor

Sponsorship/advertising
Faith Pidduck/Wayne Frost
T: +44 (0)1243 770254
E: fpidduck@wiley.co.uk

Front cover: Rome city centre. © Luigi Filetici

Subscribe to AD

AD is published bimonthly and is available to purchase on both a subscription basis and as individual volumes at the following prices.

PRICES
Individual copies: £22.99/$45.00
Mailing fees may apply

ANNUAL SUBSCRIPTION RATES
Student: UK£70/US$110 print only
Individual: UK £110/US$170 print only
Institutional: UK£180/US$335 print or online
Institutional: UK£198/US$369 combined print and online

Subscription Offices UK
John Wiley & Sons Ltd
Journals Administration Department
1 Oldlands Way, Bognor Regis
West Sussex, PO22 9SA
T: +44 (0)1243 843272
F: +44 (0)1243 843232
E: cs-journals@wiley.co.uk

[ISSN: 0003-8504]

Prices are for six issues and include postage and handling charges. Periodicals postage paid at Jamaica, NY 11431. Air freight and mailing in the USA by Publications Expediting Services Inc, 200 Meacham Avenue, Elmont, NY 11003.
Individual rate subscriptions must be paid by personal cheque or credit card. Individual rate subscriptions may not be resold or used as library copies.

All prices are subject to change without notice.

Postmaster
Send address changes to 3 Publications Expediting Services, 200 Meacham Avenue, Elmont, NY 11003

RIGHTS AND PERMISSIONS
Requests to the Publisher should be addressed to:
Permissions Department
John Wiley & Sons Ltd
The Atrium
Southern Gate
Chichester
West Sussex PO19 8SQ
England

F: +44 (0)1243 770620
E: permreq@wiley.co.uk

CONTENTS

4
Editorial
Helen Castle

6
Introduction
Anything Goes
Luigi Prestinenza Puglisi

13
Theory in Architecture:
XIII to XX Century
Francesco Proto

14
A Short History of Western Architecture from Vitruvius to Rem Koolhaas
Francesco Proto

16
Critic's Focus
junya.ishigami+associates
Joseph Grima

18
Evaporating Theory
An Interview with Yves Michaud
Luigi Prestinenza Puglisi

22
Critic's Focus
muf architecture/art
Claes Sörstedt

24
Twenty Years After
(Deconstructivism)
An Interview with Bernard Tschumi
Michele Costanzo

30
Critic's Focus
Nàbito Arquitectura
Manuel Gausa

32
Digital Morphogenesis
Neil Leach

38
Critic's Focus
Atelier Kempe Thill
Hans Ibelings

40
Meeting the New Boss:
After the Death of Theory
Christopher Hight

46
Critic's Focus
Josep Lluís Mateo/MAP
Architects
Krunoslav Ivanisin

48
The Life of Space
Derrick de Kerckhove and Antonio Tursi

54
Critic's Focus
[ecosistema urbano]
Roman Rutkowski and Lukasz Wojciechowski

56
Architecture as a Dissident Practice
An Interview with Diller Scofidio + Renfro
Olympia Kazi

60
Critic's Focus
Supersudaca
Carlos Sant'Ana

62
Club Cinemetrics: New Post-Perspectival Design Methodologies
Brian McGrath, Hsueh, Cheng Leun, Paul CHU Hoi Shan, José De Jesús Zamora and Victoria Marshall

68
Critic's Focus
Stalker/ON
Peter Lang

70
That Old Thing Called Flexibility
An Interview with Robert Venturi and Denise Scott Brown
Francesco Proto

76
Critic's Focus
The Center for Urban Pedagogy (CUP)
Bill Menking

78
Spaces of Freedom
Emiliano Gandolfi

82
'To Go Beyond or Not to Be'
Unsolicited Architecture
An Interview with Ole Bouman
Luca Guido

86
Critic's Focus
MAD
Jiang Jun

88
Cross the River by Touching the Stones: Chinese Architecture and Political Economy in the Reform Era: 1978–2008
Tao Zhu

94
Critic's Focus
Exit Ltd
Shumon Basar

96
Some Conclusions
Liberating Ourselves from the Tyranny of Architecture
Luigi Prestinenza Puglisi

98
A Not So Well-Reasoned Bibliography
Francesco Proto

104+
Interior Eye
WORK Architecture Company's Diane von Furstenberg Studio, New York
Jayne Merkel

108+
Building Profile
Vassall Road Housing and Healthcare Centre, Brixton, London
David Littlefield

112+
Practice Profile
51% Studios
Howard Watson

118+
Spiller's Bits
What Are You Looking At?
Neil Spiller

120+
Unit Factor
Algorithmic Design
Maria Bessa

124+
Yeang's Eco-Files
Nanoenergy
Ken Yeang

126+
McLean's Nuggets
Will McLean

128+
Userscape
Investigating Culture Through the Senses
Valentina Croci

132+
Site Lines
Baroque Parameters
Andrew Saunders

Editorial

Helen Castle

This is an issue that is all about juncture at a watershed moment. In the past six months while we have been compiling the publication the world has endured: environmental catastrophe (the earthquake in China and hurricane in the US); continuing war in Afghanistan and Iraq; and the credit crunch, which has rocked the very foundation of the West's financial institutions and the global economy. There have been peaks, though, as well as troughs, with the 2008 Olympics and most notably the election of Barack Obama as US president. With increasing concern about climate change and the ability for natural resources to meet the growing world population's demand, the current period can best be characterised as one of intense uncertainty and flux. There is now very little left that we can be sure of in terms of the future. Whereas the 20th century was no less turbulent with two world wars, mass genocides and the stock market crash in the 1930s, these events tended to be met with ideological absolutism or at least

confidence in architecture as well as in politics; views often polarised, but in their sureness avant-garde architects and political leaders alike continued to issue manifestos. There was an enviable sense of progress and an unfailing feeling that things could only get better. The catalyst for this title of *AD* is the underlying precept that we are currently experiencing a 'theoretical meltdown' in architecture. With the loss of conviction in the wider world, architecture has lost its borders as a discipline and theory seems to have lost its pertinence for architecture, putting into question what Christopher Hight so aptly coins in his article of how to 'act architecturally'. What has been so artful about the skill with which Luigi Prestinenza Puglisi has formulated and curated this issue is that he has invited contributions from both those who have sufficient experience to reflect on the current circumstances (it includes interviews with Bernard Tschumi, Robert Venturi and Denise Scott Brown and Liz Diller) and those who are able to signpost a way forward: 11 critics tip projects by architects who they regard as resonant of a future way forward. This approach avoids falling into that only too predictable pitfall of critiquing without actually coming up with any pointers or solutions. It also has a largely positive outcome. Much of the content implies that there is a new pragmatism in the making in design, which through its emphasis on performance, strategical thinking and problem solving is better equipped to tackle some of the most pressing and significant issues that the world is currently throwing up. ⚙

**Greg Lynn FORM, Duck Table and Eggplant Table,
Venice Architecture Biennale, 2008**
In this installation, Lynn literally melted down or
recycled kids' toys. Laser-scanned and digitised, they
are precision cut and welded with a tool used to repair
car fenders. Thus Lynn employs transdisciplinary
techniques to create objects that are 'beyond
architecture' at the cusp of art and 3-D design.

Anything Goes

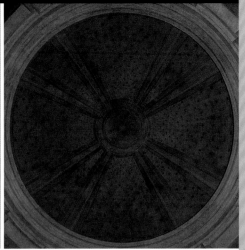

By Luigi Prestinenza Puglisi

Between the end of the 19th and the beginning of the 20th century, scientific development was boosted by a significant analytical and methodological endeavour, a process that involved a rigorous analysis of language in order to render it as univocal and factual as possible, a severe selection of fact, the construction of an impeccable syntax, founded on the rules of logic, and the search for criteria for recognising errors or, as revealed later on, for falsifying theories.[1]

The same analytical and introspective obsession also infected the world of the arts. Many of the approaches adopted by the avant-garde at the beginning of the 20th century – Abstraction, Neoplasticism, Cubism, Purism, Suprematism and so on – reveal a similar desire for clarity and logicisation focused on achieving pure art.[2]

One of the figures working along this conceptual horizon, though with antithetical and destabilising intentions, was the artist Marcel Duchamp. By the beginning of the 20th century he had already opted for a non-mimetic art, aligned with the need for abstraction typical of this period. However, it is with his readymades (ordinary manufactured products that he selected and modified) that he managed to erase traditional representation – we can think of the shovel entitled *In Advance of the Broken Arm* (1915) or the urinal signed by Mutt (1917) – replacing it with the very object that was to have been represented. Notwithstanding an excess of figuration (what does an object represent in more detail than the object itself?), the work becomes transparent; it questions the very essence of creating art and, consequently, places itself in a field of action so carefully avoided by the world of science: the point of overlap between discourse and meta-discourse.

It was during the 1960s, with his *Étant donnés*,[3] that Duchamp forced the observer to become part of the work being observed, making it impossible to perceive in its entirety. The result? Art becomes a stage that makes it impossible to construct an objective and neutral point of view outside of the object.

Luigi Filetici, I-Contaminations,
Photograph taken with an I-Phone, 2008
from above, left to right:
Detail of the ceiling of the Auditorium designed by Renzo Piano
and the coffered ceiling of the Pantheon, both in Rome.
Advertising in the Foro Italico and the dome of San Pietro
in Montorio by Bramante, both in Rome.
Sites of devotion and the MAXXI Museum in Rome
designed by Zaha Hadid.
Two scenes of domestic life.
Detail of a water pool and the Reina Sofia Museum
in Madrid designed by Jean Nouvel.
Detail of a building in the Alexanderplatz in Berlin,
and the Temple of Fortuna Virile in Rome.

While art, thanks to Duchamp, was moving 'against the method' and anticipating the happy intuitions of the scientific philosopher Paul Feyerabend,[4] in 1967 the Italian architect Giorgio Grassi published a book of writings on architectural theory entitled *La costruzione logica dell'architettura*.[5] Inspired by the axiomatic theories of science, he proposed a method that allowed for the realisation of projects capable of avoiding the contamination of the concrete events of the everyday.[6] Along a no less analytical line, even if methodologically less rigorous, we find the research of Aldo Rossi.

At more or less the same time, in 1970 to be precise, Peter Eisenman published the text *Notes on Conceptual Architecture*[7] in which he relaunched Joseph Kosuth's ideas on conceptual art. Their shared objective was the cancelling of expression, rendering the component insignificant with respect to the process of its assembly, paralysing, as brilliantly stated by Mario Gandelsonas, the semantic dimension and giving an unusual weight to its syntactic counterpart,[8] and reconstructing the purity of method, at almost any cost – including the impossibility of inhabiting the architectural object.[9] In short, the creation of an autonomous architecture.

The search for disciplinary autonomy became an obsession in architectural research in the 1970s and 1980s. The arrival of Postmodernism brought no invention, only assembly. However, as demonstrated by the exhibition 'La presenza del passato' (The Presence of the Past), curated by Paolo Portoghesi in 1980 for the Venice Biennale, this attitude only led to the constitution of a 'method' in superficial terms. In fact, as observed by Charles Jencks,[10] Postmodernism actually created two codes: a popular one, for the man on the street, and a more esoteric one, for professionals.

A rebellion against this populist and hastily assembled vision was mounted by Manfredo Tafuri and Kenneth Frampton, the latter of whom would later use tectonics to propose his idea of autonomy, intended as a system of components whose forms reveal their role in a given construction.[11]

While the search for a method occupied architects interested in autonomy, Hans Hollein declared his intentions to defend the anti-method, championing the term 'Everything is Architecture', a slogan that would become a watchword for the vast majority of radical culture from this period.

All of this took place during the 1980s, which was characterised by the 'New Spirit' - also the title of an illuminating issue of *The Architectural Review*.[12] According to Peter Cook, the main players in the New Spirit were those who returned to the heroic and experimental tradition of architecture: the continuation of the work of the CIAM (the International Congress of Modern Architecture), of Bruno Taut and, later, the Smithsons and Archigram.[13] Some of these figures, including Coop Himmelb(l)au, were educated during the period of radical architecture in the 1970s. Others studied at the Architectural Association in London: for example, Bernard Tschumi, Zaha Hadid and Rem Koolhaas. There was also the School of Graz, with its Expressionist tensions, or Cooper Union, home to the work of John Hedjuk and, finally, the architects of Los Angeles.

In an attempt to focus this explosion of energies into a style, in 1988 Philip Johnson and Mark Wigley organised the 'Deconstructivist Architecture' exhibition at the Museum of Modern Art (MoMA) in New York. However, Deconstructivism, in Johnson's conception, became a banal stylistic formula that pursued a lack of equilibrium, a caricature of the experimental anxiety that, instead, lay at the origins of the New Spirit.[14]

Anything Goes

During the 1990s, the events generated by the New Spirit, accelerated by the speed of electronic society and communication, began to wane, giving way to an uninterrupted chain reaction of mutations where, to quote Feyerabend, 'Anything Goes'.

In 1993 Deconstructivism was a distant memory.[15] Its sharp and inclined forms were replaced by the gentle sensuality of curves, anticipated by Frank Gehry in his design museum for the Vitra campus at Weil am Rhein, Germany (1989). There was also a change in the philosophies of reference: from the *différance* of Derrida to the folds of Deleuze. Soon after, this mutated into the world of blobs, made possible by the software used by a new generation of 'Natural Born CAADesigners'[16] who, since 1994, had been teaching at Columbia as part of its first 'paperless' design studios.[17]

In 1996 Rem Koolhaas published his 1,345-page *S,M,L,XL*.[18] This tome exalted the poetics of the list and the focus on reality as we knew it, presented as it was in a sort of contemporary revisitation of the famous *Learning from Las Vegas*,[19] and with its coherent absence of coherence.

Even Minimalism was subject to a process of transformation which, attacked simultaneously from the interior and exterior, upset its basic presuppositions. At the end of the 1980s, Jean Nouvel and Toyo Ito designed lightweight and transparent building envelopes to represent the immateriality of the Information Society. This form of Minimalism was in no way eschewed by Tschumi who, in 1990, designed a 'glass box' as a metaphoric space for the flows of information that crossed it. Later, in the search for the almost nothing, we find Nouvel and Ito once again, this time infused with a neo-organicism that exceeded the atmospheric effects of the Fondazione Cartier in Paris (1994) or the metaphor of the electronic aquarium of the Sendai Mediatheque, Japan (2001). The result? The Quai Branly Museum in Paris (2006) and the artificial hills of Grin Grin in Fukuoka (2005).

No less significant transformations can be found in the more orthodox Minimalism of Herzog & de Meuron. These two architects – educated at the ETH in Zurich, home to the teachings of Aldo Rossi – after reducing their buildings to aseptic volumes, were initially

NOWA (NavarraOfficeWalkArchitecture), Un sistema di padiglioni per l'agricoltura e altro (A system of pavilions for agriculture and more), Venice Biennale of Architecture, 2004
The project involves the construction of mobile structures built from the crates used to transport oranges. The objective is that of modifying the inhabitation of Sicily's agricultural landscapes.

fascinated by the infinite possibilities offered by new technologies to play with the skin of their buildings. This was followed by a progressive attraction to spatial decomposition, a period that concluded with the design of the Laban Dance Centre in Deptford, London (2003), a building whose compositional freedom has little or nothing to do with the Swiss-German rigour of which this duo were the prime exponents for many years. Even the main supporters of French and English Minimalism, Dominique Perrault and David Chipperfield, did not hesitate, when the opportunity presented itself, to make incursions into the world of complex forms.

High-Tech was in no way exempt from its own metamorphoses, reconsiderations and adjustments, resulting in its becoming something other. Santiago Calatrava transformed his structures into gigantic zoomorphic sculptures, while Norman Foster, after the Minimal-Classicist interlude of the Carré d'Art in Nîmes (1993), went on to complete London's bioclimatic Swiss Re headquarters (the 'Gherkin') in 2004 and the sculptural City Hall in 2002: two buildings that demonstrate the significant influences of an architecture of curves and computers. This period also marked the beginning of Will Alsop's Neo-Pop phase. After completing the Centre Pompidou in Paris (1997), Renzo Piano spent numerous years attempting to shed the label of High-Tech guru; his KPN Telecom Office Tower in Rotterdam (2000)

NOWA (NavarraOfficeWalkArchitecture), Image taken from the publication edited by Marco Navarra, *Repairing Cities: Repairing as a 'Survival' Strategy, Learning from Cairo*, prepared for the Venice Biennale of Architecture, 2008
In a world where everything is architecture and where strategies of globalisation are wearing thin, we can learn new strategies for survival and quality from poorer economies.

demonstrates a clear attraction to the aesthetic of the pixel, while his Auditorium in Rome (2002) reveals that even he was tempted by the blob, even if it is presented as a revisitation – in his own words – of the cupolas of Rome.

Even those who tended to favour autonomy, while looking with suspicion at the New Spirit, were unable to resist its destructive and bewitching charm.[20] Rafael Moneo, author of the Roman-styled museum in Merida (1984) and applauded for his tectonic virtues, launched himself into the exploration of an architecture of transparency with the design of the Kursaal in San Sebastián, Spain (1999). In fact, in *Inquietud teórica y estrategia proyectual, en la obra de ocho arquitectos contemporaneous*,[21] he theorises a rupture with a unitary structure of reference, presenting examples of work by

Gehry, Koolhaas, Herzog & de Meuron and Eisenman, together with the classicists Álvaro Siza and Aldo Rossi, and the mannerists James Stirling and Venturi & Scott Brown.

What is more, the search for international success began to push architects – like their contemporaries in the world of design – to seek easy recognition, leading them to progressively resemble one another, to the point of being almost interchangeable. The exuberance of a structure of reference that escapes from the canonical corresponded with a substantial hiatus in critical positions. This was made evident by the volatilisation of magazines with a strong cultural objective, or by those, such as the new *Abitare*, edited by Stefano Boeri, that prefer to replace works of critical writing with literary works. This condition is certainly not to be ascribed to a lack of critical positions. However, when architects are not stuck in the debates of the 1960s and 1970s, they are tied to a moralism that aims at exorcising rather than understanding: against the society of images, the easy effects of rendering, the dangers of the virtual, the architecture of communication, and so on. Or there is a perseverance in wishing to associate architecture with scientific and/or philosophical reflections, through correspondences that call on individual poetic choices, rather than a more general critical reasoning. However, many of these incursions into non-architectural territories appear to be more useful in characterising the image of the Archistar, rather than the evolution of the discipline. This can be ascribed to an accurate strategy of public relations: each project must be founded on an attractive narration that can be reassumed in a single concept. Today, more than ever, architects self-construct a theoretical horizon in which to locate themselves: they self-describe themselves in self-sponsored books inspired by their own work; they submit photographs and, in some cases, the critical texts, found in publications; and they make reference to theories that they have often only heard about, seeking to amaze the public and convince us of the honesty of their personal position.[22]

However, if criticism is in a hiatus, it is only because, more or less opportunistically, it is trying to escape from itself. Though it must also be said that it lacks a definite object to focus on. In fact, if Hollein's prophecy that everything is architecture has come to pass, this means that precisely because architecture has become everything, it has transformed into something else, leaving us shocked and amazed.

So what has it become? For Bruno Zevi, it has become landscape. In fact, if architecture dissolves as an object, it cannot avoid becoming a part of the context in which it is inserted.[23]

There is also a second response, which was provided to explain the explosion of new artistic phenomena, though it can also be used to help explain the transformations taking place in the discipline of architecture. The hypothesis is that art has volatilised. Indeed, a growing number of works borrow strategies from publicity, communication and everyday life, and from theatrical performances and television commercials. The philosopher Yves Michaud speaks of *art a l'état gazeux* (art in a gaseous state),[24] a reference to the work of Hans Belting and Arthur Danto who, in turn, would say that art and architecture are dead:[25] not in the sense that they have ceased to be vital activities because, now as never before, they produce an endless quantity of works, but because we have come to the end of the unifying ideal that defined them, whether this is the pre-20th-century cognitive ideal of mimesis and representation, or the self-reflexive version that pursued the idea of autonomy throughout that century. In fact, as anticipated by Duchamp, the extra something that gives aesthetic value to art or architecture is a function – and not a substance – that is progressively more evasive and evanescent and thus similar to air: lightweight and indefinable.

Theoretical Meltdown
In conclusion, we are today witnessing the dissolution of architecture into the natural and artificial landscape, the intolerance of consolidated linguistic codes and the gaseous state in which it is progressively more difficult to identify the margins between art and life, because the first has lost its disciplinary autonomy, and the second has been aestheticised. At this point it is easy to imagine that the state of uncertainty in which we live will be anything but transitory. In fact, if the 20th century was characterised by powerful theories and claims that were no less important, often expressed as manifestos, we can imagine that the current century will be characterised by an endemic state of 'theoretical meltdown', dominated not by the logic of borders, but by that of hypertext: the rapid shift from one sequence to another. This will result in an obvious realisation that art is tied to publicity, that architecture borrows its techniques from the world of communication, that politics relies on sophisticated techniques of communication and thus rediscovers architecture as a medium, that sculptors dedicate themselves to the creation of inhabitable spaces, and that architects such as AMO[26] create structures focused on inventing lifestyle programmes capable of generating new business and perhaps – and this is a big perhaps – new building programmes.

Anything goes. However, in all cases, when we broaden the frontiers of opportunities and freedom, there is also an increase in the danger of the irrelevant, the arbitrary and the banal. The weaker the system of disciplinary rules, the more we require a strong orientation that can no longer depend on simple value judgement.

Thus the question raised in this issue of *AD* seeks to identify the critical opinions capable of orienting us during this phase of theoretical meltdown. Are new ones being created, or do we have to rely, for the most part, on older ones?

To attempt a response we developed a list of questions regarding the field of contemporary architecture that were forwarded to respected scholars and theoreticians.

The first set of questions has to do with the possible terms for the consideration of a theory after theory. Under what terms can we make a proposal? What – other than the dangers already highlighted by the vast literature in opposition to the architecture of spectacle and communication – are the opportunities offered by the rupture of disciplinary confines? In a world dominated by fashion, advertising and concepts, is it possible to imagine, and under what conditions, a new ethic of artistic and architectural writing?

The second set of questions deals with the fallout, in terms of architectural opportunity, of the new technologies that, as we are well aware, have erased the static qualities of perspectival space, exposing the boundaries between the animate and the inanimate, between interior and exterior, between here and there, and between natural and artificial.

Finally, the third set of questions asks how the events of 11 September 2001 – which marked the end of an excessively optimistic way of looking at globalisation and new technologies – have led us to consider new relations between architecture, the body, ecology and the different geopolitical situations that now characterise our planet. In other words, is it correct to imagine that a new architecture can produce, other than the progressively flashier, yet banal and standardised constructions of the Star System, other projects capable of criticising existing relationships, above all those between space and power?

The result was a composite framework of answers that demonstrates the promising qualities of an operative approach marked by the idea of theoretical meltdown. Disorientation may, in fact, represent not only a danger, but also an opportunity. Proof can be found in the 11 particularly significant projects featured in this issue. These were selected by an equal number of critics from around the globe, all of whom are particularly attentive to the changes taking place in our world today.

These projects are interleaved throughout the issue, and respond to to the question that generated it: How, in our current era, is it possible to anticipate new and convincing working hypotheses for tomorrow's architects? ∆

Translated from the Italian version into English by Paul David Blackmore

Notes

1. This scientific research was pursued, though from different positions, by philosophers, scientists and epistemologists: from Bertrand Russell to Ludwig Wittgenstein, from Rudolf Carnap to Alfred Julius Ayer, from Alfred North Whitehead to Norbert Wiener, and Karl Popper and Imre Lakatos.
2. Even in this case, the objective is that of clarifying language and redefining a disciplinary corpus, stripping it of all overtly empirical aspects, or metaphysical beliefs – such as the correspondence between representation and what is represented, or the poetic of similarity and mimesis – that impede the artistic practice from becoming a structured and self-sufficient autonomous universe. Having exhausted his first avant-garde period, the theoretician Clement Greenberg went on to pursue a more radical approach in this direction, becoming one of the critical references for the world of art during the 1940s and 1950s. His decisive preference for a painting-painting or a sculpture-sculpture, one of which moves in the realm of pure two-dimensionality and the other in that of three-dimensionality, was the working hypothesis for an entire generation of abstract artists who, like many of their contemporaries in the field of science, wanted to focus their efforts within a discipline that was autonomous from the others, with its own particular problem, coherent with the tools – above all linguistic – available for its development.
3. The work was inaugurated in June 1969, almost a year after his death. Designed between 1944 and 1966, it was conceived of as a posthumous work and, for this reason, accompanied by detailed instructions left with the artist's wife.
4. Paul K Feyerabend, *Against Method: Outline of an Anarchist Theory of Knowledge*, New Left Books (London), 1975. The book's theses circulated from at least the beginning of the 1970s as a manuscript or in other publications. Italy's Lampugnani Nigri Editore, for example, published the almost definitive text in 1973 under the title *Contro il Metodo*.
5. Giorgio Grassi, *La costruzione logica dell'architettura*, Marsilio (Venice), 1967.
6. According to Grassi, architecture can do this only when presented on two levels: first, as the development of a syntax that combines the piece in the most aseptic way possible in order to escape the trap of compositions marked by expression and individualism, exactly like that which takes place in the world of science when it combines facts using neutral operations of symbolic logic; second it must choose its own elements, selecting them from a historical repertory – in particular the classical – in order to avoid external suggestions that may disturb the purity of the game of combination that must take place entirely within the discipline.
7. Peter Eisenman, *Notes on Conceptual Architecture: Towards a Definition*, self-published by the Institute for Architecture and Urban Studies (1970).
8. Mario Gandelsonas, 'Linguistics in Architecture', *Casabella*, No 374, 1971, p 22.
9. This can be seen in House VI, where the clients must accept a series of situations resulting from geometric rules – rotations, projections, translations, doubling – that no longer have anything to do with real life.
10. Charles Jencks, *The Language of Post-Modern Architecture*, Academy Editions and Rizzoli International Publications (London and New York), 1977.
11. Kenneth Frampton, *Studies in Tectonic Culture: The Poetic of Construction in Nineteenth and Twentieth Century Architecture*, MIT Press (Cambridge, MA), 1996.
12. *The Architectural Review*, No 1074, *The New Spirit*, August 1986.
13. Peter Cook, 'At last! Architecture is on the Wing Again', in ibid, pp 34–9.
14. This is proven by the fact that the seven architects invited to partake in the exhibition, after opportunely reaping the benefits in terms of notoriety resulting from having been invited to display their work in the sanctuary of contemporary artistic culture, have all, on more than one occasion, declared that they feel no belonging to Deconstructivism.
15. 'Deconstruction has done its job,' declared Kenneth Powel in 'Unfolding Folding', *AD Folding in Architecture* (revised edition), 2004, p 23.
16. Christian Pongratz and Maria Rita Perbellini, *Nati con il computer. Giovani architetti americani*, Testo&Immagine (Milan), 2000. Published in English under the title: *Natural Born CAADesigners*, Young American Architects, Birkhäuser (Basel, Boston, Berlin), 2000.
17. In 1994 Bernard Tschumi, Dean of Columbia University's Graduate School of Architecture, Planning and Preservation in New York since 1988, introduced the first 'paperless' design studios, entrusting them to Greg Lynn, Hani Rashid and Scott Marble. The story of the paperless studios can be found in Ned Cramer and Anne Guney, 'The Computer School', *Architecture*, September 2000, pp 93–8.
18. Rem Koolhaas, Bruce Mau and the Office for Metropolitan Architecture, *S,M,L,XL*, The Monacelli Press and 010 Publishers (New York and Rotterdam), 1995.
19. Steven Izenour, Denise Scott Brown and Robert Venturi, *Learning from Las Vegas*, MIT Press (Boston, MA), 1972.
20. It is interesting to note that, vice versa, the promoters of the New Spirit sought in turn to recover autonomy. This would appear to be the approach pursued by Patrik Schumacher, partner of Zaha Hadid Architects, in his book *The Autopoeisis of Architecture: A Conceptual Framework for Architecture* (to be published by Wiley in early 2009), which reclaims a new tectonic of forms within disciplinary discourse.
21. The book was published in Spanish (Actar), Italian (Electa) and English: *Theoretical Anxiety and Design Strategies in the Work of Eight Contemporary Architects*, MIT Press (Cambridge, MA), 2005).
22. We must thus consider the softening of the media resulting from the economic pressures that mean that professional publications are largely funded by industry advertising. The consequence of this situation is that large companies and high-profile architects often have sway/control over what is said about them.
23. This was the reason for the conference 'Paesaggistica e linguaggio grado zero dell'architettura' organised by Zevi in Modena in 1997. The conference proceedings were published in *L'architettura, cronache e storia*, Nos 503–06, 1999, in Italian and English under the titles: 'Paesaggistica e linguaggio grado zero dell'architettura' and 'Landscape and the zero degree of architectural language'.
24. Yves Michaud, *L'art à l' état gazeux. Essai sur le triomphe de l'esthétique*, Éditions Stock (Paris), 2003.
25. Michaud's point of view, as he unashamedly admits, refers back to the theories of Hans Belting and Arthur Danto, who dealt with this topic at the beginning of the 1980s. Hans Belting, *The End of the History of Art*, trans Christopher S Wood, University of Chicago Press (Chicago, IL), 1987, and Arthur Danto, *After the End of Art: Contemporary Art and the Pale of History*, Princeton University Press (Princeton, NJ), 1997.
26. Koolhaas' intuition when, during the 1990s, he founded AMO, was that it was necessary to create a new structure to accompany OMA, the existing technical one. Thus, 'while OMA remains dedicated to the realisation of architectural projects, AMO applies architectural thinking in its pure form, to questions of organisation, identity, culture and program, and defines ways – from the conceptual to the operative – to address the full potential of the contemporary condition.' (From the OMA-AMO website: www.oma.eu)

1230	Villard de Honnecourt	Codex
1464	Filerete	Codex Magliabechiamus
1542	Leon Battista Alberti	De Re Aedificatoria Libri Decem
1547	Jean Martin	Architecture ou Art de Bien Bastir
1548	Walter Rivius or Ryff	Vitruvius Teutsch
1550	Hans Blum	Von den Fünff Sülen
1452	Cesare Cesariano	De Architectura di Lucio Vitruvio Pollione
1556	Daniele Barbaro	I Dieci Libri dell'Architettura di M Vitruvio
1561	Philibert de l'Orme	Nouvelles Inventions Pour Bien Bastir et a Petits Fraiz
1561	Philibert de l'Orme	Le premier Tome de l'Architecture
1562	Vignola	Regola delli Cinque Ordini d'Architettura
1563	John Shute	The First and Chief Grounds of Architecture
1570	Andrea Palladio	I Quattro Libri dell'Architettura
1598	Wendel Dietterlin	Architecuçra von Au_theilung, Symmetria und Proportion der Fünff Seulen
1615	Vicenzo Scamozzi	L'idea della Architettura Universale
1619	Sebastiano Serlio	Tutte l'Opere d'Architettura et Prospettiva
1623	Pierre Le Muet	Manier de Bien Bastir Pour Touttes Sortes des Personnes
1647	Pierre Le Muet	Augumentation de Nouveaux Bastiments Faits en France
1650	Roland Fréart de Chambray	Parallele de l'Architecture Antique et de la Moderne
1673	Claude Perrault	Le Dix Livres d'Architecture de Vitruve
1677	Abraham Leuthner von Grundt	Grundtliche Darstellung Der Fünff Seüllen
1683	François Blondel	Cours d'Architecture
1683	Claude Perrault	Ordonnance des Cinq Espèces de Colonnes Selon la Méthode des Anciens
1691	Augustin Charles d'Aviler	Cours d'Architecture Qui Comprend les Orders de Vignole
1713	Domenico de' Rossi	Disegni di Vari Altari e Cappelle nelle Chiese di Roma
1716	Paulus Decker	Fürstlicher Baumeister Oder: Architectura Civilis
1721	Domenico de' Rossi	Studio d'Architettura Civile
1721	Johann Bernhard Fischer von Erlach	Entwurff Einer Historischen Architectur
1725	Colen Campbell	Vitruvius Britannicus
1728	James Gibbs	A Book of Architecture, Containing Designs of Buildings and Ornament
1728	Robert Morris	An Essay in Defence of Ancient Architecture
1732	James Gibbs	Rules for Drawing the Several Parts of Architecture
1736	Robert Morris	Lectures on Architecture
1756	Jacques-François Blondel	Architecture Françoise
1756	Isaac Ware	A Complete Body of Architecture
1759	William Chambers	A Treatise on Civil Architecture
1761	Giovanni Battista Piranesi	Della Magnificenza ed Architettura de' Romani
1765	Marie-Joseph Peyre	Ouvres d'Architecture
1777	Jacques-François Blondel	Cours d'Architecture ou Traité de la Dècoration, Distribution & Costrution des Bâtiment
1781	Francesco Milizia	Principi di Architettura Civile
1800	Giovanni Battista Cipriani	Indice delle Figure Relative ai Principi di Architettura Civile
1800	Jean-Nicolas-Louis Durand	Recueil et Parallèle des Edifices de Tout Genre Anciens et Modernes
1804	Claude-Nicolas Ledoux	L'Architecture Considèrrèes Sous Rapport de l'Art, des Moeurs et de la Legislation
1805	Jean-Nicolas-Louis Durand	Précis des Leçons d'Architecture
1817	Jean-Baptiste Rondelet	Traité Théorique et Pratique de l'Art de Bâtir
1819	Friedrich Weinbrenner	Architektonisches Lehurbuch
1822	Leo von Klenze	Anweisung zur Architectur des Christian Cultus
1826	Heinrich Hübsch	In Welchen Style Sollen Wir Bauen?
1827	Johann Gottfried Gutensohn + Johann Michael Knapp	Denkmale der Christlichen Religion
1828	Joseph Futtenbach il Vecchio	Architectura Civilis
1834	Gottfried Semper	Vorläufige Bemerkungen Über Bemalte Architektur und Plastik Bei den Alten
1836	Augustus Welby Pugin	Contrasts
1840	Karl Fridrich Schinkel	Sammlung Architectonischer Entwürfe
1842	Augustus Welby Pugin	The True Principles of Pointed or Christian Architecture
1844	Christian Carl Josias Bunsen	Die BAsiliken des Christilichen Roms
1847	Guillame Abel Blouet	Supplément
1845	Friedrich Hoffstadt	Gotisches A-B-C Buch
1851	Gottfried Semper	Die Vier Elemente der Baukunst
1852	Carl Alexander Heideloff	Der Kleine Altdeutsche (Gothe)
1863	Gottfried Semper	Der Stil in den Technischen und Tektonischen Künsten
1864	Georg Gottlob Ungewitter	Lehrbuch der Gothinschen Konstruktionen
1868	Eugène-Emmanuel Viollet-le-Duc	Dictionnaire Raisonné de L'architecture Française du XIe au XVIe Siècle
1872	Eugène-Emmanuel Viollet-le-Duc	Entretiens sur l'Architecture
1898	Ebenezer Howard	To-morrow: A Peaceful Path to Real Reform
1910	Frank Lloyd Wright	Ausgeführte Bauten und Entwürfe
1917	Tony Garnier	Une Cité industrielle: Étude pour la Construction des Villes
1919	Bruno Taut	Die Stadkrone
1919	Bruno Taut	Alpine Architektur
1923	Le Corbusier	Vers une Architecture
1925	Le Corbusier	Urbanisme
1925	Walter Gropius	Internationale Architektur
1932	Henry R Hitchcock + Philip Johnson	The International Style: Architecture since 1922
1932	Paul Schmitthenner	Das Deutsche Wohnaus
1943	Le Corbusier	La Cherte d'Athènes
1950	Ministerrat der DDR	Gründsatze des Städtebaus
1961	Archigram	Archigram
1966	Aldo Rossi	L'Architettura della Città
1966	Robert Venturi	Complexity and Contradiction in Architecture
1972	Robert Venturi, Denise Scott Brown + Steven Izenour	Learning from Las Vegas
1977	Kisho Kurokawa	Metabolism in Architecture
1977	Charles Jencks	The Language of Post-Modern Architecture
1978	Rem Koolhaas	Delirious New York
1995	Rem Koolhaas	S, M, L, XL

Compiled by Francesco Proto

Text © 2009 John Wiley & Sons Ltd

A SHORT HISTORY OF WESTERN ARCHITECTURE FROM VITRUVIUS TO REM KOOLHAAS

1. Vitruvius, *De Architectura Libri Decem*
(this edition translated by Marchese Berardo Galliani, published in Venice, 1854)

Marcus Vitruvius Pollio (*c* 80–15 BC) was the first Roman architect to have written surviving records of his field. In *The Ten Books on Architecture*, the only major book on architecture from classical antiquity, he famously asserted that a structure must exhibit the three qualities of *firmitas*, *utilitas* and *venustas* (durability, usefulness and beauty). According to Vitruvius, architecture is an imitation of nature. This concept is exemplified by the *Vitruvian Man*, of which Leonardo da Vinci provided a universally known drawing: the human body is inscribed in the circle and the square as a rule following the fundamental geometric patterns of the cosmic order.

2. Leon Battista Alberti, *Della architettura: Libri dieci*
(original translation by Cosimo Batoli, published in Milan, 1833)

Alberti (1404–72) patterned *The Ten Books on Architecture* after *De Architectura* by the Roman architect and engineer Vitruvius. The work was the first architectural treatise of the Renaissance. It covered a wide range of subjects, from history to town planning, from engineering to the philosophy of beauty. *De Re Aedificatoria*, however, was not fully published until 1485, after which it became a major guide for architects in spreading theories and ideals of the Florentine Renaissance to the rest of Italy. The first Italian edition is dated 1546; the standard Italian edition, by Cosimo Bartoli, 1550.

3. Vignola, *Regola delli Cinque Ordini d'Architettura*
(this edition printed in Siena by Bernardino Oppi, 1635)

In 1562, Giacomo Barozzi, often simply called Vignola, wrote the treatise entitled *Canon of the Five Orders of Architecture* (probably in Rome), which was immensely successful throughout Europe right up until the 19th century. Alongside *Due Regole della Prospettiva Pratica/Two Rules of Practical Perspective* (Bologna, 1583), the *Canon of the Five Orders* helped formulate the canons of classical architectural style without theoretical obscurities. In particular, the posthumously published *Two Rules of Practical Perspective* favoured the diffusion of one-point perspective rather than two-point methods such as bifocal construction.

4. Andrea Palladio, *I Quattro Libri dell'Architettura*
(original edition published in Venice by Domenico de' Franceschi, 1570)

The importance of the *The Four Books of Architecture*, in which Andrea Palladio (1508–80) acknowledged the authority of Vitruvius and Alberti, lies not only in the improvements brought about by the ancient models, but also in the 'declaration of independence' established by modern constructions. One of the most innovative configurations Palladio introduced to architecture was the interlocking of two architectural orders, delineating a hierarchy of a larger order overriding a lesser order, which he applied to the design of Roman Catholic churches. This idea of two superimposed systems paralleled the setting of the rules of illustration in modern architectural representation as based on the exact juxtapositions of plans and facades. Interest in Palladio's style was renewed in later generations to such an extent that Palladianism became a new architectural trend that was fashionable all over Europe.

5. Giovanni Battista Piranesi, *Della Magnificenza ed Architettura de' Romani*
(this title page from *Antichità di Albano e di Castel Gandolfo*, first released in Rome, 1764)

In *Roman Magnificence and Architecture* (Rome, 1761), Piranesi (1720–78) triggered a harsh polemics with Johann Joachim Winckelmann (1717–68), a staunch supporter of the primacy of Greek art over Roman architecture. The result was a learned *tractatus* in the guise of a dialogue whose novelty is to be found in the application of the dialect of Enlightenment to establish a new, modern style based on the combinatorial eclecticism of past forms. Piranesi gave a brilliant sample of his innovative conception in more than 1,700 drawings and engravings by faithfully imitating the missing parts of Rome's remains that he so meticulously used to depict. Piranesi's work, which heavily influenced Neoclassicism by anticipating the historical revivalism affecting Postmodernism, also influenced a number of disciplines outside of architecture, including cinema (for example, Sergei Eisenstein's invention of the cinematic cut).

6. Eugène-Emmanuel Viollet-le-Duc, *Dictionaire Raisonne de L'Architecture Francaise du XIe au XVIe Siècle* (this edition published in Paris by VA Morel & C, 1875)

In 1948, Sir John Summerson considered that 'there have been two supremely eminent theorists in the history of European architecture – Leon Battista Alberti and Eugène Viollet-le-Duc' (1814–79). Viollet-le-Duc's 'restorations' of ancient buildings frequently combined historical fact with creative modification, and his 'updating' of the church of Notre Dame in Paris influenced the architecture of the 19th century to such a degree that it led to a massive revivalism of Gothic architecture everywhere. By applying the lessons he had derived from Gothic architecture, Viollet-le-Duc saw beneath its historical allure. Pushing forwards what he conceived to be its rational structural systems, he thus opened the way for Modernism by opposing the set rules of its time: Gothic against classical, construction against decoration, truth against lie, progress against academism, etc. This he did via a remarkably innovative kind of architectural representation, as expressed in his *Dictionaire*, which first appeared in Paris between 1854 and 1868.

7. Le Corbusier, *L'Esprit Nouveau* (Paris, Issue 1, 1920)

In the hope that politically minded industrialists in France would lead the way with their efficient Taylorist and Fordist strategies, adopted from American models, to reorganise society, Charles-Edouard Jeanneret, better known as Le Corbusier (1887–1965), began a new journal entitled *L'Esprit Nouveau*. The journal advocated the use of modern industrial techniques and strategies to transform society into a more efficient environment and with a higher standard of living at all socioeconomic levels. Le Corbusier forcefully argued that this transformation was necessary to avoid the spectre of revolution that would otherwise shake society. His dictum 'Architecture or Revolution', developed in his articles in the journal, became his rallying cry for the book *Vers une Architecture* (*Towards an Architecture*), which included selected articles from *L'Esprit Nouveau* between 1920 and 1923, and was first released in 1923.

8. Aldo Rossi, L'Architettura della Città (Marsilio Editori, Padua, 1966)

Aldo Rossi (1931–97) became extremely influential for the theories he promoted in his 1966 book *The Architecture of the City*. In his writings, Rossi criticised the lack of understanding of the city in current architectural practice by arguing that a city must be studied and valued as something constructed over time; of particular interest in this respect are urban artefacts that withstand the passage of time. Rossi in fact held that the city 'remembers' its past in the shape of 'collective memory', and that therefore we use that memory through monuments. In other words, monuments give structure to the city. In Aldo Rossi we can therefore find an 'iconist' *avant-la-lettre*, for the spreading of his treatise paralleled the growth of iconic buildings capable of rejuvenating the economy of forgotten quarters of a city or the whole city itself.

9. Robert Venturi, Denise Scott Brown and Steven Izenour, *Learning from Las Vegas: The Forgotten Symbolism of Architectural Form* (this edition published by in Cambridge, MA, by MIT Press, 1986)

A controversial critic of the purely functional orthodoxy professed by Modernist architecture, Robert Venturi's 'gentle manifesto' in *Complexity and Contradiction in Architecture* (1966) was described by Vincent Scully as 'the most important writing on the making of architecture since Le Corbusier's *Vers une Architecture* (1923)'. In 1972, with Denise Scott Brown and Steven Izenour, Venturi wrote *Learning from Las Vegas*, a further rebuke to elite architectural tastes. By coining the terms 'Duck' and 'Decorated Shed' as applied to opposed architectural building styles, the book compared the 'expressionism' of late-Modernist architecture with a new architectural trend of treating the building's facade as an advertising billboard exhibiting the 'forgotten' symbolism of American imagery rather than commercials. This highly influential treatise also broadened the ongoing debate about the 'skin' of the architectural organism, which became central to architectural practice in replacing old-fashioned concerns about 'style' or 'shape'.

10. Rem Koolhaas, *Delirious New York: A Retroactive Manifesto for Manhattan* (this edition published in New York by Monacelli Press, 1994)

With *Delirious New York* (1978), Koolhaas emphatically embraced the contradictions of two disciplines – architecture and urban design – struggling to maintain their humanist ideals in a rapidly globalising world. Rather than material honesty, human scale and carefully crafted meaning, architecture now has to face material economy, machine scale and random meaning. For this reason, Koolhaas celebrates the 'chance-like' nature of city life, an approach already made evident in the Japanese Metabolist Movement of the 1960s and early 1970s. He therefore interrogates the notion of 'programme', first raised by Modernism in the 20th century, as the pretext of architectural design epitomised in the maxim 'Form Follows Function'. The latter is in fact replaced by a new design method called 'cross-programming', which Koolhaas derived from high-rise architecture in Manhattan and (unsuccessfully) proposed for the Seattle Public Library project (2003) through the inclusion of hospital units for the homeless.

Compiled by Francesco Proto

junya.ishigami+associates

Facility of Kanagawa Institute of Technology, Atsugi, Kanagawa, Japan, 2008

The Executive Director of Storefront in New York **Joseph Grima** tips off the young Japanese architect Junya Ishigami for our attention. Ishigami's extension to the Kanagawa Institution of Technology might at first glance resemble a humble greenhouse. Stripped back far beyond the bare essentials, it has a finely tuned structure that enables it to be supported on pillars alone and elevates it to the poetic.

Joseph Grima

Like it or not, it would seem that lineage is almost as important in architectural practice as in horse racing. If this is so, then Junya Ishigami is unquestionably a thoroughbred of the contemporary era, being a direct descendant of the Shinohara-Ito-Sejima bloodline. Does he have the intelligence to innovate and not simply replicate? This remains to be seen, but the promise is undeniably there.

His first major commission to be completed is the extension to the Kanagawa Institute of Technology. The new university building contains offices, workshops, study and relaxation areas, but not a single wall or partition, and has been described by some who have visited the facility as an anticlimactic experience – one is left with the sensation that there is almost nothing to be seen. To seek a jaw-dropping experience is to miss the point. While it is true that experiencing Ishigami's architecture is akin to an intellectual exercise, there is also – and more importantly – an emotional component: it is *uplifting*. It is designed to speak to the soul rather than the mind. It alludes to patterns present in nature, but almost imperceptibly, certainly less explicitly than in Toyo Ito's work; it is

evanescent, but does not brag about it. More than in its Minimalism, it is profoundly Japanese in its restraint.

To achieve the effect that inspired the original design (the roofplate is supported by the forest of pillars, without any lateral bracing and no interior partitions) required years of experiments, revisions and research, and even the development of a special software application. Yet there is nothing spectacular about the Kanagawa Institute of Technology. This, however, makes it all the more remarkable: that such pains were taken to realise a very simple idea, a subtle effect, despite the fact that the extent of the efforts might well go unnoticed, is a testament not only to remarkable determination, but also to the belief that the pursuit of an unspectacular architectural poetic is worthwhile. And ultimately, it is the tenacity necessary to rigorously pursue an idea – however simple it may be – that sets the few great architects apart from the many good architects. ⚠

Text and images compiled by Anna Baldini
Captions translated from the Italian version into English by Paul David Blackmore

top: The insertion of natural elements creates an artificial forest that is home to both man-made and natural elements.

above: Seen from the exterior, the building also resembles a greenhouse. The slender structural elements, its white colour and the large transparent surfaces give it an abstract, almost Platonic quality.

left: Aerial view. The building plate has a distorted square base. Light enters from the sides and through rooftop skylights.

Evaporating Theory
An **Interview** with Yves Michaud

Is architecture evaporating and losing its distinct status as a discipline? In pursuit of an answer to this question, **Luigi Prestinenza Puglisi** spoke to Yves Michaud, Professor of Philosophy at the University of Paris and author of *L'art à l'état gazeuz* (Art in a Gaseous State), 2003.

In 2003, Yves Michaud wrote a book that met with considerable success in France. In *L'art à l'état gazeux. Essai sur le triomphe de l'esthétique*[1] he claims that it is now almost impossible to identify a demarcation line between the examples of high art on display in museums and supported by large cultural institutions,[2] and the various products with strong aesthetic impacts produced by advertising and fashion.

'Art,' Michaud tells us, 'in the sense of visual or sculptural art, has dedifferentiated itself within itself. This means that there are no longer artistic genres so to speak (painting, sculpture, photography, and so on). It has also dedifferentiated itself from many other social activities, such as advertising or cooking: for example, when Nan Goldin creates publicity campaigns for the SNCF [the French National Railway Company] or when Ferran Adria represented Spain at Kassel's Documenta in 2007. In this sense art leaves its defined domain and extends itself in a gaseous manner or like an aesthetic vapour that colours or tints other domains and other practices: fashion, design, politics, entrepreneurship, humanitarianism, the environment.'

Michaud develops a number of considerations advanced by Hans Belting and Arthur Danto regarding the so-called death of art:

'I don't say that art is dead, but that a certain form of art, the modern form, is dead. Between the 1800s and the 1980s there existed a certain regime of art that characterised itself by a fetishism of works, an avant-garde position of the artist, formal preoccupations in the artist or in the spectator, a great seriousness in the aesthetic attitude. All this has been replaced by other things: hedonism, spectacle and emotions. From a historical and cultural point of view, a form of art cedes the path and from it we arrive at other experiences, certain of which have already been made in the past, notably in architecture, the decorative arts or music. Thus I don't support the thesis of the death of art, but only of a certain form of art.'

This has significant consequences, for example, on the autonomy of the arts:

'Effectively this implies the end of the autonomy of art, in the sense that art once had its own domain of values and norms and could, from this position, claim to influence other aspects of social life. It is clear, for example, that artists are no longer politically influential. It's the politicians, the stars, the singers or actors who lead the show. By the same token, advertising is more effective than art; we need only mention the ads by Benetton or the campaigns for NGOs.

'If one were to cite a great ancestor, this was the role of Marcel Duchamp, who created works of art from any object (his 'readymades'). He used everyday objects and advertising, was not politically engaged, and insisted on the non-aesthetic and non-artistic character of his artworks. However, he is still modern because he continues to claim to formally inscribe his creations in the history of modern art, even if to subvert it.'

Much like art, architecture now seems to be blurring its boundaries. It is difficult, for example, to distinguish between a work of architecture and a sculpture, between a sign and a building facade, or between a work of art and a commercial. In *L'art à l'état gazeux*, Michaud mentions only two buildings, perhaps because architecture now plays a marginal role in this process.

'My book *Art in a gaseous state* dates from 2003 and is the beginning of a diagnostic. Since then I've expanded this diagnostic to include architecture and music – without mentioning cooking and the like. Architectural projects are, in effect, simultaneously functional works and sculptures, monuments and constructions, places of commerce and places of artistic attraction. Architecture is also a work of art, and at the same time an atmosphere, ambience and environment: one perceives it from far away, either from an aeroplane or in a model, as a symbol; but close up and in reality it is an environment, for example a shopping centre, large train station or airport. It is even clearer that in music, especially in electronic music, the acoustic ambience replaces the acoustic object being listened to.'

The gaseous state, nonetheless, has its own force and effectiveness.

'I don't at all say that the gas or vapour is nothing, a void. It is rather another sort of experience that is proposed and that conveys something other than concepts, ideas or identifiable sensations. How would one speak of a perfume or a visit to a city? In fact, one renews ties with the aesthetic themes broached and largely popularised in the 19th century by Schopenhauer, Baudelaire or Stendhal. From this point onwards we must imagine that we are dealing with a non-objective aesthetic, with experiences. There is, therefore, no transmission of ideas, but only of experiences, of ways to feel, of breaths of sensations, of emotions.'

So which artists currently manage to take advantage of the vaporisation of art to develop approaches that Michaud considers to be important?

'If one remains at the interior of art, I believe that this type of experiment was inaugurated by Minimalist artists, often also by the artists of the Arte Povera movement, and today these experiments are produced by those who create complex installations or who attract attention to … nothing. I cite, in any order, Jason Rhoades, Francis Alÿs, Teresa Margolles and James Turrell. Outside of the so-called art world there are many rivals: designers, architects, chefs, couturiers, artistic directors of luxury brands, DJs and VJs.'

MaO-emmeazero, Piazza Risorgimento, Bari, 2002–05.
A public space from which architecture has disappeared: the new seating is composed of rotating benches that are hinged at one end. Members of the public are free to rearrange the seating as they wish.

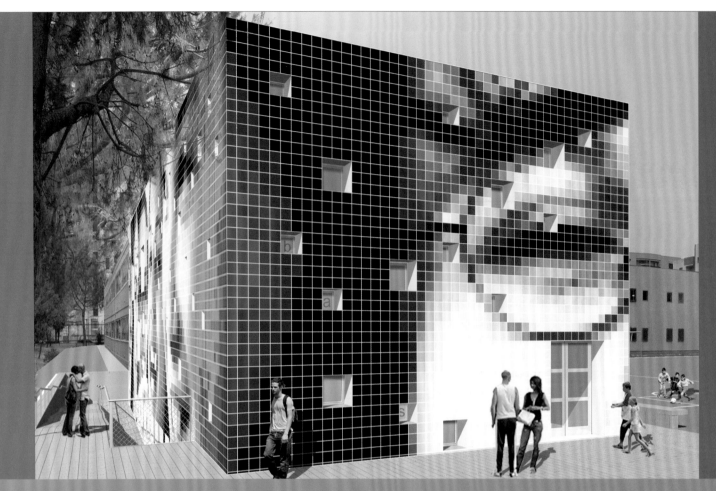

MaO-emmeazero, Addition to the Lombardi High School, Bari, Italy, 2003–04
Photographs become architecture. Ten of the school's students were invited to participate in a workshop run by architects
MaO-emmeazero to develop the design of the school's facade based on their photographs. The images were transformed into
architecture by a system inspired by the logic of pixels, translated into different-coloured ceramic tiles.

Criticism, Self-Promotion and Philosophy

Criticism currently finds itself in a state of crisis. Artists
seek a direct relationship with the market, skipping the
mediation of the critic. Vice versa, many critics abdicate
their role as theoreticians and thinkers, choosing to act as
simple promoters – as instruments of the market.

'Evidently, since art no longer constitutes an
autonomous domain, artists no longer need criticism to
assure the mediation of their work. They need diffusers,
communicators, to make themselves heard among other
producers of aesthetic experiences. The critic becomes
quite naturally and logically an events organiser, a
manager, a *buzz* producer.'

Naturally there are connections between the
philosophies or techniques of self-promotion employed by
star-artists or star-architects.

'The situation is no different for the artist than the
architect by nature. What is very different now are the
economic conditions. Architects need to mobilise
investments that are so consequential that they are obliged to come
into contact with important political and economic decision-makers.
Artists, even if they are famous and expensive, are, in comparison,
inexpensive and therefore less influential.'

The crisis faced by architectural critics can be observed in the case
of magazines, which more and more rarely choose to confront
theoretical discourses, limiting themselves instead to acting as
soapboxes for the Star System or the launching pads for future stars.

'The situation renders theoretical discourse practically useless. It is
difficult to create a theoretical discourse on emotions. There is
therefore no place for theoretical discourse in the first degree, only for
meta-discourses of the type to which I associate the new relationship
between art and culture. Koolhaas' theoretical discourses are of this
type, as are those of Sloterdijk or Bruno Latour. I notice in France that
new art criticism is made under the name of "Fresh Theory" by young
philosophers or essayists who speak of other things besides art, who
speak next to it.'

If critics do not want to lose their role, they must focus on
providing valuable opinions.

'Paradoxically, it seems to me that between the media buzz and the theoretical meta-discourse, there is still room for value judgements, though they will not necessarily be very theoretical because they reference mostly traditional criteria. For architecture, this would be the coherence of the project, the elegance of the solution, the beauty of the object. For works of visual art, this would be criteria of the same order, plus the capacity of emotion and sensitivity. If I mention Rhoades, Alÿs, Margolles and Turrell this is because they possess qualities of this order, as opposed to purely pompous artists like Bill Viola or Jeff Wall. If we use the example of the architecture of Jean Nouvel, there is the best and the worst according to which Nouvel takes the project seriously, choosing whether or not to play with his own technical resources, mastering urban inscription or not. These are not values of the past, but aesthetic values present in all sorts of experiences.'

For Paul Virilio, the spectacularisation of communication and the increased speed imposed by new media are leading us towards an aesthetic of the catastrophe. Yet it would seem that, above all for the younger generation of architects and artists, there is a desire to avoid the fetishisation of new technologies, to combine them with other, simpler ones, in some cases archaic and local, in order to develop new approaches that are ecological, socially or politically relevant, or ethical.

'I believe that Virilio is convinced that technological development is heading towards a catastrophe. I believe it and I don't believe it – for there are always technologies of precaution or reparation. It seems to me, from this point of view, that we are partially witness to an evolution due somewhat, for certain people, to the need to innovate or distinguish themselves in relation to proponents of technology, including turning towards the archaic and the local. There is also a partial development of a clear consciousness that all human activities have an environmental and ecological imprint, a *fortiori* architecture; this is equally true when it pertains to the arts. If the first response appears a bit anecdotal, the second corresponds to the fact that the arts are no longer outside of the social. One could tolerate the horror of totalitarian architectural gestures when art dominated society – for example the urban projects of Le Corbusier. Today, the artist and the architect toe the line and they must therefore account for their carbon footprint or coexistence with the environment.

'In recent decades many architects have been inspired by philosophers such as Martin Heidegger, Jean-François Lyotard, Gilles Deleuze and Jacques Derrida. This process has not been without its misunderstandings: it is one thing to speak of the Postmodernism of Lyotard, another to speak of that of Charles Jencks; and Derrida's Deconstructivism has little to do with that of Peter Eisenman. However, these misunderstandings, even while they can be criticised from an exclusively theoretical point of view, have had positive effects on the creation of new formal universes. I ask myself whether one of the characteristics of this gaseous state, in which all elements mix together, is not precisely that of creative misunderstanding. In other words, whether this is not an astute practice of individual disciplines that, instead of enclosing themselves in a self-referential world, decide to invade neighbouring territories, in order to feed off of them, metabolising them and, in turn, developing them.

'Creative misunderstandings aren't as creative as that. I imagine what Eisenman would have done if he wanted to without Derrida. I don't know any examples of Lyotardian or Deleuzian architecture. In reality, artists often need theoretical subjects that serve as rhetorical ornaments, to feel less alone. On the other hand, Lyotard and Derrida in reality had incredibly ordinary and even petit-bourgeois aesthetic tastes. The same applies to Baudrillard. This takes nothing away from their merits as philosophers. However, I am perfectly in agreement with you that the expansion and the redefinition of the experience in the process of the vaporisation of art renders possible collaborations, imaginations and inventions. The majority of current inventions in science appear at the interfaces – between mathematics and economics, between biochemistry and computer science, between archaeology and genomics. This applies equally in our domains. The good architectural specialists I know are close to geography, which is in itself a discipline of open contours.'

So after the gaseous state, is it still possible to imagine a strong theory of architecture, or should we resign ourselves to its demise?

'One strong theory of architecture could be, I would bet, a simultaneous theory of the city and of architecture, with two very different poles: one concerning the absorption of architecture by the city, the other the transcending of the city by a few hyper-monuments functioning as symbolic attractors. It is very curious to observe that, today, the city eats architecture and architecture saves itself by transforming itself into hyper-symbol.' ◮

This interview has been compiled from email correspondence between Luigi Prestinenza Puglisi and Yves Michaud from January to June 2008.

Translated from the Italian and French versions into English by Paul David Blackmore and Karri Campbell

Notes
1. Yves Michaud, *L'art à l'état gazeux. Essai sur le triomphe de l'esthétique*, Editions Stock (Paris), 2003.
2. We can mention three examples, ranging from the fashion shows/performances of Vanessa Beecroft, Damien Hirst's bulls preserved in formaldehyde, or Maurizio Cattelan's sculpture of the pope hit by a meteorite.

muf architecture/art

Barking Town Square, Barking and Dagenham, Greater London, 2008

Claes Sörstedt

Barking, in east London, has become the unlikely site for a regeneration project by muf that dissolves art, architecture, landscaping, psychogeography and instant mythology. Swedish architect and critic **Claes Sörstedt** highlights the 'attractive combination of mystery and utility' that he finds in this reinvented piazza.

Barking Town Square was once a less than unarticulated space behind the main street in Barking town centre, in Barking and Dagenham – a bleak, sprawly and ungentrified suburb in the outer periphery of Greater London. Previously famous only as the borough whose second largest political party is the BNP (British National Party), Barking and Dagenham is now home to a regeneration and renewal project that convincingly merges strategies from art discourse with methods more often talked and written about than realised within the architectural realm: psychogeography, relational aesthetics, participatory design, eclecticism, architectural tuning and so on. muf architecture/art's reinvention of the area in front of the Barking and Dagenham town hall is actually only the smaller part of an ambitious 35,000-square-metre (376,737-square-foot) project. Allford Hall Monaghan Morris (AHMM) has designed some 200 new flats built on top of the old, but now refurbished, library (now a learning centre). Nevertheless, slick contemporary architecture is available everywhere, though muf's attractive combination of mystery and utility is not.

The layout of the town square is a series of four adjacent, interlocking and differently themed spaces. In front of the town hall there is a quite straightforward formal space, and next to it is an arboretum with a collection of 40 trees of 16 different species. Parallel to the trees and carved out of the ground floor of the remodelled library runs an 80-metre (262.5-foot) long and 8-metre (26.2-foot) high arcade of north Italian grandeur (Bologna or Piazza San Marco.) Above the arcade's chequered terrazzo floor hang 13 golden chandeliers designed by Tom Dixon. The fourth, and most picturesque, feature of the scheme is the backdrop of the town square: a folly. Made of salvaged 19th-century brick and sculptures, it has at once freed the place from its previous life as junk space with an injection of history and instant mythology. ⌂

Text and images compiled by Anna Baldini

top left: The new arcade is 80 metres (262.5 feet) long and 8 metres (26.2 feet) high.

top right: The folly wall is made of salvaged 19th-century brick and sculptures.

above: The arboretum has a collection of 40 trees of 16 different species.

left: In front of the town hall, muf has created a relatively straightforward formal space.

Twenty Years After (Deconstructivism)
An **Interview** with Bernard Tschumi

Michele Costanzo interviews Bernard Tschumi about his work and his vision of the changing field of contemporary design research. How do the younger generation of students receive Tschumi's seminal theoretical works? Is a lack of time merely the current scapegoat for a more considered conceptual approach? How does Tschumi view the proliferation of architectural fetishes in the urban landscape? How is his own theoretical landscape shifting?

In the early 1990s, there was a significant schism in architecture. This was triggered in the recently globalised world of design by a simultaneous crisis in theoretical thought and a growing shift towards the formal. As the preoccupation with form developed through the decade it concurred with a burgeoning international economy, which paved the way for the exponential rise of the signature architect. Elevated by the association with the gilded world of the global brand, the architectural doyen inevitably became separated from the spatial concerns of the city. However, with the current economic slowdown and an acute growing awareness of wider issues, such as the imminent shortage of water, food and energy as well as climate change, the reconsideration of the architect as merely a marketing instrument or branding package has become pressing. It is now time to re-evaluate how the architect might become an operative figure in the world of aesthetics while being attentive to social and urban objectives.

The fact that Bernard Tschumi is both a theoretician and a designer is key to understanding his distinctive approach to architecture. After completing his degree at the Federal Institute of Technology (ETH) in Zurich, Tschumi moved to London in 1970 to teach at the Architectural Association (AA) under the directorship of Alvin Boyarsky. In 1976 he moved to the US where he taught at the Institute for Architecture and Urban Studies, founded by Peter Eisenman, and the University of Princeton, before taking up a position as a visiting professor at Cooper Union in New York in the early 1980s.

In the late 1970s, Tschumi began to focus on identifying a different and more direct relationship with architecture through a series of drawings known as *The Screenplays* (1977), in which he used collages of images from *film noir* to experiment with the technique of cinematic editing and montage. This research was expanded in *The Manhattan Transcripts* (1981) with its three simultaneous levels of reality:[1] the event (represented by documentary-style news photography); movement (re-created by diagrams of movements from choreography and sport); and space (explored through photography, and building and site plans). This effectively placed the architectural experience in close proximity on three different levels.

In 1983 when Tschumi won the competition to design the 50-hectare (125-acre) Parc de la Villette in Paris, he entered the world of professional practice and started to build a series of highly iconic projects, pervaded by a profound theoretical investigation. His ties with academia, however, remained strong, and in 1988 he was appointed Dean of the Graduate School of Architecture, Planning and Preservation at Columbia University in New York. His 15-year term at Columbia testifies to his efforts in the field of education, an activity that provided him with a great deal of stimulation and an important outlet for his ongoing speculative, intellectual reflections on the making of architecture.

Between 2001 and 2002, the drawings from *The Manhattan Transcripts* were included in a significant retrospective exhibition that travelled to four US cities. Curated by Jeff Kipnis, 'Perfect Acts of Architecture' displayed the graphic work that Peter Eisenman, Rem Koolhaas and Elia Zenghelis, Daniel Libeskind, Thom Mayne and Tschumi all produced in a 10-year time period – from 1972 to 1982.[2] Paper architecture, Kipnis notes, can have a role in the history of architecture provided that it is innovative and if its main purpose is the drawing in itself.[3] In other words, it must suggest new research trends and have an objective value. Work was selected from that particular era in order to consider these points by highlighting their internal values. However, although supported by a profound theoretical content, they all subsume the historical momentum in which they were produced. By encapsulating the social context and the economic transformations typical of their time, they stress their affiliation to a period of great communication changes. This incontrovertibly led to the profusion of computer-aided design with its almost inexhaustible potential.

In his selection of the six projects for the exhibition, Kipnis captures a renewed confidence.[4] There is a strong sense that the featured architects are poised to pass on something important to ensuing generations. In a similar way that it was apparent in other cultural and artistic forms at the time, such as cinema and rock music (think of *2001: A Space Odyssey* from Stanley Kubrick, or *Electric Lady Land* from Jimi Hendrix).

Transcending History and 'Concept-Form'
Interviewing Tschumi provided the unique opportunity to ask him whether he shares Kipnis' interpretations of the featured projects. Does he think that *The Manhattan Transcripts* continue to have a theoretical value to emerging generations, providing a catalyst for new ideas?

'While the mode of communication and the general sensibility of *The Manhattan Transcripts* clearly belong to the period, the issues they explore always had the ambition to transcend the historical conditions

Bernard Tschumi, Concert Hall and Exhibition Centre, Rouen, France, 2001
This cultural complex is located at the gateway to Rouen, close to the National Route 138. The concert hall plays host to various musical and sporting events, and the new exhibition centre accommodates large conventions and trade fairs. The concept involves two envelopes, with a large 'in-between' area which, animated by the various routes to the hall itself, becomes one of the project's key spaces.

Bernard Tschumi, Blue Residential Tower, Manhattan, New York, 2007
This 17-storey residential and commercial tower in the Lower East Side of Manhattan includes 32 apartments.
The strategy was to create a highly specific architectural statement that responds to the eclecticism of the historic
neighbourhood. Its original, pixellated profile is a new presence in the Manhattan urbanscape.

of their time. My interest at that time (as well as today) was to try to contribute to – or potentially alter – the generally accepted definition of what architecture is. Hence issues of movement and event, together with their mode of notation, were first of all an investigation into the nature of architecture.

'Had I engaged in the work today, it is likely that the use of computers would have radically changed the appearance of the work. Would it have changed the content itself? Probably up to a point, yet the questioning would have remained fairly comparable, due to the larger issues at hand. Would the new generations be able to draw from them? I have always been suspicious of the notion of generations. I rather believe in a certain periodicity of themes, returning to haunt us at certain moments of history.'

Tschumi's generation was able to dedicate a great deal of time to further research and careful consideration of

conceptual design. Is this, however, now a justifiable scapegoat for the loss of any conceptual approach to design?

'There have always been periods of conception and periods of consumption. This is due to economic or social forces way beyond the control of architects. I would say that, as opposed to the1970s, the early 21st century is characterised by a faster cycle of production and consumption. This raises conceptual as well as political issues. I hope these will soon be investigated.'

Given Tschumi's association with Deconstruction, I was keen to find out what his understanding of the 'formalistic' is vis-à-vis the current hedonistic attitude affecting architecture now:

'What is "form"? The problem is that both media and dictionaries define it in the most reductive and banalising way: "form as the outline of an object against a background". So does the architectural dictionary of received ideas. I find more pleasure in what I would call "concept-form", bringing a high level of abstraction in orchestrating together a complexity that includes materials, movement and programmes in the definition of architectural form.

Bernard Tschumi, Parc de la Villette, Paris, 1983–98
The aim of this project, which marked the starting point of Tschumi's career as a theorist and designer, was to create a new model for the urban park, in which programme, form and ideology all play integral roles. The image represents, as the architect asserts, the idea that the importance of architecture 'resides in the ability to accelerate society's transformation through a careful agency of spaces and events'.

Bernard Tschumi, Lindner Athletic Center, University of Cincinnati, Ohio, 2006
Representing the epicentre of the university's athletic and academic activities, the unusual curvilinear shape of this building takes advantage of the tight constraints of the site to create dynamic residual spaces between the existing stadium, sports fields and the recreation centre.

'I suppose it is the same distinction as between pornography and eroticism. They are both okay, but one is substantially more complex and more abstract.'
    Spectacle?
    'I also would not completely condemn the production of spectacle. After all, it can also be theorised … '

Context, Place and Theory

Designers cannot avoid including in their work the changes occurring in their everyday lives, whether it is a matter of interpretation or mirroring their own inner thoughts. With this in mind, how can we view the proliferation of architectural fetishes in the urban landscape; that is, the uncontrolled diffusion of architectural objects that are indifferent to the environment they are part of?
    'This indifference is more problematic. Exporting the same "shapes" to Bilbao, Los Angeles or Abu Dhabi may on the one hand raise interesting questions about a new form of architecture, yet on the other signify an impoverishment of architectural thought and invention. I personally like the challenge of different geographical or social contexts as a stimulus to new architectural concepts.'

Given the distractions and difficulties of executing work, do you think it remains important to establish the 'theoretical core' around which architecture is to rely on in the near future? 'Probably not one single synthetic core, but four or five anchor points, around which issues revolve and occasionally intersect: space, programme, body, envelopes, global versus local, economy of means, typology versus topology, concept-form, etc.'

Given this, can the theoretical/conceptual nucleus of a project safeguard architecture from the market?
    'Architecture does not need to be safeguarded: commerce has also been a driving force of progress throughout history. Yet it is commercialism that is problematic – when market forces begin to control every aspect of architectural thinking.'

Bernard Tschumi, New Acropolis Museum, Athens, 2009
The distinctive characteristic of this new museum structure is its relationship with the ancient Acropolis and celebrated monuments which sit on a plateau overlooking the city. The building highlights the individual elements on the site by focusing on the creation of broad and inspired views from the different vantage points within the museum.

Bernard Tschumi, School of Architecture, FIU Miami, Florida, 2003
The Florida International School of Architecture is a place in which social exchange, discussion and debate between students and teachers are key. Its buildings are thus generators of events and interactions. According to Tschumi: 'The project can be described as the sobriety of two wings defining a space activated by the exuberance of three colourful generators. The sober wings are made of precise yet user-friendly precast concrete; the three generators are, respectively, varied yellow ceramic tiles, varied red ceramic tiles and nature.'

Bernard Tschumi, Concert Hall, Limoges, France, 2007
Like the Rouen Concert Hall and Exhibition Centre, the Limoges Concert Hall is based on the idea of a double envelope. The inner envelope, which delineates the perimeter of the performance space, is clad entirely with wood, while the exterior envelope is composed of polycarbonate panels. The concept responds to the dramatic site: a clearing in a large forest at the edge of the city, surrounded by 200-year-old trees.

Tschumi's buildings tend to be vital places open to a range of human activities and exchanges: places committed to the satisfaction of social needs. However, in the third volume from *Event-Cities*,[5] the identification of the 'Concept, Context, Content' triad seems to have removed the role of the user from architecture's original aim. What has caused such a change in the understanding of strategic planning?

'To move from "Space, Event, Movement" to "Concept, Context, Content" is by no means a negation of the first triad. On the contrary, my goal is to expand the earlier issues by inserting the unavoidable complexity that reality entails. To bring context and content to event and movement is a way to confront them with the realities of both culture and production.'

In recent times, words like 'event' and 'space' in Tschumi's work have been replaced by others like 'concept' and 'context'. This seemed to start happening with the project for the New Acropolis Museum. Does this shift in terminology represent a critical reassessment of the work?

'The project for the New Acropolis Museum had a profound effect on my thinking. After we won the competition and for a couple of years, I was not sure what to make of it. It did not fit neatly into the argumentation around my earlier projects. So I would rarely talk about it. And yet I knew the project was important. It took me a while to realise that this project brutally confronted issues that I had been able to sidestep before, such as the issue of context. Rather than a reassessment of the work, it became a means to expand thought about the overall work, a case where practice feeds theory.'

The last consideration, in which Tschumi asserts that it is possible in defined circumstances to arrive at a theory through practice, explains and analyses more thoroughly what he affirmed at the beginning of his studies and reflections on the project: that 'concept, context and content are part of the definition of contemporary urban culture and therefore of architecture. Theory is a practice, a practice of concepts. Practice is a theory, a theory of contexts.'[6] ∆

This interview has been compiled from email correspondence between Michele Costanzo and Bernard Tschumi from April to June 2008.

Translated from the Italian version into English by Paul David Blackmore

Notes
1. *The Manhattan Transcripts*, *Architectural Design* (London), 1981; 2nd edition, Academy Editions (London), 1994.
2. For an overview of the exhibition see http://www.sfmoma.org/exhibitions/exhib_detail.asp?id=42.
3. Jeffrey Kipnis, *Perfect Acts of Architecture*, The Museum of Modern Art (New York) and Wexner Center for the Arts (Columbus), 2001.
4. The six featured series of drawings in the exhibition were as follows: Rem Koolhaas and Elia Zenghelis, *Exodus* or *The Voluntary Prisoners of Architecture*, 1972; Peter Eisenman, *House VI Transformation Collages*, 1976; Bernard Tschumi, *The Manhattan Transcripts*, 1976–81; Daniel Libeskind, *Micromegas*, 1978, and *Chamber Works*, 1983; Thom Mayne (Morphosis Studio), *Sixth Street House*, 1986–87, and *Kate Mantilini Restaurant*, 1986.
5. Bernard Tschumi, *Event-Cities 3*, MIT Press (Cambridge, MA, and London), 2005.
6. *Event-Cities*, op cit, p 3.

Nàbito Arquitectura

Masterplan for the Poljane area of Ljubljana City: The Rainbow Tower, Ljubljana, Slovenia, 2007–

Manuel Gausa

The complexity of contemporary sites and situations requires architects' design skills to exceed the single object and to expertly negotiate between competing forces at both a global and local level. Nowhere is this more apparent than in the city, where a multitude of tensions and scales must be played out. Barcelona-based architect and author **Manuel Gausa** locates in the work of Nàbito Arquitectura the ability to develop 'real connective landscapes', as explicitly expressed in their scheme for the Poljane area of Ljubljana.

One of the most important scenarios of investigation at the beginning of this century is to be found in the unexpected leap in scale of the new multicity and the possible leaping between scales of contemporary design (or, if preferred, an interscalar shift between the city, the site and the architectural object).

In reality, if the current vocation of architectural design is that of functioning as an authentic 'relational/emotional surrounding' or a 'field of forces' between tensions, information, vocations and solicitations – global and local, rather than an aesthetic object – then there are only a few groups such as Barcelona-based Nàbito Arquitectura with the ability to define – with a relaxed and natural talent that is rich with solutions and ideas – a necessarily extroverted condition of contemporary architecture. While this holistic motivation, combined with a significant control of the formal, can be found in most of Nàbito's projects, perhaps their more recent works in Rome (the Meno é più operation) and Slovenia (the urban masterplan and implementation plan for Ljubljana) are those that most clearly express this relational vocation. Such works both conceptually and expressively synthesise and materialise the specificity of the urban context in relation to the city, place in relation to context, building in relation to place, and landscape in relation to building as part of a unique architectural intervention.

This can be seen as much in the use of one resourceful model capable of creating patterns and blueprints for programme and space, building and landscape (for example, the five-leaf geometries of the school and park of the Colle delle Gensole in Rome), as in the explicit materiality of an a-scalar instrument – the uniting arch of the urban spaces designed for Ljubljana (an anti-typological skyscraper planted on its site, renouncing its naturally rigid totemic and vertical condition, bending itself in the search for somewhere else, and uniting linear development with a topological liaison). Such a 'glocal' concept becomes particularly intense, invoking another, fundamental level of interaction between architecture, infrastructure and landscape.

Given these considerations it is worth noting that Nàbito's current work develops and designs, specific to each project, real connective landscapes used to structure geometries and answers, abstract logics and arranged actions, imposed orders and exposed forms and, above all, concept and poetry, sense and sensitivity, pure strategy and formal/plastic pleasure, spatial quality and, most definitely, human quality. Such terms seem to refer to our (un)conscious search for enjoyment, desire, motivation and exchange, and a desire for interaction, as optimistic as it is uninhibited, and as communicative as it is expressive. ⚐

Text and images compiled by Anna Baldini
Translated from the Spanish version into English by Joao Sobral

PROJECT SITE

WATERGATE AND THE CORNER

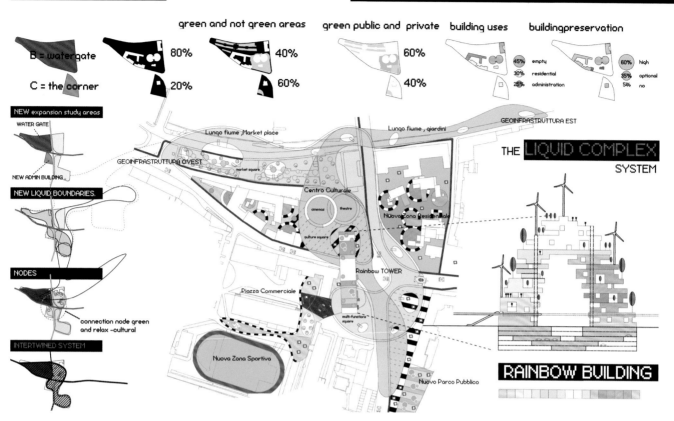

B = watergate

C = the corner

green and not green areas
80%
20%

40%
60%

green public and private
60%
40%

building uses
45% empty
30% residential
25% administration

building preservation
60% high
35% optional
5% no

NEW expansion study areas
WATER GATE
NEW ADMIN BUILDING

NEW LIQUID BOUNDARIES.

NODES
connection node green and relax –cultural

INTERTWINED SYSTEM

THE LIQUID COMPLEX SYSTEM

RAINBOW BUILDING

top: An open and liquid system with fuzzy borders, the aim of Nàbito's masterplan is to host all activities in a compact construction to free up space for public uses. Poljane area of Ljubljana could therefore become an advanced district of services immersed in a large green area.

above and right: Model of the Rainbow Tower and plans for the residential units. The tower deals with both the vertical and horizontal dimensions simultaneously. The numerous activities within it transform it into a container which is both an attractor and a distributor of energy.

Digital Morphogenesis

Taking its inspiration from biology, digital morphogenesis operates through a logic of optimisation. Departing from the notion of architecture primarily as form-finding that privileges appearance, **Neil Leach** describes how morphogenesis places emphasis on 'material performance' and 'processes over representation'.

Monika Bilska and Marta Naganska, Environmental Ornamentation proposal, Hong Kong, 2007
The design of this tower was inspired by a biomimetic study of the Cactaceae family. The plant's self-shading logic was then combined with a camera diaphragm mechanism. This drove the form-finding logic for a double skin, which was populated on the facade through scripting according to an analysis of sun exposure during different times of the day and seasons of the year.

Within contemporary architectural design, a significant shift in emphasis can be detected – a move away from an architecture based on purely visual concerns towards an architecture justified by its performance. Structural, constructional, economic, environmental and other parameters that were once secondary concerns have become primary – are now being embraced as positive inputs within the design process from the outset. Architecture, it would seem, is no longer so preoccupied with style and appearance. It is as though a new paradigm has emerged.

This new paradigm can be understood as an attempt to overcome the scenography of Postmodernism. It aims to locate architectural discourse within a more objective framework where efficient use of resources supersedes the aesthetic indulgences of works that previously came under the broad heading of Postmodernism, which might include not only the somewhat conservative movement noted for its decorative use of applied decorative motifs – as Postmodernism is understood most commonly within architectural culture – but also more progressive movements such as Deconstructivism, all of which privilege appearance over performance.

This development is by no means universal. Many areas of architectural production remain deeply rooted in Postmodern concerns for appearance, and no doubt architectural culture would be poorer if all architects were to subscribe to the same approach. However, it does represent a significant shift not only in the various 'hot spots' of architectural production – cities such as London, New York, Rotterdam and Los Angeles – but also in other cities where the designs of various progressive architects from around the world are now being built. The structural logic that informs the Bird's Nest, Water Cube and CCTV headquarters building in Beijing, no less than the environmental logic that is beginning to inform various developments in Dubai, suggests that this is a global phenomenon.

We might describe this privileging of performance within the design process as an interest in 'morphogenesis'.[1] Used initially in the realm of biological sciences, the term refers to the logic of form generation and pattern-making in an organism through processes of growth and differentiation. More recently it has been appropriated within architectural circles to designate an approach to design that seeks to challenge the hegemony of top-down processes of form-making, and replace it with a bottom-up logic of form-finding.[2] The emphasis is therefore on material performance over appearance, and on processes over representation.

We need to recognise, then, that though there may be an apparent formal similarity between the 'nonstandard'

Kristina Shea, Neil Leach, Spela Videcnik and Jeroen van Mechelen, eifFormStructure, Academie van Bouwkunst, Amsterdam, 2002
The design of this temporary structure was generated using the eifForm program, a stochastic, non-monotonic form of simulated annealing. This was the first 1:1 prototype of a design produced using eifForm and, almost certainly, the first architectural structure built where both the form and related structure were generated by a computer via design parameters and conditions rather than by explicitly described geometry.

forms of architects like Frank Gehry and other, more contemporary architects such as FOA with their increasing interest in the morphogenetic questions of performativity and form-finding, there is an enormous difference in terms of design methodology. For example, Gehry represents a more traditional, 'Postmodern' approach towards design, where the architect is perceived as the genius creator who imposes form on the world in a top-down process, and the primary role of the structural engineer is to make possible the fabrication of the designs of the master architect, as close as possible to his or her initial poetic expression. Meanwhile, the more contemporary architects operating within the new morphogenetic paradigm can be seen more as the controllers of processes, who facilitate the emergence of bottom-up form-finding processes that generate structural formations.

The difference, then, lies in the emphasis on form-finding over form-making, on bottom-up over top-down processes, and on formation rather than form. Indeed the term 'form' should be relegated to a subsidiary position to the term 'formation'. Meanwhile, 'formation' must be recognised as being linked to the terms 'information' and 'performance'. When architecture is 'informed' by performative considerations it becomes less a consideration of form in and of itself, and more a discourse of material formations. In other words, 'form' must be 'informed' by considerations of 'performative' principles to subscribe to a logic of material 'formation'.

However, the logic of morphogenesis in architecture is not limited to questions of design methodology; it also extends into the ethical arena.

If we can find forms that operate more efficiently from a structural point of view, then we can use fewer materials. Equally, if we can devise forms that perform more efficiently in terms of energy consumption, we will consume less energy in heating or cooling our buildings. In either case morphogenetic design will help to preserve the world's resources. As such it can be taken not only as a critique of the scenography of Postmodernism, but also as an ethical argument in terms of the environment.

Material Computation

Biology provides one of the major sources of inspiration for research into morphogenesis in architecture. Nature operates largely through a logic of optimisation, and can therefore offer important lessons for architects. Biomimetics – the study of what we can learn by replicating the mechanisms of nature – has therefore emerged as an important field of research. It is not simply that nature can inspire products such as Velcro or recent fabrics used in the manufacture of swimwear that are based on the hydrodynamic properties of shark's skin; rather, nature itself can teach us important lessons about the efficiency of certain structural organisations. Following on from the early experimentation of Gaudí, Frei Otto has become a champion of observing the behaviour of certain structures in nature, and reapplying their principles through analogue modelling. Thus spiders' webs and soap bubbles can provide deep insights into the behaviour of form-finding lightweight structures.

These observations come under the heading of 'material computation'. They offer us analogue forms of computation, which – despite the apparent crudeness of the modelling process – are actually highly sophisticated means of understanding structural performance. To describe them as a form of computation is not to undermine the role of digital computation; rather it is to recognise that computation is everywhere in nature. 'Computation' – a term derived from the Latin 'computare' (to 'think together') – refers to any system where individual components are working together. But it is equally important to recognise that digital computation has its limitations. It necessarily involves the reduction of the world to a limited set of data that can be simulated digitally, but it can never replicate the complexity of a system such as a soap bubble whose internal structural computation involves an intricate balance between highly complex surface material organisations and differential atmospheric pressures.

A number of contemporary architects have re-examined the works of Gaudí and Otto, and found in them sources of inspiration for the new morphogenetic generation of form-finding research, often coupling the lessons of their analogue experimentation with more contemporary digital techniques. Mark Goulthorpe of dECOi Architects describes his work as a form of 'post-Gaudían praxis', while Mark Burry, as architectural consultant for the completion of Gaudí's Sagrada Família church in Barcelona, has been exploring digital techniques for understanding the logic of Gaudí's own highly sophisticated understanding of natural forces. Meanwhile, Lars Spuybroek of NOX has performed a number of analogue experimentations inspired by the work of Frei Otto as a point of departure for some innovative design work, which also depends on more recent software developments within the digital realm.[3]

This work points towards a new 'performative turn' in architecture, a renewed interest in the principles of structural performance, and in collaborating more empathetically with certain progressive structural engineers. However, this concern for performance may extend beyond structural engineering to embrace other constructional discourses, such as environmental, economic, landscaping or indeed programmatic concerns. In short, what it amounts to is a 'folding' of architecture into the other disciplines that define the building industry.[4]

Digital Computation

Not surprisingly in an age dominated by the computer, this interest in material computation has been matched by an interest in digital computation. Increasingly the performative turn that we have witnessed within architectural design culture is being explored through new digital techniques. These extend from the manipulation and use of form-generating programs from L-Systems to cellular automata, genetic algorithms and multi-agent systems that have been used by progressive designers to breed a new generation of forms, to the use of the computer to understand, test out and evaluate already designed structures.

The seemingly paradoxical use of the immaterial domain of the computer to understand the material properties of architecture has spawned a new term in architecture: 'digital tectonics'. In other words, the old opposition between the highly material world of the tectonic and the immaterial world of the digital has broken down. What we have instead is a new tectonics of the digital or 'digital tectonics'.[5]

A certain genealogy can be detected in the use of the computer in architecture. What distinguishes this new digital paradigm from early uses of the computer in the architectural arena is that it reinterprets the computer not simply as a sophisticated drafting tool – an extension, in other words, of the possibilities of the previous paradigm of ink on tracing paper – but also as a device that might become part of the design process itself. With this we see a development in the very nature of the architect from the demiurgic 'form-giver' to the architect as the controller of generative processes, where the final appearance is a product not of the architect's imagination alone, but of the generative capacities of computer programs. It is not that the architect here is any less imaginative; rather, the architectural imagination has been displaced into a different arena – into the imaginative use of various processes.[6]

But even within the logic of digital tectonics there is a certain genealogy of development. Computational methodology had first been

IwamotoScott Architecture, Voussoir Cloud installation,
SCI-Arc, Los Angeles, August 2008
Voussoir Cloud explores the structural paradigm of pure compression coupled with
an ultra-light material system. The overall design draws from the work of
engineer/architects such as Frei Otto and Gaudí who used hanging chain models to
find efficient form. The hanging chain model was here coupled with vaulted surface
form-finding to create a light, porous surface made of compressive elements.

used as a means of testing and thereby verifying and
supporting the initial designs of the architect. The
objective here was simply to use the computer to make
the designs of the architect realisable. The only
significant contribution to the design process occurred
when findings of this process influenced the original
design and forced minor amendments to it. Examples
here would include the use of software to test out the
acoustic performance of the Greater London Authority
building by Foster + Partners.[7] Occasionally, also, a more
precise structural definition of a loosely formulated
architectural concept could be made by the computer, for
example the use of algorithms to define the form of the
glass canopy to the British Library on the part of Chris
Williams, and the 'dynamic relaxation technique' to
define the precise vectorial layout of the mullion system.[8]

A second generation of computational methodology,
however, can be detected in the work of Kristina Shea,
whose eifForm program serves to generate structural
forms in a stochastic, non-monotonic method using a
process of structural shape annealing.[9] The 'designer'
merely establishes certain defining coordinates, and
then unleashes the program, which eventually
'crystallises' and resolves itself into a certain
configuration. Each configuration is a structural form
that will support itself against gravity and other
prescribed loadings, and yet each is different. Such is
the logic of a bottom-up, stochastic method.

It is programs such as this that reveal the true potential of the
digital realm in influencing the process of design itself, by opening up
fields of possibilities. The computer, then, emerges not only as a
prosthetic device that extends the range of the architectural
imagination, but also – much like a calculator – as a tool of
optimisation that offers a more rigorous means of searching out
possible options than what could be described as the pseudo-
computational logic that often dominates contemporary practice.

New Theoretical Paradigms
This interest in digital production has also prompted a broad shift in
theoretical concerns. If the 1980s and 1990s were characterised by
an interest in literary theory and continental philosophy – from the
Structuralist logic that informed the early Postmodernist quest for
semiological concerns in writers from Charles Jencks to Robert Venturi,
to the post-Structuralist enquiries into meaning in the work of Jacques
Derrida that informed the work of Peter Eisenman and others – the first
decade of the 21st century can be characterised by an increasing
interest in scientific discourses. It is as though the dominant logic of
today has become one of technology and material behaviour.

This is not to endorse the position of architectural theorist Michael
Speaks who claims that we have witnessed the 'death of theory'.[10] For

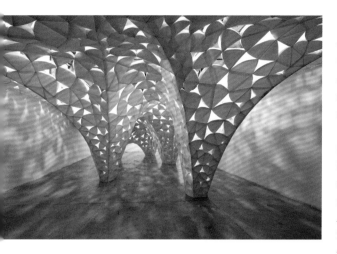

such a theory, it could be argued, is merely an anti-theory theory in that there is surely no position that stands outside theory. Any form of practice must be informed by a theoretical impulse, even if it is a positivistic one that purportedly disdains theory. Rather, what we are witnessing is the ascendancy of a new branch of theory, one that engages with science, technology and material behaviour.

As such, one can detect a waning of interest in literary theories and literary-based philosophies, and an increase in interest in scientific thinking and in philosophies informed by scientific thinking and an understanding of material processes. So it is that just as the work of Jacques Derrida is fading in popularity, that of Gilles Deleuze is becoming increasingly popular. Indeed it has been through the work of secondary commentators on Deleuze, such as Manuel DeLanda, that the relevance of Deleuze's material philosophies has been championed within architectural circles.[11]

DeLanda has coined a new term for this emerging theoretical paradigm: 'New Materialism'. This should be distinguished from Marx's 'Dialectical Materialism' in that the model is extended beyond mere economic considerations to embrace the whole of culture, and yet the principle behind Marx's thinking – what we see on the surface is the product of deeper underlying forces – remains the same. Here we might understand cultural production not in symbolic terms, but in terms of material expressions. It is not a question of what a cultural object might 'symbolise' – the dominant concern in the Postmodernist quest for interpretation and meaning – but rather what it 'expresses'. The concern, then, is to understand culture in terms of material processes – in terms of the actual 'architecture' of culture itself. Within this new configuration the economist, the scientist and the engineer are among the reassessed heroes of our intellectual horizon, and figures such as Cecil Balmond have become the new 'material philosophers' – to use another term adopted by DeLanda – of New Materialism.

To some extent this can be read as a highly positive development within architectural circles in that the domains of science and technology, for so long neglected at the expense of history and theory and treated as largely positivistic domains, have now been reappropriated and recognised as offering a highly relevant and rich domain of intellectual enquiry.

But it is not just materialist philosophies that have seized the imagination of architectural theorists. So, too, has scientific thinking itself begun to find its place in the architectural curriculum, from the early observations of D'Arcy Thompson on growth and form to more recent theories – such as 'emergence', popularised by Steven Johnson, and Stephen Wolfram's discourse of 'A New Kind of Science', both of which deal with complexity emerging from a simple set of initial rules.[12]

If we add to these the developing interest in computational methodology – the possibility of scripting, parametric modelling and performance-based generative techniques such as multi-agent systems or genetic algorithms – we can begin to define a broad shift that has already appeared in certain progressive schools of architecture and that is beginning to spread into mainstream architectural culture. ⚙

Notes
1. Morphogenesis is derived from the Greek terms 'morphe' (shape/form) and 'genesis' (creation).
2. See Michael Hensel, Achim Menges and Michael Weinstock's issues of *AD: Emergence: Morphogenetic Design Strategies* (July/August 2004) and *Techniques and Technologies in Morphogenetic Design* (March/April 2006).
3. See Mark Burry, 'Virtually Gaudí'; Mark Goulthorpe, 'Gaudí's hanging presence'; Lars Spuybroek, 'Softoffice', all in Neil Leach, David Turnbull and Chris Williams (eds), *Digital Tectonics*, John Wiley & Sons (London), 2004.
4. As Alejandro Zaera-Polo and Farshid Moussavi comment, their interest is to recognise the other disciplines in the building industry not simply as offering a service that should be treated as an afterthought in the design process, but rather as an important range of design considerations that should be embraced and incorporated into the early stages of the design process itself. Farshid Moussavi and Alejandro Zaera Polo (Foreign Office Architects), 'Rollercoaster construction', in Neil Leach (ed), *Designing for a Digital World*, John Wiley & Sons (London), 2002, pp 80–7.
5. See 'Introduction', in *Digital Tectonics*, op cit, pp 4–12.
6. See Manuel DeLanda, 'Deleuze and the use of the genetic algorithm in architecture', in *Designing for a Digital World*, op cit, pp 117–20.
7. See Michael Weinstock and Nikolaos Stathopoulos, 'Advanced simulation in design' in *AD Techniques and Technologies in Morphogenetic Design*, op cit, p 56.
8. See Chris Williams, 'Design by algorithm', in *Digital Tectonics*, op cit, pp 78–85.
9. See Kristina Shea, 'Creating Synthesis Partners', in *AD Contemporary Techniques in Architecture*, No 72, March 2002, pp 42–5.
10. Michael Speaks, 'No Hope, No Fear', *ARQ*, 6/3, pp 209–12.
11. See Manuel DeLanda, *War in the Age of Intelligent Machines*, Zone Books (New York), 1992; *A Thousand Years of Nonlinear History*, Zone Books/Swerve Editions (New York), 1997; and *Intensive Science and Virtual Philosophy*, Continuum (New York and London), 2002.
12. D'Arcy Wentworth Thompson, *On Growth and Form*, Dover Publications (New York), 1992; Steven Johnson, *Emergence: The Connected Lives of Ants, Brains, Cities and Software*, Penguin (London), 2001; Stephen Wolfram, *A New Kind of Science*, Wolfram Media (London), 2002. On emergence, see also Eric Bonabeau, Marco Dorigo and Guy Theraulaz, *Swarm Intelligence: From Natural to Artificial Systems*, Oxford University Press (New York and Oxford), 1999; and John Holland, *Emergence: From Chaos to Order*, Oxford University Press (Oxford), 1998. ⚙

Atelier Kempe Thill

23 Town Houses, Osdorp, Amsterdam, 2008

Hans Ibelings, Editor of *A10 – new European architecture*, locates the future of architecture in a Dutch practice, Atelier Kempe Thill, who embrace pragmatism with their elegant solutions. Rather than resisting modern building practices, they accept their logical consequences as exemplified by the glass terminations of the tunnel formwork in their Osdorp row houses.

Hans Ibelings

The work of Rotterdam architectural firm Atelier Kempe Thill is becoming an *oeuvre* of considerable proportions. In the first half of 2008 alone, four new works were completed. Bit by bit, it is becoming ever clearer why the architecture of founders André Kempe and Oliver Thill creates such a powerful impression: they consistently accept the logical consequences of modern building practices. A leads to B leads to C and so on. In other words, they take an axiom from current building practices and apply it as fully, consistently and logically as possible – like mathematicians.

The most obvious example of their approach is the way in which they deal with tunnel formwork, the dominant method of concrete construction in Dutch housing. The construction of a housing project in the Netherlands almost always starts with this method. The row of houses designed by Kempe Thill in Osdorp is exactly that: a repetition of tunnels whereby the front and back ends of each dwelling consist simply of glass. Instead of ending in thick facades – built of outer sheeting, insulation material, a cavity and inner sheeting, all composed of

various materials – theirs are the simplest possible termination of the concrete tunnels.

The direct approach adopted by Atelier Kempe Thill in searching for the most logical and consistent answer to the question being posed is evident in all of their buildings. Their architecture is not cluttered with aesthetic conventions or stylistic niceties, in the same way that the Helvetica font remains far removed from all typographical mannerisms and styles and makes its own simple statement: a font with an unmistakable aesthetic elegance, but at the same time the most neutral letter possible. The architecture of Atelier Kempe Thill is the architectural equivalent of the Helvetica font. They succeed in creating buildings whose beauty is based on the elegant way in which they make it crystal clear that their design, and no other, is the most logical and simple solution possible. ∆

Text and images compiled by Anna Baldini

Captions translated from the Italian version into English by Paul David Blackmore

top: View of the main facade. With respect to traditional row houses, the dwellings designed by Atelier Kempe Thill are less introverted and more open to a relationship with urban space.

above: The walls are built using industrially produced materials that enclose the tunnel structure in the simplest manner.

left: The houses are characterised by a Modernist design and the use of large glazed surfaces.

Meeting
After

Exit

the New Boss
the Death of Theory

Christopher Hight, Control Spaces: Exit, George Bush Intercontinental Aiport, Houston, Texas, 2006
Photograph from an ongoing series documenting the spaces being constructed by the biopolitical formations within the contemporary built environment. Engaging such territories as sites for design research requires theory, since they are undefined within our existing repertoire of concepts or, at best, are seen as negatives of known models (for example, SUB-urb). In understanding these super-modern conditions as positivities rather than bad copies of now historical formations, the traditional roles of theory and 'material' knowledge switch roles, with the former being pragmatic and the latter speculative.

Christopher Hight seeks to find out what might be left over after the death of theory. Have theoretical questions become merely replaced by reproducible techniques and business plans? How should architects think and practise if they no longer – in the wake of Koolhaas – solely think architecturally?

The death of theory should be treated as history. The anthologies are already being compiled, preparing the ground for the exhumation by future doctoral students.[1] We – and let us be clear that the matter is laughably Ameri-Eurocentric – can consider the death certificate to have been signed in the last issue of *Assemblage* in April 2000. That document made official what had been known for a while; we had all seen the corpse, like one of Warhol's suicides exquisitely smashed into a car bonnet. The vehicle, of course, was a GMC (Global Management Capital) SUV. Black with tinted windows.

Instead of the typical format of long essays and a few projects, this last issue was filled with more than three-dozen one-page statements – eyewitness reports from an inquest into the death. The exception was an appended essay by the court's appointed coroner, RE Somol: a longer piece in a smaller font (which in *Assemblage* graphic semiotics meant 'serious'). Somol began by playing the naughty boy, declaring that he had read only 12 of the articles from the entire run of *Assemblage*, half of those by himself and his compadres. He then proceeded to describe the injuries and probable cause of death. If critical theory was once surprising, disruptive and experimental – a way to 'develop interests' – it had become all too 'academic' in the worst sense: ubiquitous, predictable, normative, even moralising. Yet the 'murder-suicide' of *Assemblage* and its cousin from the Big Apple, *ANY*, did not mark their obsolescence, but the establishment of the 'critical … as the almost exclusive idiom for the disciplinary identity of architecture'. Like 'Elvis', critical theory may have left the building, but living off 'now dominant cultural institutions … the impersonators will be as effective'.[2] Enjoy the wake, Somol concluded, and bring some uninvited guests.

Architects were, as usual, last to arrive at the party. The 'death of theory' was a transdisciplinary phenomenon. For example, 'Post-Theory' emerged most obviously in film studies, where it was argued that overused theoretical armatures need to be displaced by empiricism and the now dated 'cognitivism' (the quantitative analysis of the way the eye and mind process information). But Post-Theory is not a coherent movement beyond a shared rejection of Big Theory, whatever the flavour: psychoanalytic, post-Structural, post-colonial, Postmodern or critical. The last, at least in architecture, often stands for any of the other forms of theory.

Although architects arrived late, we have lingered into the evening. Michael Speaks, who implicated himself as a 'person of interest' in that last *Assemblage*, has continued to declare through a series of archly sound-bite-sized articles that theory is obsolete in the global marketplace. His brand of Post-Theory resonates with Fukyama's *post-historie*. Somol and Sarah Whiting have manifestoed to manifest 'projective practices' that would replace the critical practices of the 1980s and 1990s.[3] In the cakewalk shuffle of Ivy League deanships, Stan Allen has shifted Princeton into the 'material practice' mode he witnessed in the last *Assemblage*, while under Mark Wigley Columbia has become a haunt of critical theory. There, Reinhold Martin, the co-editor of *Assemblage*'s heir-apparent (*Grey Room*), has dismissed the entire Post-Theory movement. Martin argues explicitly against Somol in a classical rhetorical reversal that we cannot be post-critical because architecture never became critical, that the challenges presented by critical theory or post-Structuralism were never really engaged. Architects appropriated their slogans while neglecting their implications. For Martin, the Post-Theorists are smug 'yuppies reading Deleuze'.[4]

While it is surely true that the critical was erected as the straw man, largely to sublimate oedipal anxieties towards Peter *Familias* Eisenman,[5] too often it seems like theory is defended by treating designers as punchbags. This, hyperironically, lends credence to Somol's caricature of the critical as a cynical don policing the halls rather than seeking to develop interests.

There is a farcically Tafurian echo in this back and forth, especially for those who claim to have rejected him, such as Somol and Michael Speaks, whose dialectical cartographies of contemporary architectural thought seem indebted to Modernist and Tafurian logics.[6] Interestingly, neither camp ever invokes empirical evidence or systemic analysis (much as I am restricted from here). In that respect, they conform to the form of polemical debate throughout Modern architecture's history. Every 'yuppie reading Deleuze' dances with a post-Marxist wearing Prada.

Therefore, as night becomes dawn we have become a bit hungover on the cheap stuff. Amid the stupor, the question posed to me by the guest-editor of this issue, Luigi Prestinenza Puglisi, and which might be asked of the generation drinking the leftovers, is: What do we do in the morning, after the death of theory?

This question is strikingly similar to that posed by that Martin Heidegger almost half a century ago in his article 'The End of

Philosophy and the Task of Thinking', when he claimed the historical problem of philosophy had ended. The question this begged was: 'What task is reserved for thinking at the end of philosophy?'[7] Today we are being asked: What is left over for us after the end of the Big Theory, which replaced philosophy no small thanks to Uncle Martin.

'End' here intones not just 'over', but also something accomplished and, moreover, in the sense of a shift in teleology. For Heidegger, the social-psychological and biological sciences (which Foucault argued precipitated the modern human subject) had largely supplanted the historical function of metaphysics because they had diffused its problems into what Heidegger called 'cybernetics'.[8] That is to say, problems of knowledge such as had existed since Kant had become technical difficulties of information transmission and feedback. The arts became 'instruments of information'.[9] Heidegger was not the only one to have suggested that a dramatic shift had occurred. George Canguilheim also argued that with the discovery of DNA an informational model of life has replaced previous models. The problem of life became a problem of knowledge, which became a problem of information transmission and productive errors (mutations).

Today, Post-Theory in architecture or film claims that the job of theory has been replaced by a further wave of cybernetic sciences, from management studies to biotechnology, to empirical cognitive sciences, or literally cybernetic informational infrastructures that suggest a fundamental realignment or even diffusions of boundaries between subject and object, and of knowledge itself. For Somol and Speaks, what were once autonomous theoretical questions have become reproducible techniques and business plans for a world in which design has become a ubiquitous agent for the fashioning of lifestyles. With this comes anxiety that the historical problems of architecture as a discipline have more or less ended, or its 'ends' displaced by other fields. This is a logical step after critical theory rendered the traditional concerns of the discipline and authorship rather problematic. For example, in a opening Post-Theory skirmish, Peter Eisenman (Daddy Critical) once recounted a 'desk crit' he offered Rem Koolhaas (Prodigal-Son Projective) during his days at 'The Institute':

Peter: Rem, you know what your problem is? You just don't think like an architect. You think like a filmmaker or journalist.

Rem: Yes, Peter, and that is why I will be the greatest architect in the world!

Whether the story, or my memory of it, is true,[10] it nevertheless highlights what underlay the 'end of theory' phenomena: it is an ethical problem, not in the common sense of moralism, but of how one constitutes oneself as an architect, of acting architecturally, of the possibility of doing so today, of whether the ways in which we have done so – including institutions and familial lines of descent – are somehow inadequate so that the 'world's greatest architect' is so because he does not think architecturally. As with Heidegger's questions, today's global economic transformation, the environmental pressures of a realised technological world, as well as intellectual developments, all suggest the need for transformation at the level of disciplinarity.

Heidegger's answer (or at least the blunt version I am going to use here) was to shift from the 'representational' thinking about meaning that dominated the philosophical tradition, to that which had been obscured by this traditional emphasis; and paramount among these, a shift from questions about the subject to questions of the conditions of his or her thought. If philosophy had become history, it could be treated as such so that what it avoided could now be engaged.

Similarly, Post-Theory/post-critical thought seems to really be an attempt to shift from a reliance on the meaning of objects constructed by practice, to the problems of constructing a practice – of being an architect. This is clearest in Stan Allen's claim that architecture becomes rather 'inert' and boring when understood as what the critical Mark Wigley called a 'built discourse' because this ignores the 'specificity' of architecture.[11] As an alternative, Allen asked of theory what Robin Evans once asked of history: an account of architecture focusing on specific conventions and transformations in architects' manners of working rather than representation or signification.[12] Of course, Evans claimed that a great deal of such a history would be focused on the drawing and other tools of representation within architecture, just as the diagram plays a central role for Allen not as a place for storing ideas from elsewhere, but as a way of (re)producing architectural ones.

For what it is worth, as architects have bickered, landscape architects have leveraged exactly this ethical problem by theorising a shift from the dominance of the scenographic to socioecological processes. The latter, of course, have always been integral to the tradition of the pictorial in landscape, but remained 'un-thought' as concepts because they were seen as technical manners of working. James Corner's work – before and with Stan Allen for a time – combined theories of mapping with mechanical and digital technologies of reproduction in order to transform the sorts of question that could be asked through landscape design to give it renewed agency. In parallel, Charles Waldheim argued that this suggested a disciplinary reconfiguration in which landscape takes the place of architecture and urbanism as the way to think and intervene within the post-Fordist environment exactly because this landscape urbanism was able to engage what remained un-thought by the architectural, urban or planning disciplines.

Christopher Hight, Control Spaces: Extopia 3, Unknown flyover state, 2007
This city, set in the middle of the American desert, could be the locale for a series of novels that JG Ballard never wrote.
At its entrance might be a sign: Welcome to the Reale of the Desert. The abstract grid overlays the terrain without regard
to topography, echoing the rationalist Jeffersonian dream of settlement, while the crossroads of meandering paths recall
romantic nomadic vectors. What as-yet-unknown music will the devil provide for us at this intersection?

None of this is antagonistic to Reinhold Martin's suggestion that actor-network theory developed in part by Bruno Latour to understand scientific practices (as opposed to theoretical method) might be adapted to understand those of architects.[13] Following Latour, however, the doctrines of critical theory will not help because they rely on modern-esque dialectics such as nature/culture and subject/object. While a useful distinction in Kantian critiques, Latour argues, they have become reified by subsequent waves of critical thought leaving un-thought the simultaneous and unprecedented promiscuous mixings of natures/cultures and cyborg assemblages that now dominate our world, but which we have scarcely begun to understand.[14] We do not even have the proper language for them, relying instead on colliding the terms of, as it turned out, not-so-modern thinking.

Similarly, the modern discipline of architecture, as well as urbanism and landscape for that matter, was formalised through educational and professional institutions and regulatory bodies calibrated to the now historical conditions of the 19th-century European and American metropolis, industrialisation and post-Kantian epistemological and aesthetic contexts. The post-Second World War built environment and the rise of biopolitical economic power may seem to make that matrix history, but it was born out of its dynamics, and much of our thought and work clings to the debris. We need to explore how current conditions present opportunities not just to innovate the objects of practice, but to open territorialities and reconfigurations of practice immanent yet latent to modern – and critical – dialectical structures.

All these are theoretical issues that cannot be so much appropriated by design as developable through close entanglements with it because the conditions of acting 'architecturally' are in question. Interestingly, the design fields seem uniquely able to provide figurations of the mixtures that surround us and are thus made accessible as intellectual and political objects exactly because design practices and their instruments constantly integrate conflicting information with simultaneously analytic and synthetic modes. When Bruno Latour attended one of my studio's reviews at Rice last year, in which we were mapping and designing for the biopolitical territories along the Gulf coast, his response to the work was that architects seem better able to articulate through design the problems and opportunities of our present than can so-called theorists.[15] Yet within the design fields, theory is eminently pragmatic to the question of constituting, or reconstituting, practices that seek to operate across the conventional boundaries of the design disciplines, treating what Sloterdijk calls technological, natural and cultural entanglements as a site of design research.

Moreover, one might turn attention to the historicity of the instruments and institutions of the discipline as constituted in modernity. We need to provide accounts of the history of our discipline that no longer rehearse the same dialectics, but take account of their role in architectural discourse and design's conditions of possibility. Rather than declare or dismiss a great break with the past, we continue to need something like what Foucault called a history for our present in order to find the hybridity and complexity already immanent to our practices and which might be mobilised. To actually develop such accounts would displace the increasingly cumbersome oedipalisations that result from naturalising their construction as our inheritance. Perhaps this remains a critique, but not in the sense of treating architecture as a fixed and remote territory that requires representation, and instead as what in Heidegger's wake Irigaray called an 'interval' of transformation.

The question before us is therefore not so much what remains – one expects, literally, the leftovers – so much as what has opened the possibility for thought in architecture, an architecturally specific mode of theorisation, one that is not so much distanced from design as anamorphic to it.[16] As we cease conflating the discipline with articles a few score Anglo-Europeans apparently do not even read, the 'death of theory' appears a domestic dispute: a tempest in a teacup stuck in a melting ice sheet. ⚿

Notes
1. Most notably William Saunders (ed), *The New Architectural Pragmatism*, University of Minnesota Press (Minneapolis), 2007, which gathers essays on the topic mostly from *Harvard Design Magazine*.
2. RE Somol, 'In The Wake of Assemblage', *Assemblage*, No 41, April 2000, p 92.
3. RE Somol and Sarah Whiting, 'Notes around the Doppler Effect and other moods of Modernism', *The New Architectural Pragmatism*, op cit, pp 22–33. First published in *Perspecta*, No 33, 2002, pp 72–7.
4. A phrase he takes from Slavoj Zizek. Reinhold Martin, 'On theory: Critical of what?', *The New Architectural Pragmatism*, op cit, p 154. First published in *Harvard Design Magazine*, No 22, Spring/Summer 2005, pp 1–5.
5. As George Baird detailed in '"Criticality" and its discontents', in *The New Architectural Pragmatism*, op cit, pp 136–49. First published in *Harvard Design Magazine*, No 21, Fall 2004/Winter 2005.
6. As I argued in Christopher Hight, 'Preface to the multitude', *AKAD 01: Beginnings*, AXL Books (Stockholm), 2004.
7. Martin Heidegger, 'The end of philosophy and the task of thinking', *On Time and Being*, University of Chicago Press (Chicago, IL), 2002 [1972], p 55. First published in *Zur Sache des Denkens*, Max Niemeijer (Tübingen), 1969.
8. Ibid, p 58.
9. Ibid.
10. Peter Eisenman, Lecture at Rice University School of Architecture, Houston, Texas, late 1994 or 1995.
11. Stan Allen, *Assemblage*, No 41, April 2000, p 8.
12. Robin Evans, 'Translations from drawing to building', *Translations from Drawing to Building and other Essays*, AA Publications (London) 1997, pp 153–94.
13. Martin, op cit, p 154.
14. Bruno Latour, *We have Never Been Modern*, Harvard University Press (Cambridge, MA). 1993, p 154.
15. Paraphrased from Latour's comments during a review of a studio taught by myself and Michael Robinson at the Rice School of Architecture, spring 2007. Latour recounted this experience in an interview in *New Geographies*, Issue 0, 2008.
16. Somol and Whiting use a similar metaphor of the Doppler effect to contrast with the distancing effect of critical theory, but I favour 'anamorphic' as it requires a bit less metaphorical work.

Josep Lluís Mateo/MAP Architects

Camp Nou Stadium, Barcelona, 2007

By focusing on a 'scientific approach' that emphasises the importance of cause and effect, Josep Lluís Mateo/MAP has developed a design for the Camp Nou Stadium in Barcelona that is less about spectacle and more about the people it accommodates. Croatian critic and architect **Krunoslav Ivanisin** admires the structure for the 'inherent logic of its parts', but also for its prioritisation of communal life.

Krunoslav Ivanisin

MAP's proposal for the new Camp Nou football stadium (home to Barcelona Football Club) works well as a sound critique of the current 'creationist' approach to understanding architecture-related problems. Shunning the now popular practice of creating iconic buildings, it was instead developed following a logical chain of causes and effects. First, it addresses the singularities of the given situation: a dense asymmetrical setting from the outside, and an asymmetrical structure and its particular tectonic aspects from the inside. Second, it apprehends, in architectural terms, what a stadium is actually about – about structure, about flow of people, about the transparency of its roof, about specific aspects of its programmatic arrangements. It is not only about the spectacle in its centre and the representation of this spectacle on its envelope. The project thus focuses on the 'bones' and not the 'skin'.

Respecting and reacting to these singularities, the communal aspects of the stadium are emphasised and numerous relationships between its parts established. The existing stadium is approached archaeologically, as if a precious ruin, with new structures built on to, around and within it. A series of 'scientific' projections and decisions resulted in a sequence of spaces in between, thus the surrounding area is consolidated, and the interior layering exposed.

'Scientific' here does not mean utilitarian or restricted to any sober engineering logic. Quite to the contrary, the logical distinctions between the different programmatic parts of the new stadium are not blurred in order to create a homogenous appearance in a situation where no homogeneity exists. In other words, the materiality of architecture has not been denied here, as is the case in many contemporary 'creations'. In fact, this is a *project*, and not a *creation*, and it requires little explanation. Complex, but not complicated, it is self-explanatory through the inherent logic of its parts and the relationships they establish. By stressing the exceptions to the rules followed, some of the archaic qualities of a stadium, not an arena, are here reinstated. It is a public monument bound to its setting, and is thus capable of integrating communal life both in and around it. ◬

Text and images compiled by Anna Baldini

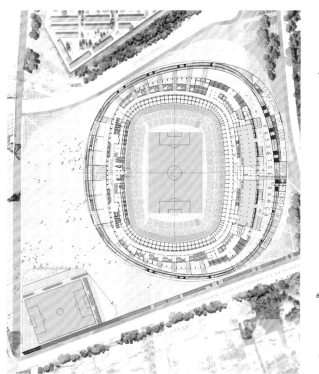

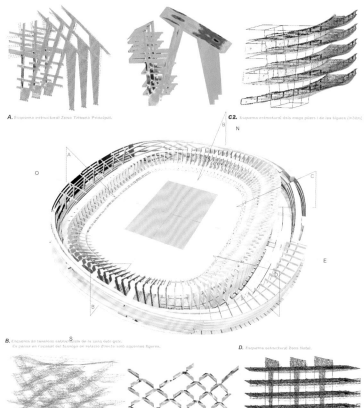

A. Esquema estructural Zona Tribuna Principal.

C2. Esquema estructural dels mega pilars / de les figures (h30m)

B. Esquema de tensions estructurals de la zona dels gols.
Es pensa en l'acabat del formigó en relació directa amb aquestes figures.

D. Esquema estructural Zona Hotel.

top left: Site plan.

top right: Structural schemes.

above: The large entrance concourse organises both general admissions and more monumental entrances.

left: The new roof follows the slant of the old stadium.

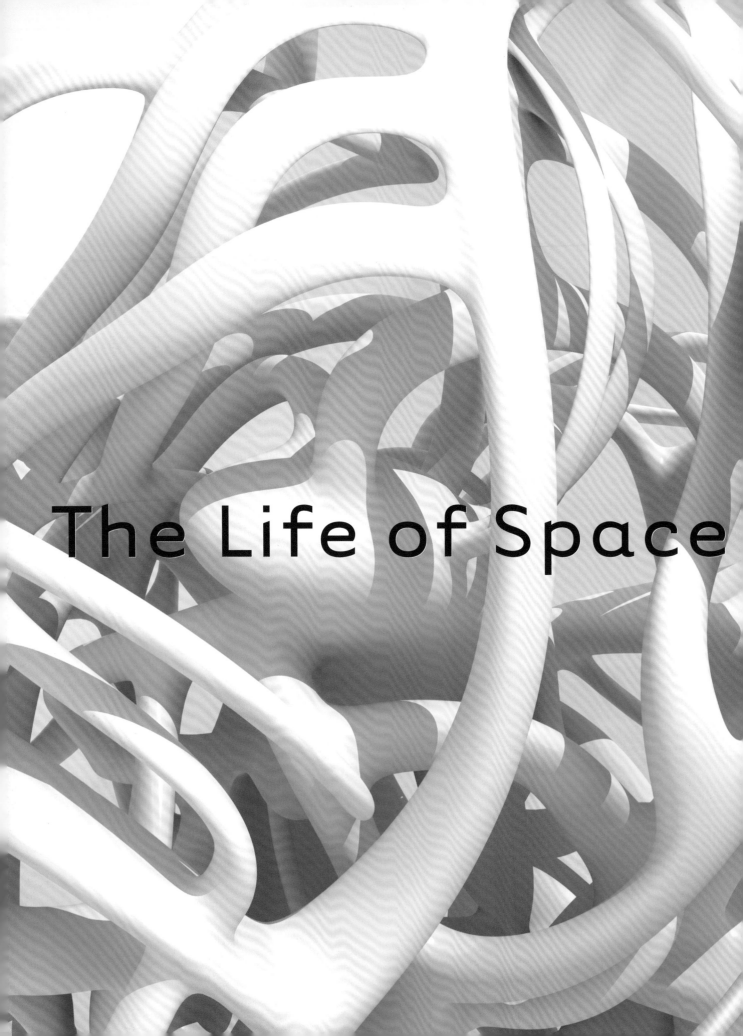

The Life of Space

The digital has revolutionised the notion of space that was formulated on the two-dimensional page in the Renaissance with the discovery of perspective and the printing press. **Derrick de Kerckhove** and **Antonio Tursi** explore how our ideas about space have been overturned since the onset of the computer and the many different ways that architects are reinterpreting them.

How can we change our idea of space and what are architects doing to interpret this profound departure? How do we inhabit post-perspectival space and what are its defining characteristics? What, in fact, constitute the spaces of contemporary dwelling? To ask and attempt to answer these questions requires observation and interpretation of the role and function of communication technologies. Just as printing was tied to the world of perspectival space, so today computer networks continually immerse us in the world of cyberspace. What is more, cyberspace has erupted into the very spaces of our everyday lives. So pervasive is the nature of digital media and networks that architecture cannot afford to remain indifferent to it.

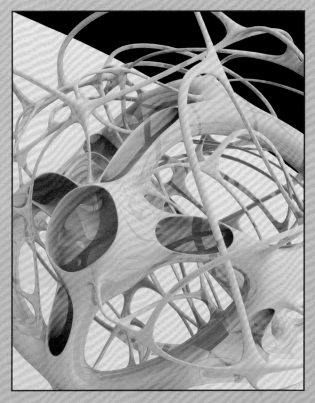

Marcos Novak, Turbulent Topologies, Istanbul, 2008
Organic forms from a recent installation by American artist, trans-architect and theorist Marcos Novak created by modelling regions of mathematical inequalities within perturbed fields. Among other things, this is an exploration of how objectively generated 'quanta' (algorithmic processes, specific quantities) can be made to yield subjectively significant 'qualia' (humanly meaningful qualities).

The World in Perspective

The humanist Renaissance witnessed the imposition of a mediascape composed of the printed word, the theatre and perspectival art. Together, they created an environment characterised by the predominance of vision and linearity; together, they led us to accept the succession of time and a homogenous, uniform space defined by the temporal relation between foreground and background.

However, to understand time as composed of aligned, regular elements and space as a void and neutral container required a process of significant abstraction of the bodily experience. Not the body in terms of the totality of its senses, but that part of it that defines what it sees – the eye – has determined the experience of modern man. Perspective represented an immediate demonstration of the working of this process of abstraction, based as it was on the complete mathematisation of space. In this way, it established an indisputable 'symbolic form'.[1]

This abstraction imposed on the spectator a fixed and predetermined role, placing him or her outside the spectacle. Perspectival space completes the 'epistemological-geometric-mathematical *Raumgestaltung* (space configuration) that pre-establishes and anticipates, and thus renders apparent the movement of those who inhabit works of architecture. In the temple, the theatre, the *polis*, the church, the castle and the fortified city, inhabitants do not actually move because their movements have already been established beforehand, and once and for all, by the architectural structure and configuration of space.'[2]

The neutralisation of space dominated the modern era, reaching its apotheosis in the 20th century, something clearly demonstrated by the work of Le Corbusier: the aseptic qualities of his buildings pursued the objective of predetermining the lifestyles of their inhabitants.

Electrical Con-tacts

At the end of the 19th century, and above all during the 20th, this environment of services and dis-services was modified by the advent of communication technologies, initially electric and, later, electronic. They have invaded and permeated global space and gradually, over time, helped us to develop an understanding of space and an experiential practice, both of which are richer and more involving than anything that has gone before. Space is no longer an empty and neutral container that can be described on a flat surface using the arithmetic–geometric relations of perspective. Rather, it is continuously generated and regenerated by the networks that structure it, by the conflicts that vivify it, by the living beings that inhabit it.

This new definition of space is naturally tied to the development of 20th-century physics and its notion of the 'field': space becomes a field of forces and counterforces, a field that emerges from the actions taking place within it.

The electronic media, as mentioned, play a fundamental role in raising our awareness of the global, interconnected space in which we are constantly immersed, and from which we cannot separate ourselves. We no longer observe nature as if through a window (*item perspectiva*); now we ourselves are immersed in a new, artificial landscape. And this immersion encompasses every one of our senses, not just the eye: we enter into con-tact (both digitally and physically) with space, no longer limiting ourselves to looking at it from afar.

This process of re-involvement in our environment began, at the very latest, with the networks of the electric telegraph, the first externalisation of our nervous system, as McLuhan has shown.[3] Through television, and above all computer networks, this process underwent a decisive acceleration. The rate of travel of these networks has sped up to the point of annulment (real time). Clicking a link is no longer akin to the linear succession of the pages of a printed book. We have conquered a new time, one composed of leaps backwards as well as forwards. Computer networks have enabled the emergence of a new space – cyberspace, itself a term coined by the authors of science fiction to describe the spatialisation of our hallucinations. Cyberspace is now a common term and, above all – precisely as William Gibson forecast – a part of each and every one of our daily lives.[4]

We surf the electronic waves, seeking information, news and, above all, con-tacts. Web 2.0 has only rendered more obvious what we could and should have noticed from the beginning of the explosion of computer networks: they are vectors of a new sociality, a new emotivity – a connective emotivity. These con-tacts, these explorations, continuously regenerate cyberspace, the space of our signs. Its virtual quality lends itself to this continuous regeneration, to this boundless metamorphosis.

The Game of Architecture

The principle of a space in continuous mutation defines the challenge to which architects are now called upon to respond. We are faced with a new dimension, the successor to that to which Renaissance perspective attempted to provide a response. This latter imagined the world in three dimensions, while presenting it on a flat, two-dimensional surface. It was a challenge faced not only by the era's great painters, but also its great architects who, in the wake of Leon Battista Alberti, designed their buildings according to the principles of perspective.

People at a party in Second Life. Avatars in SL meet together to discuss, socialise and party.

A historic Sardinian building (a *nuraghe*) from the Nuragic Civilisation, Sardinian Bronze Age (1600 BC), part of Unesco's World Heritage, rebuilt in its original form in Second Life, and avatars wearing traditional Sardinian dress.

Networks now create the *n*-dimensional space in which we are immersed. However, above all they make possible an uninterrupted process of metamorphosis of this space. It is the life of this space, its 'fourth dimension' that challenges contemporary architects.

No longer is their brief to design imperishable buildings that will define our landscape, for centuries if not millennia, independently of its social, political or environmental evolution. Today architects are aware of the need to design buildings intended to last, at most, only a few decades, or to create those that will be subjected to a continual process of adaptation (domestication) by their users.

A decisive role is thus attributed to the cyber conception and practice of space. An entire generation of architects (from Hani Rashid to Greg Lynn, from Lars Spuybroek to Kas Oosterhuis) has not only grown up with a computer in their hands, devouring computer drawing programs, but has also attempted to draw this new space of immersion generated by technologies of communication.

Peter Bohlin, Apple Store, Fifth Avenue, New York City, 2006
The Bohlin building generates instability of perception and introduces the experience of a mixed reality to those who enter.

Naturally, architecture has always been subjected to a process of adaptation by its users. However, a different, entirely new situation arises when architecture is perceived as an obstacle, a resistance to this process, and when architecture itself promotes this process. Currently, like all pioneering artists, architects must understand that they are merely the developers of games, games that become real only through the contribution of their players. 'Once the game has been started, the building/game is investigated by many users, in many styles and with different skill levels. … Architecture becomes a game played by its users.'[5]

Inhabiting Second Life
Today the challenge of 4D is forcefully present in different scenarios. Let us consider three particularly important ones: 1) Second Life (SL); 2) the Internet of Things; 3) bioarchitecture. The space of flows has fully demonstrated its immersive character, its depth and its sensorial richness, secreting the online world that offers us a 'second life', a world inhabited by millions of self-created avatars and the spaces in which they interact with one another.

In the world of Linden Lab,[6] we investigate to the full the spatialisation of the quantity of data processed by our computers. We are in this space, we inhabit it and we create relationships with landscapes, situations and alterity. All of this requires a concerted effort from architects, focused in at least two directions. First of all, we must design the land, the buildings that sit on it and the landscapes in which we move. That SL operates beyond perspective is more than evident, and emblematically represented by the function that allows for 360-degree vision. At present, the majority of SL's builders re-propose the spaces of real life. Perhaps, however, it is precisely thanks to worlds like SL that we can understand the trend towards a new sort of 'mixed reality', one in which we confuse the boundaries between atoms and bits. Let us take as an example the Apple Store on Fifth Avenue in New York, designed by Peter Bohlin. This glass cube, almost 10 metres (32.8 feet) high, creates a significant instability of perception. It has its double in SL. In short, Apple offers its clients different spatial experiences, which overlap and fuse with one another. This is the same mixed reality that a team at the McLuhan Program in Culture and Techonology has imagined in the Global Village Square project: a virtual public square, created using giant screens installed in galleries and shopping malls and capable of uniting, for example, Toronto and Naples by transmitting images and the voices of visitors as they walk around the screens.

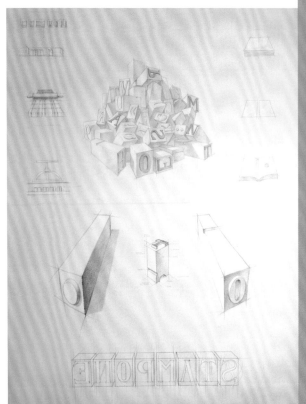

Giuseppe Stampone, *Dispositivo per la diffusione del pensiero*, pencil on paper and acrylic, 180 x 113 cm, Rome, 2007
Italian artist Giuseppe Stampone here re-creates the printing era view, which was bounded by the dictates of Renaissance perspective and the human eye, in an exhibition of his works: 'Maestro Stampone's 18 Inventions + 1 That Will Change the World'.

Stelarc, The Third Hand, Tokyo/Yokohama/Nagoya, 1980
Highly innovative Australian artist Stelarc here implanted a third, artificial hand to create a cyborg. This electromechanical feature, capable of independent motion, is also invested with a partial sense of touch. The artist thus explores space through bodily adaptation.

Second, SL also calls on architects and designers to participate in something that is a profound part of our identity. The first project that we must complete before entering SL has to do with our body, our avatar. We must design ourselves and the masks that we wish to wear; we must design our senses.

Marcos Novak defines the avatars as 'projects used to populate projects'. For Novak, the future role of architects lies in the design of avatars: 'providing virtual senses as today's designers provide physical senses. However, the senses belong to the body, and thus providing virtual senses means, first and foremost, inventing virtual bodies complete with virtual senses. ... The design of the future is that of avatars and their senses.'[7]

Designing the inhabitants of new spaces, designing ourselves, designing a body-cyborg-avatar continuum, a biochemical-electromechanical-televirtual continuum: this is our identity. This is the identity that the other mutants place before us. Stelarc, Orlan, Steve Mann and Kevin Warwick have all turned their bodies into 'objects of design', moving beyond the de-finite and fixed body, towards a hybridisation of alterity.

Technological Hylozoism

The recognition of media as environment and of environments as media has pushed engineers (computer, electronic, civil) and architects to work on what we could call the pulverisation of communicative microtechnology in our spaces of dwelling: from ubiquitous computing to the smart house, from Internet Zero to the Internet of Things. This latter expression refers to the spread of electronic labels in the objects of our everyday lives. RFID technology (radio frequency identification) is designed to substitute for the bar codes on purchased products (from food packaging to books, from clothing to technological devices). These new labels are capable of communicating not only with the cash register scanner, but with one another and, remotely, with the computers that designed them, gathering information on all the various uses and abuses of the products to which the labels are attached, and developing their own sensibility. A smart bicycle is capable of sending information to its manufacturer about how it is used by its owner, and perhaps even the state of wear of certain of its parts.

To function as effective architects in this new dimension, we must make ourselves aware of how the diffusion of the intelligent microchip irreversibly alters our environments. It has been said that 'we are currently on the threshold of an era in which animals, trees and even inanimate objects can interact by the Internet'.[8] We could speak of 'technological hylozoism'. Hylozoism is an ancient doctrine that affirms an animation, a movement and a sensibility towards living matter. The proliferation of the microchip renders the everyday spaces of our existence alive, capable of interacting and reacting to our passage. The very air that we breathe is pervaded by and dense with the uninterrupted action of these small elements. We must be aware that we are immersed in living fields of communication, just as we are immersed in the electric fields and smog of the metropolis. Space is growing progressively denser and the Internet of Things offers further proof.

Designing with Bios

From the life of space to living space, the passage is a brief one. Integrating living elements and using bios in design represents the extreme frontier of a post-perspectival comprehension of space, of a bioarchitecture. Eduardo Kac, with his famous fluorescent rabbit Alba, Oron Catts with his laboratory-bred frog steaks, Marta de Menezes with her fake butterflies and George Gessert with his selections of ornamental plants; all have explored the boundaries between expressive form, biotechnologies and living matter. This exploration, in turn, has generated hybrid entities, chimeras, monsters that at first sight scare us, but which, in the end, raise questions about our very selves, about the shifting and permeable borders of what we have chosen to call 'human'.[9]

For some time now architects have captured the importance of exterior surfaces; they have returned to the notion of the skin, of the membrane, designing and structuring exteriors. As part of the current focus on eco-sustainability, we can imagine the use of organic materials as integral to the design of our buildings. What better insulation to reduce heat loss and protect us against the cold than our own skin? Today, thanks to biotechnologies it is possible to cultivate cartilaginous tissues, bone tissues and other cells that are useful in the world of architecture. In addition to their environmental advantages, these materials are also capable of responding fully to the challenge of the fourth dimension. In fact, it is thanks to these materials that we are able to create forms that grow, that move, that transform: forms impossible to capture in a static perspective.

The Mutating Spaces of Contemporary Dwelling

After perspective we thus inhabit a space of flesh, a space of our own flesh. After perspective, space can be understood and investigated as an extension of our bodies. After perspective, we are space, we are

Eduardo Kac, GFP Bunny: Alba, the green fluorescent rabbit, 2000
Working with bio-engineers, Brazilian artist Eduardo Kac has created a transgenic artwork that involves the genetic mutation of a rabbit. The project was embarked on with great care and appreciation for the complex ethical issues involved – and a profound commitment to nurture the life produced.

expanded beings in a post-human horizon. The observation of media has thus led to a recognition of the spaces of post-human dwelling that appear to have nothing to do with the media themselves. In reality, media are an extension of our senses, tying them indissolubly to the needs of our bodies. Just as printing, accompanied by the concept of perspective, emphasised and isolated the eye, so computer networks involve and profoundly modify all our senses. Through the imagination and the practice of media we have arrived at a post-human horizon, one that is implemented by biotechnologies.

Digital and network media, post-perspectival spaces and post-human bodies together challenge architecture to redesign the mutating spaces of contemporary dwelling. △⃝

Translated from the Italian version into English by Paul David Blackmore

Notes
1. See Erwin Panofsky, *Die Perspektive als 'Symbolische Form'*, Vorträge der Bibliothek Warburg 1924–25, B-G Teubner (Leipzig-Berlin) 1927.
2. Emanuele Severino, *Tecnica e architettura*, Raffaelo Cortina (Milan), 2003, p 92.
3. Marshall McLuhan, *Understanding Media: The Extension of Man*, McGraw-Hill (New York), 1964.
4. William Gibson, *Neuromancer*, Ace Books (New York), 1984; William Gibson, *Spook Country*, Penguin Putman (New York), 2007.
5. Kas Oosterhuis and Lukas Feireiss (eds), *Game Set Match II: On Computer Games, Advanced Geometries, and Digital Technologies*, Episode Publishers (Rotterdam), 2006.
6. The Linden Lab is the software house, founded in 1999 by Philip Rosedale, that designs and manages Second Life. The group also owns SL, a public space that is also private: it can be accessed only after accepting the rules and conditions dictated by Linden Lab.
7. Marcos Novak, *Babele 2000*, 'trax', 2000: http://www.trax.it/marcos_novak.htm.
8. Ernesto Hofmann, 'Verso l'internet delle cose', Istituto per le imprese di beni di consumo, 2004: http://www.indicod-ecr.it/punto/archivio/hofmann.php.
9. Jens Hauser (ed), *L'art biotech. Le lieu unique*, Filigranes Éditions (Nantes), 2003; Jens Hauser (ed), *Sk-Interfaces: Exploding Borders – Creating Membranes in Art, Technology and Society*, Liverpool University Press (Liverpool), 2008.

[ecosistema urbano]
Eco-Boulevard, Vallecas, Madrid, 2006

Polish architecture tutors and critics **Roman Rutkowski** and **Lukasz Wojciechowski** identify a new kind of architecture in [ecosistema urbano]'s ingenious temporary tower pavilions for a sterile new housing estate in Madrid. Contributing power to the local electricity grid, these towers are explicitly designed to provide shelter from the unmediated heat of the harsh external environment through their cooling effect and in so doing to stimulate communal activities and events.

Roman Rutkowski   Lukasz Wojciechowski

At the 2006 Venice Biennale, curator Richard Burdett, Centennial Professor in Architecture and Urbanism at the London School of Economics, and chief adviser on architecture and urbanism for the London 2012 Olympics, demonstrated the unpleasantness and chaotic development of the contemporary city that all too rarely produces architecture and urban spaces that are appropriate for good living. [ecosistema urbano]'s Eco-Boulevard in Madrid is a project that pacifies this phenomenon. Neither a presentation of the newest technologies, nor a simple application of nature, the proposal instead merges the two, focusing rather on the creation of a social space for a newly built and, thus, harsh and sterile housing estate.

The simple yet impressive composition of three tower pavilions can be quickly dismantled and moved to another site, reflecting the changeability, temporality and dynamics of the contemporary world. They are not untouchable, solid and heavy monuments erected for the sake of the architects' fame, but light and portable urban machines to be located and used where needed.

Energetically self-sufficient, and even contributing extra power to the local electricity supply, the structures are perfect examples of architectural sustainability.

The project is not a formal attempt to build a strange and eye-catching form, or to illustrate any sophisticated theory. Unpretentious, almost anonymous, the buildings are just city devices erected to improve community life in the area. They challenge potentials of technology and nature in order to trigger some very basic and natural effects: simple social activities are stimulated not by programme/function of the architecture or by any special occasions, but by climatic conditions: temperature, humidity, shadowing and so on. In this way the project reaches to the very core of nature, not so much by redefining its structural (morphologies) or formal (surfaces) qualities, but by exploring its operational potential to stimulate the social activities of different species (humans, birds and so on). This is a new type of space that is delineated not by tangible partitions, but by intangible micro-weather ingredients. ⌂

Text and images compiled by Anna Baldini

Media Tree Pavilion

top left: View of the interior space with vaporised cloud generated by water atomisers and LED screens conected to weather stations.

top right: Neighbourhood associations organise rock concerts during the summer months.

Air Tree Pavilion

above: The outer skin/exterior thermal shield is made from high-density, multilayer polyethylene films and aluminium.

Ludic Tree Pavilion

left: Night view of the pavilion which has an artificial lighting system made of 12-millimetre (0.47-inch) thick fibre-optics connected to LED RGB lamps.

Architecture as a Dissident Practice
An **Interview** with Diller Scofidio + Renfro

Diller Scofidio + Renfro, Blur Building, Lake Neuchâtel, Switzerland, 2002
An artificial cloud created by thousands of mist nozzles, the building is an architecture of atmosphere, an ephemeral mechanism to test the boundaries of our perception of space.

For three decades architect Liz Diller and artist Ricardo Scofidio have been collaborating on projects that test the boundaries between art and architecture. They have done more than any other practice to champion interdisciplinary research and to advocate architecture as a wider form of cultural production. **Olympia Kazi** went to talk to Liz Diller to ask her if she thinks theory could really be dead, or merely in a 'lull'.

Diller Scofidio + Renfro (DS+R) is an unconventional architectural firm. For about three decades now it has practised architecture in a most unusual way. On its website it defines itself as 'an interdisciplinary firm straddling architecture, urban design, visual arts and the performing arts'. That definition is about right: it captures the erratic trajectory the firm has been pursuing, the constant shifting of scales of their projects, the ease with which they move between architecture and art. Indeed, the redefinition of the boundaries of architecture as a discipline is possibly the most critical contribution of DS+R.

Since the late 1970s, architect Liz Diller and artist Ricardo Scofidio have toyed with both the physical and conceptual limits of architecture. In a series of experiments with art and electronic media installations, set designs for the theatre, and buildings, Diller and Scofidio have explored and tested the boundaries of cultural and architectural conventions. For example, their Blur Building, a project built for the 2002 Swiss Expo on Lake Neuchâtel, challenges the way we think of matters of perception: supported by a lightweight structure, the building is made up of thousands of mist nozzles which create an artificial cloud. Architecture, for centuries associated with ideas of permanence, stability and monumentality, is here defined by the most impermanent of materials – water. The building is ultimately an architecture of atmosphere, an ephemeral mechanism to test how we see and perceive space.

In recent years the studio of Diller and Scofidio has grown. Commissions have increased in scale and complexity, and a new partner, architect Charles Renfro, has joined the firm. Its work is more explicitly architectural: after the completion of the Institute of Contemporary Art in Boston, the firm is currently at work on two key projects in New York City: the transformation of the High Line (an elevated train line that cuts through Chelsea and the West Village) into an urban park, and the renovation and expansion of the architectural complex of the Lincoln Center. Throughout this evolution, the firm has maintained its distinctive commitment to interdisciplinary research. Above all, DS+R continues to champion a critical approach to architecture, an understanding of architecture not merely as a professional activity, a practical endeavour, but as a form of cultural production.

Last May I sat down for a talk with Liz Diller at DS+R's studio in New York. We discussed the firm's recent work, the role of research in its practice, and contemporary architectural discourse. The premise of our conversation was Luigi Prestinenza Puglisi's proposition which forms the basis of this issue of *AD* – the idea that we are now witnessing a sort of 'theoretical meltdown'. The collapse of the certainties and orthodoxies of previous generations seems to have created a condition for the discipline which is at once liberating and extremely disorienting. In explaining such a transitional moment for architecture, Puglisi insists on three 'afters': after theory, after perspective and after the Twin Towers. Diller is sceptical:

'Everything that the structure of this issue talks about presumes that there is a shift, so where does that come from? What's the hypothesis? Clearly this seems to start from the back, it seems to start from 9/11 and go forward. I am very suspicious of the "after theory" and "post-critical" discussion. No one has yet explained precisely what that means. It seems that everyone is so desirous of having a theory, even if it's "after theory" as a theory. That seems like a desperate measure. I am still trying to figure out how post-critical is different from pre-critical. I kind of take it all with a grain of salt. Architects that came out from a certain generation of studies were affected by cultural theory and other fields, so they will for ever incorporate that kind of thinking into architecture. For me, it was the very reason I became interested in architecture. I thought of it as a cultural discipline, totally integrated, not autonomous.'

This understanding of architecture's fundamental heteronomy is at the core of DS+R's research. Diller uses a beautiful expression to define their approach: 'thick understanding'. They position themselves vis-à-vis the discipline with 'an understanding of its involvement, its networks, its complexities, its ties into the political, economic, social, into different disciplines within the arts, different modes of expression whether it's writing or architectural installations, permanent/temporary, small/large.'

In her analysis of contemporary architectural discourse, Diller insists on the fundamental role of cultural theory in shaping the discipline in the past decades. 'Cultural theory was such a big part of learning and thinking in the 1990s, and at that point everything was opened to be rethought. It was not a historicism like architectural Postmodernism, but Postmodernism in a different sense, one which engaged a lot of thinking from cultural studies and other fields. That's where we first started thinking about gendered space, that's when we started thinking about politics of space. Then the whole Derridean stream came, and we were all very involved and engaged in practices at that time which continue to filter through our work. ... I don't think all

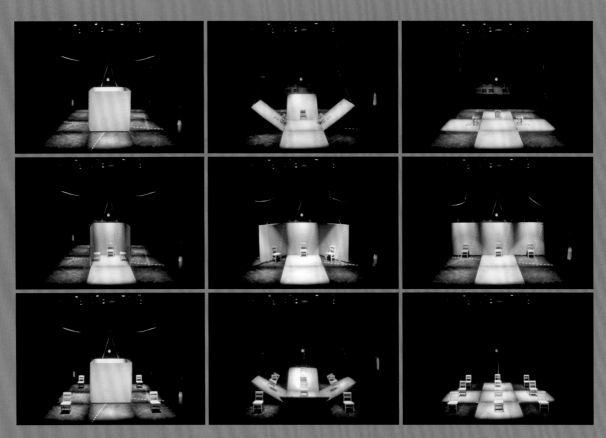

Diller + Scofidio, Scenography for *American Mysteries*, La MaMa Experimental Theater Club, New York, 1983
The set design here is an exploration of the conventions of the stage: the mechanics of the set, the scenic apparatus that conventionally would be hidden, becomes the set itself.

that is over, theory is not over. Maybe what's happening right now is a kind of lull. No one has anything polemical to say right now, and I think that part of the problem is that there is nothing to react against because a lot of the people of my generation hold positions of power in a lot of institutions, universities, publications, museums, in all sorts of cultural institutions, even in the government, and maybe soon even more so, hopefully. It's like we are finally getting what we wanted, so, what is there to react to? One can say that the discipline has to internally transform, it has to do that autonomously, within itself; and I never saw architecture as autonomous, so it's hard for me to think in that way.'

The relationship with institutions, and more generally the critique of architecture as an institution, has been a leitmotif of the firm's research. 'Everyone says that the institutional critic is dead. I don't think that is possible because even though we are the institutions now, still, literally, when you look at every single institution, it is dominated by people whose power comes from money, and it's usually disconnected from a specific cultural

interest. So, what happens with the institutions, who builds them, what they sow, what they present, reflects typically the ones with power/money. It also reflects the need to produce and generate income for institutions simply because there is less and less money coming from the government for the arts, so the arts are more sustained by private money and therefore you get into this conundrum. I don't see how it's possible to ever think that the institutional critic is dead. We have to be vigilant about our institutions, we have to constantly look out for their interests. Sometimes it takes stealthy, undercover work, to be able to be part of them, but also to not let them go along the course that they would go naturally.'

How much of the theoretical backbone of DS+R's projects does it think is actually readable by the users? 'It doesn't really matter,' says Diller. 'Fundamentally, if something is good, it's going to be good for grandmas and people with no education and little kids. It doesn't matter if you'll get every single idea of it, how much you can cross-reference to what's been written and other experiments. For me it's not a prerequisite to understand the theory behind in order to have a great architectural experience. At the same time for us to be able to produce interesting work, we work on parallel paths. We write and we work in a visual and a textual world. One comes out of the other. It sounds like they are running separately, but they are totally connected to one another. Sometimes it's an idea that is expressed, and usually ideas don't come from out of space, they come from a discourse, and then an image comes into it and one critiques the other; and then we work on an idea and ultimately we present it in different forms, we present it as the thing, as writing about the thing. ... Do all interesting architectural works come with a kind of parallel theory? I don't know. I do think that that's the way that change happens. People situate themselves within a discourse and that discourse is what propels the discipline forward. That's ultimately what produces good and interesting work that's vital in transforming the discipline. I think, yes, the answer is: theory is good.'

The 'after perspective' proposition, too, leaves Diller cold: 'I don't really think of space in perspectival terms. I also don't think of it in flat terms. I think of space in temporal terms: the dimension that interests me is time and movement. It's interesting what Ric [Scofidio] says often: "When you stop moving, space flattens." One has to accept that there is more to architecture than space-making: architecture is event-making, it's always thinking about perception, and space, use, choreography, setting up relations and so forth.'

The anomaly of DS+R within contemporary architectural practice is especially surprising when one considers the way the firm has maintained its experimental character even while the scale of its interventions has kept growing. Diller explained what drives its experiments: 'We have a research-based studio. That kind of inquiry is going on all the time anyway and it feeds into our larger projects that have a client and a budget and all that. It doesn't really matter that the research filters into that. The research takes on different forms. We are kind of writing and want to do a feature film. We are doing nine installations right now and the work with theatre persists. There is a deep interest in keeping that stuff alive. In our studio there are people who are working with us on this – it's almost like the money-losing department of our studio – and on larger-scale commercial projects, which by the way is a money-losing one too. They are supposed to feed one another.'

Those 'money-losing' experiments, and especially DS+R's numerous collaborations with playwrights and theatre directors, offer some of the best examples of its oblique approach to architecture. 'Virtually all the pieces that we've done for theatre,' says Diller, 'undermine perspectival space, undermine classical theatre, and undermine the relationship between the audience and performers in many different ways.' I asked her about some of the scenographies and set designs that the firm has conceived since the 1980s; for example, *American Mysteries*, a piece written and directed by Matthew Maguire and presented by the Creation Production Company at the La MaMa Experimental Theater Club in New York City in February 1983: 'Instead of having a stage and a backstage, everything is right in front of you; all the mechanics of the set are part of the set. The set is simply divided into nine spaces, nine acts, nine characters, nine stories. It's just a division of nine, it's not linear, it doesn't have a classical arch and a great ending. It's not set up as a story that way, both in time and space, but is serial in its physical structure and serial in its development.'

Of *Moving Target*, a project conceived by Frédéric Flamand and presented in Charleroi, Belgium, in 1996, Diller says: '[There was] a 45-degree mirror above the stage where everything that was on the stage was reflected to the audience – we called it an interscenium rather than a proscenium. The audience saw the stage turned through 90 degrees. It [produced] different conditions of gravity and [split] the focus of the audience into two registers, sometimes combining the two spaces in very virtual, optic and unusual ways.

'Each one of our theatre pieces is explicitly about conventions of the stage – stage space, storytelling, fiction, nonfiction – and each one of them undermines it and produces new opportunities for theatre. Another major theme [in our research] is liveness and mediated experience, taking conventions of stage and screen and combining them into another kind of experience. That's our interest in theatre, because we can actually work on undermining conventions of space and time in real time in a way that we can actually understand how the audience is responding to it. It's very different, an ephemeral event; it's there, it's not there. It offers a really interesting way of seeing and observing the kind of appreciation or the shock or the disorientation of the audience at once because it's all about spectatorship.'

In a monograph published recently on the firm's work, Scofidio is quoted as saying that he is afraid of the radical thinking of today because it will become tomorrow's orthodoxy.[1] Diller: 'I don't even like to think in terms of radical and not radical. Our work has always been outside these things, we make our own context, in a way. At the same time, we are learning how to work the network because we are getting a lot of things done. That's permanent, it's going to make a difference to people's lives. The academic system is kind of predisposed to send out something new every three years so that there is a refresh of the system. I am very wary of newness just for the sake of newness. It wears thin. Obviously we are all interested in our next idea, but whether that can be characterised as newness, who knows? It's new for us.' ∆

This interview took place on 27 May 2008 in the New York office of Diller Scofidio + Renfro

Note
1. Guido Incerti, Daria Ricchi and Deane Simpson, *Diller + Scofidio (+ Renfro): The Ciliary Function: Works and Projects, 1979–2007*, Skira (Milan), 2007, p 127.

Supersudaca

Al Caribe, Mayan Riviera, Caribbean, 2008

The simultaneous move towards specialisation and generalisation has opened up the way for 'new fields of action' and 'strategical approaches to design'. Portuguese architect and critic **Carlos Sant'Ana** describes how urban Latin American think tank Supersudaca epitomise what is best about this new 'Pragmatopian' thinking with their Al Caribe project.

Carlos Sant'Ana

Architecture is living in confusing times. We can look for plenty of reasons and excuses, but the main one is that society is becoming more and more specialised. Categorisation, classification and labelling are becoming an inevitable part of our daily routine. People, groups, trends, ideas, *modus operandi*, techniques, formal and conceptual approaches are made recognisable so that society can have a sense of control over them.

New branches of applied sciences or artistic developments appear every day, thus augmenting the confusion of who is able to do what. Architects, by in-definition, live divided somewhere in between these extremes. Professional practice requires great technical skills, while academic environments favour critical and conceptual approaches closer to artistic methods.

Architecture becomes paradox. We are specialists in coordinating specialists, leaving us in an awkward position of being nonspecialists, or of being specialists in absolutely nothing.

This ambiguity – apparently mining the grounds of our profession – is leaving us in a precarious condition, but it also provides fertile land for innovation and creativity, often used by young architects to explore new fields of action, where strategical approaches to research and design become the norm. This is most apparent in the work of urban think tank Supersudaca, which was founded in 2001 by a group of young Latin American architects who met and studied at the Berlage Institute in Rotterdam. The driving force behind its collaborations has been its aspiration to bring together the previously fragmented Latin American architectural scene. This it has done through a series of art installations and actions in public spaces, and also by engaging students in workshops across the world.

The most notable of Supersudaca's projects is Al Caribe, which explored the impact of tourism in the Caribbean, winning Best Entry Award at the II International Architecture Rotterdam Biennale in 2005. Despite not being specialists in the field, Supersudaca here used its architectural analytical and research skills to highlight the accumulative effects of tourism. In 2007, Supersudaca transferred its abilities directly to architectural practice and at the International Competition on Social Housing in Ceuta, Spain, won the commission to build 170 housing units.

Architects can do everything – or at least we want to believe that – and we end up entering into fields that are totally foreign to our knowledge. However, this can be the true advantage we bring to a theoretical view of the world. No more ideologies or impossible quests for a better world, nor simple functional solutions with no added value. We want it all, and we want to do everything at the same time.

Utopia, our desire for a perfect world, meets pragmatism, the reality show of daily life. Pragmatopia thus becomes the new keyword of architecture, providing an answer to all the present dichotomies of the profession. ⟑

Text and images compiled by Anna Baldini

SUPERSUDACA collaborators on Al Caribe: Elena Chevtchenko (NL) based in Rotterdam; Juan Pablo Corvalan (CHILE) based in Talca; Stephane Damsin (BL) based in Brussels; Martin Delgado (UY) based in Montevideo; Victoria Goldstein (ARG) based in London; Pablo Guerrero (COL) based in Washington; Felix Madrazo (MEX) based in Rotterdam; Ana Rascovsky (ARG) based in Buenos Aires; Manuel de Rivero (PERU) based in Lima; Sofia Saavedra (BOL) based in Curacao; Juan Alfonso Zapata (RD) based in Barcelona; and Max Zolkwer (ARG) based in Buenos Aires.

top left: The picture here reveals one of the most subtle strategies: that of buffer zones between the low-density tourist sprawl of Punta Cana in the Dominican Republic and potential development nearby. A precise green strip has been declared a reserve zone for potential floods and works simultaneously as a perfect background to an illusion of natural wilderness.

centre left: Despite serious concerns about the impact of cruise tourism, many countries still want to jump on board and are currently rushing to upgrade their oceanside infrastructure to bring these moving resorts to their shores. Yet the cruise ships are getting bigger and bigger, making investment for local ports increasingly unaffordable.

bottom left: Under the alibi that the cays are the most sensitive areas for development, the Cuban government has decided to keep a notorious special segregation policy between workers and tourists. Everyday workers commute to the cays on newly built 'terraplenes', with their use of space also controlled at their final destination.

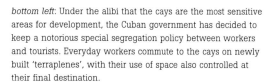

top right: Massive destruction of jungle is replaced by massive architectural schemes. There are two key principles of tourism development: 1: More than 700 rooms are required to make the logistics profitable. 2: The investment must pay for itself within just five years.

bottom right: Euphemistically called '*pueblos de apoyo*', the workers' settlements next to the Mayan Riviera highway are both a product of land invasions and the result of enabling the workers to avoid tedious commuting to and from Cançun.

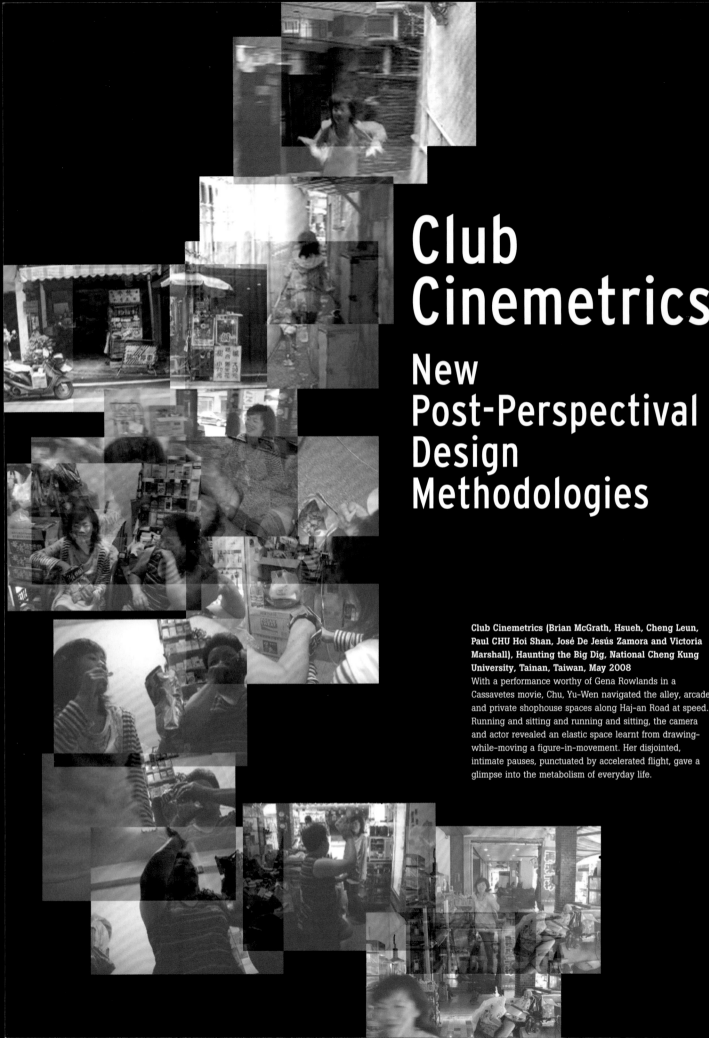

Club Cinemetrics

New Post-Perspectival Design Methodologies

Club Cinemetrics (Brian McGrath, Hsueh, Cheng Leun, Paul CHU Hoi Shan, José De Jesús Zamora and Victoria Marshall), Haunting the Big Dig, National Cheng Kung University, Tainan, Taiwan, May 2008
With a performance worthy of Gena Rowlands in a Cassavetes movie, Chu, Yu-Wen navigated the alley, arcade and private shophouse spaces along Haj-an Road at speed. Running and sitting and running and sitting, the camera and actor revealed an elastic space learnt from drawing-while-moving a figure-in-movement. Her disjointed, intimate pauses, punctuated by accelerated flight, gave a glimpse into the metabolism of everyday life.

Cinemetrics is a post-perspectival, cinematically inspired drawing system that encourages a way of working that is multilayered and multiscalar, responding to the complexities of contemporary life and the city. Here **Brian McGrath**, in collaboration with **Hsueh, Cheng Leun, Paul CHU Hoi Shan, José De Jesús Zamora** and **Victoria Marshall**, demonstrates how in field work in the US, Thailand and Taiwan, Cinemetrics enabled them to adopt an interdisciplinary process addressing transdisciplinary issues.

Club Cinemetrics (Brian McGrath, Hsueh Cheng Leun, Paul CHU Hoi Shan, José De Jesús Zamora and Victoria Marshall), Haunting the Big Dig, National Cheng Kung University, Tainan, Taiwan, May 2008
Cybernetic architect Ting-fu Chang used his laptop, digital camera and tripod to frame intervals in flowing matter flux, day and night, at Hai-An Road in Tainan. With his partners, he followed the methodology of Japanese film director Yasujiro Ozu in order to reveal the blind spots in static perspectival projections by documenting key places in the site simultaneously from three distinct vantage points.

The enormous social and environmental challenges of today demand a departure from linear design methodologies that reinforce architecture as an autonomous discipline, and a move towards open-ended processes that engage design in systemic relationships with the everyday world around us. This is equally true for the emerging Asian megacities, from Dubai to Shanghai, as well as for the sprawling edge cities of North America and Europe.

Cinemetrics: Architecture Drawing Today[1] is not a threat to the critical relevance and role of drawing in art and design, but provides post-perspectival digital design methodologies for an expanded field within which architects can operate critically. With such theories and tools, designers can begin to address the 'wicked problems' of globalisation, emancipatory movements and climate change.[2] The book calls for an architecture that transforms, mutates, generates and regenerates urban-life worlds at different speeds and scales. As such, Cinemetrics is a mode of thinking, working and drawing that continually reflects on the existence of multilayered and multiscalar urban relationships in contemporary cities, and a research methodology that opens up the possibility for a more comprehensive framework to perceive and explain the complexity and contradiction in contemporary urbanscapes.

The Club Cinemetrics social network and urban design collaborative emerged out of a series of drawing workshops at Chulalongkorn University Faculty of Architecture (CUFOA) in Bangkok, Thailand, Parsons The New School for Design (PNSD) and Syracuse University School of Architecture (SUSOA) in New York, and the National Cheng Kung University (NCKU) in Tainan, Taiwan. At Parsons, José De Jesús Zamora began to explore Cinemetrics as a way for using handmade drawing in new and revitalised ways, and most recently, in Taiwan, Victoria Marshall explored the technique as a way to direct landscape architecture methodologies towards engaging urban ecosystem processes, while architect/artist Paul CHU Hoi Shan demonstrated his use of Cinemetrics for reinforcing disappearing social practices in Hong Kong. The following field experiments are organised around three conceptual fragments: Architectural Blind Spots, Disappearance and Apparitions, and Changing States of Matter Flux. Design students and practitioners on both continents have quickly embraced these new methodologies with a creative optimism in the innate ability of human beings to create positive environmental change once given the right tools and access to information.

Architectural Blind Spots

Post-perspectival cybernetic design must reach beyond the blind spots of traditional perspectival architectural design methodologies. Instead of a linear process of projecting forms from static ideal conceptions, designs emerge from moving 'centres of indeterminacy' within worlds of changing states of flowing matter flux.[3] Perspective itself was developed as a 15th-century urban field experiment when Brunelleschi deployed his famous mirrored drawing device in front of the Baptistry in Florence and Alberti developed a concept of a 'physical picture frame' on which the viewer draws the shapes observed when looking through the glass.[4] Students at Parsons and NCKU learnt to understand the concept of visual perception by deconstructing perspective through modern cinematic interpretations of these tools. Instead of perpetuating the 'static' imagery that makes perspective drawing and digital walk-throughs appear dead, Cinemetric drawing demands deciphering our sensorial perceptions through reiterative analyses of movement and time in relation to space and form.

Cinemetric tools and field experiments point towards new directions, not just in the way we draw, but in the way we live, think and how we inhabit our urban planet. The methodology first seeks to uncover the six blind spots in any single architectural perspectival projections: the space behind the viewer, the space on top, below and on either side of the frame, and the space behind the building or scene depicted. Japanese film director Yasujiro Ozu maintains a fixed camera position within any single shot in order to frame changing states of matter flux. He then repositions his camera within key moments in a scene to reveal the blind spots behind, around and in front of any single framed image. His subtle altering of the distance between his camera in relation to building surfaces, performers or scenes produces very different qualities of images: a close-up view produces an image of affection or feeling, a medium shot emphasises human action, while a long shot gives a perception image of the spatial location of a scene. In a post-perspectival Cinemetric design methodology, this succession of simultaneous immobile cuts from distinct vantage points at different distances of a moving scene produces a new multidimensional architectural space beyond the blind spots of perspectival projection.

Disappearances and Apparitions

French film-maker Jean-Luc Godard uses the slow panning, tracking and tilting movements of the mechanical camera of the classical cinema to great effect in his cinemascopic epic *Contempt* (1963). His film is an elegiac lament on the disappearance of classical

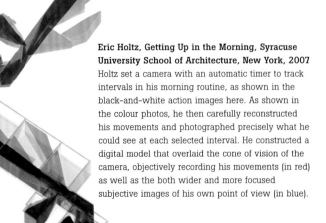

Eric Holtz, Getting Up in the Morning, Syracuse University School of Architecture, New York, 2007
Holtz set a camera with an automatic timer to track intervals in his morning routine, as shown in the black-and-white action images here. As shown in the colour photos, he then carefully reconstructed his movements and photographed precisely what he could see at each selected interval. He constructed a digital model that overlaid the cone of vision of the camera, objectively recording his movements (in red) as well as the both wider and more focused subjective images of his own point of view (in blue).

| Long Distance: Perception Image | Medium Distance: Action Image | | Close-up: Affection Image |

José De Jesús Zamora, Jean Gardner and Brian McGrath, Cinemetrics Workshop, Parsons The New School for Design, New York, 2008
Seven Parsons students here drew a moving yoga model from three 90-degree angles, as well as from three different distances. Each student had a viewfinder with layers of acetate – a hybrid tool combining Alberti's Renaissance drawing machine and the transparent surfaces used by early Disney cartoon animators to create moving characters across background spaces. The assemblage of their drawings constitutes a collective moving image without the blind spots of singular perspective drawing.

Club Cinemetrics (Brian McGrath, Hsueh Cheng Leun, Paul CHU Hoi Shan, José De Jesús Zamora and Victoria Marshall), Haunting the Big Dig, National Cheng Kung University, Tainan, Taiwan, May 2008
In order to begin to create spaces generated out of 'any instant whatever' instead of privileged poses, students simulated French film-maker Jean Luc-Godard's mechanical panning, tracking and tilting. Using wheelchairs from the faculty of medicine, they created moving action images of t'ai chi instructor Hau-Ting Huang.

European culture and the rise of American media-fed consumerism. Club Cinemetrics' work in Tainan, Bangkok and Hong Kong relates to both the form and content of *Contempt*. Moving vehicles, such as buses, motorcycles, skateboards, wheelchairs and handcarts extend the range of Godard's mechanical shooting through everyday objects. The slow and mechanically bound observer objectively scans the various flows of life – material, informational, as well as the habitual movements of human routine – without privileging any action, pose, gesture or view. Instead people, things and qualities appear, disappear, leave traces and reappear as apparitions. The content of Godard's film – the politics of cultural disappearance – is clearly present in Asian cities today.[5] Cinemetrics enabled the students in Bangkok and Tainan, as well as Paul CHU Hoi Shan in Hong Kong, to discover and document both the architecture of the social disappearance of older cultural practices in alleys, sidewalks, markets and temples, as

well as the phantasmagoric landscape of apparitions of a new urban space of media advertisement and consumerism.

Club Cinemetrics considers architecture as the space generated within the intervals of flowing matter flux. In addition to being a situated material object constructed as an idealised projective space, architecture is constituted by disappearances and apparitions of site, programme, building, energy, earth, light, air, water and human life. These systems of flows are disturbed and re-sorted through the creation of architectural space. Cinemetric exercises situate architecture within the uncertain psycho-socioecological flows of globalisation, where a site is understood as constituted by states of flux and we are moving centres of indeterminacy within an a-centred world. As Walter Benjamin has pointed out, especially in an era of mechanical reproduction architecture is experienced in a state of distraction.[6] Henri Bergson's conception of human cognition based on circuits of automatic and attentive reflection also forms the basis of considering architecture as experienced within a world of changing states of flowing matter flux – whether the melting of solid

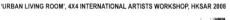

Paul CHU Hoi Shan, Urban Living Room, Hong Kong, 2008
Artist/architect Paul CHU Hoi Shan documented the social disparities in rapidly gentrifying Hong Kong and commissioned local hand-trolley makers in Sham Shui Po to create a movable architecture as a community art project.

Piyawut Kidmungtangdee, Bangkok Commute, Chulalongkorn University Faculty of Architecture, Bangkok, 2007
For a week, Piyawut Kidmungtangdee carefully recorded his daily trip to the workshop from the back seat of a bus. His camera tilts up then slowly tilts down the rear exit stairs to give an unusual point of view of the steamy activity on a Bangkok sidewalk below. His commute revealed a strange torquing helix space generated from his movement coming and going to school.

Club Cinemetrics (Brian McGrath, Hsueh, Cheng Leun, Paul CHU Hoi Shan, José De Jesús Zamora and Victoria Marshall), Haunting the Big Dig, National Cheng Kung University, Tainan, Taiwan, May 2008
Carving through and below old Hai-An Road in Tainan is an 800 x 40 metre (2,625 x 131 foot) empty shopping mall that was never completed. Lively neighbourhoods and markets constitute the daytime city, while the logistics of car and motorcycle parking in the middle of the street, and the social appropriation of the sidewalk concrete bulkheads of the underground world, animate the night-time environment.

to liquid perception in Bangkok, or the crystallisation of a frozen world in upstate New York.[7]

The Hong Kong 4 X 4 International Artists' Workshop made use of one of the city's oldest districts, Sham Shui Po, as a platform to promote creative exchange and community experimentation among artists and residents. For his Urban Living Room project, Paul CHU Hoi Shan commissioned local hand-trolley makers to create a movable architecture that revealed the new social disparities in rapidly gentrifying Hong Kong. He documented the conceptual, design and fabrication process as well as the social interactions on the street outside the shop. The notion of spatial authority, community identity and traditional sustainability in a rapidly transforming district was reflected through the coincidental interactions between dwellers with different levels of education, income and age. Cinemetric descriptions go beyond the physicality of urban artefacts and question the permanence of things created by the rapid and crude urban redevelopment processes today. CHU attempted to relate more to intangible values such as social identity and personal affection in the contemporary world and hopes to highlight the importance of maintaining a compact and harmonious social network in an old district of Hong Kong undergoing renewal.

Changing States of Matter Flux

In director John Cassavetes' *Faces* (1968), pure optical images emerge with the breakdown of our sensory motor schema as a multifaceted time image replaces action. Transposition in space is replaced by transformation in time. A new crystalline regime of memory and reflection emerges beyond linear narrative time. Students in Bangkok and Syracuse both documented their routines of getting up in the morning for the workshop. While in Bangkok it might involve the swelteringly slow process of a public bus, at Syracuse University it involved elaborate routines of fortifying for the brutal cold and often the need to clear a pathway through drifting snow. Contemporary ecosystem science points to several new recognitions that come from the fact that nature can no longer be considered as a force seeking equilibrium. First, ecological systems are open to material exchange with other systems; second, factors from outside a specified system can regulate system behaviour; third, disturbance can be part of the dynamics of the system; fourth, succession in response to disturbance can be highly unpredictable or probabilistic; and finally, humans, including their institutions and behaviours, are an integral part of ecological systems. In other words, ecosystems are seen as nonlinear and dynamic, as spatially heterogenous flow structures.[8]

Architecture, landscape architecture and urban design can assist new states of perception to emerge after the beneficent image of nature melts down. Landscape architecture has recently emerged from the divorce of its association with scenographic landscape painting and a post-colonial critique where mapping is no longer understood as innocent measuring but as an instrumental relational system. The practice of landscape design is now tied to the staking out of new urban ecosystem processes. However, what happens when the constantly new, which is the outcome of a sensory-motor schema breakdown, is cinemetric rather than territorial?

Like cybernetic seeds, students explored Hai-Ân Road in Tainan using hand-held cameras, themselves as performers, 'any instant whatever', with a continuum of affection and perception images. Sensing both the unseen visible world as well as invisible urban design contexts they created shots constructed by performance rather than the Cartesian geometries of the spaces in which they filmed. The above-ground alley network, arcades, road surfaces and the underworld mall merged as a space where ghosts, eddies of buried coastlines, ice cream, breath and television constituted a type of life where spirits and shopping are linked.

Cinemetrics generates an understanding of the relationship between space, human bodies and architecture as a means of reframing flowing matter flux. Each student, in his or her own way, explored the self-reflective aspect of cinema by finding a way to draw not by representing architecture as a material object, but by framing images in movement and generating architectural space as flowing matter flux. Crucial to this were their own ways of choosing framed images of flowing matter flux within the infinite possibilities of creatively inhabiting our mediated world. With the expansion of Club Cinemetrics to include hand drawing, product design, fabrication and landscape architecture, it is clear that 'people with expertise in specific disciplines work together in multidisciplinary teams in an interdisciplinary process, in order to better address the complexities of a transdisciplinary issue or problem'.[9] ∆

Notes
1. Brian McGrath and Jean Gardner, *Cinemetrics: Architectural Drawing Today*, John Wiley & Sons (London), 2007.
2. Tim Marshall, 'Discipline', in Michael Erlhoff and Tim Marshall (eds), *Design Dictionary: New Perspectives on Design Terminology*, Birkauser (Basel), 2008.
3. Gilles Deleuze, *Cinema 1: the Movement Image*, University of Minnesota Press (Minneapolis), 1986.
4. See also 'The Mind of Leonardo', Institute and Museum of the History of Science, Florence, Italy, January 2007.
5. Akbar Abbas, *Hong Kong and the Culture and the Politics of Disappearance*, University of Minnesota Press (Minneapolis), 1997.
6. Walter Benjamin, 'The work of art in the age of mechanical reproduction', in Hannah Arendt (ed), *Illuminations*, Harcourt Brace Jovanovich, Inc (New York), 1968.
7. Henri Bergson, *Matter and Memory*, Zone Books (New York), 1991.
8. Steward Pickett and Mary Cadenasso, *Designing Patch Dynamics*, Columbia Graduate School of Architecture, Planning and Preservation (New York), 2008.
9. Marshall op cit, p 136.

Stalker/ON

Campus Rom, 2008

How might we 'reboot' architecture and 'regain the critical'? American architectural critic and professor **Peter Lang** finds in Stalker's interactive field study of a Romany community around Rome a trigger for a re-energised way of thinking that questions how we might effectively live communally and economically.

Peter Lang

Organised by the Stalker/ON collective over the summer of 2008, and bringing together Roma III University, TU Delft, KTH Stockholm and the Faculty of Architecture at the University of Belgrade, the Campus Rom project was developed around a set of travelling workshops, the main objectives of which were to experience, document and interact with a series of Rom (gypsy) nomad camps located around Rome. The community dynamics and forms of the settlements were observed, and these were then traced back to their origins in Serbia and Macedonia. Campus Rom was thus a significant instructional model for understanding alternative forms of collective living, offering examples that could be considered more informative than the canonic visions of architecture still prevalent today.

This begs the question as to where the emancipatory forces of architecture have gone. Such a question seems almost crude today, at a time when nations govern by realpolitik, and no society is willing to sacrifice a privileged position for the global good. Resources are hoarded, rivers deviated, impoverished communities ignored – all for the sake of a driving image of prosperity and glamour. Architects frequently play to this formula, selling their talent and expertise to construct dazzling yet substance-less monuments. They rarely recognise the obvious traps until it is too late: what can a 'starchitect' do when he or she realises that his or her monument to a national television network is the nexus of violent political censorship and repression? It is too easy to decry the fact that these practices are prevalent everywhere and skip on to the next regime's bountiful commission.

The waning of the Modernist impulse, as Jürgen Habermas noted, may yet be countered by the increasing role of the people in reasserting their rights in the face of the 'media of money and power'.[1] Socially conscious design is not a new phenomenon – if one thinks back to the utopian projects of the 19th century – but certainly its most eclectic dissemination emerged during the 1960s 'teach-ins' and 'sit-ins' that were part of the mythical heyday of the communes and 'summers of love' of youth movements worldwide. If somewhat narcissistic, the period nonetheless introduced a battery of interactive trials and errors, of living experiments and community constructs which, after some decades of incubation, are again proving valuable resources for renovating today's over-glossed architectural practices.

The challenge, of course, is not to suspend architectural practice until the world changes, but to find the triggers embedded deep inside the profession that can be used to reboot the process, to regain the critical, to recover so much of the lost contemporary meaning. This is a call not to impersonate the 1960s but for a serious consideration of what is happening now, for the ground perspective, the mud on the boots and willful time to share with others. What has emerged from Stalker's interactive field studies is a way of giving new definitions to today's humanity while learning how to live collectively, economically and strategically. Tomorrow's monuments will be places of coexistence, community and mutual understanding. It is hard to imagine sticking to old habits any longer. ⚭

Text and images compiled by Anna Baldini
Captions translated from the Italian version into English by Paul David Blackmore

Note

1. Jürgen Habermas, 'Modern and Postmodern Architecture', in K Michael Hays, *Architecture Theory Since 1968*, Columbia Books of Architecture/MIT Press (New York), 2000, p 425.

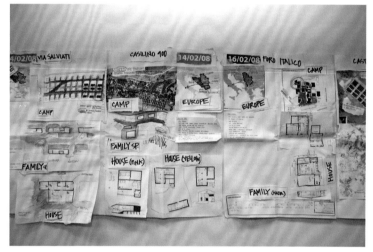

top left: Various initiatives, including convivial meetings with the Rom communities around Rome, preceded the 2008 workshops. Lunch at the Campo Boario nomad settlement, Rome, 2006.

top right: The Campo Boario nomad settlement in Rome.

centre left: Rom camps in Castel Romano, Rome.

centre right: A lesson at the Faculty of Architecture at the University of Belgrade.

bottom: A shanty town in Gazela, Belgrade.

That Old Thing Called Flexibility
An **Interview** with Robert Venturi and Denise Scott Brown

Robert Venturi and Denise Scott Brown hold an unrivalled position within architecture. Now written several decades ago, their classic books *Learning from Las Vegas* and *Complexity and Contradiction* remain unsurpassed for their ability to shock and overturn current architectural thought. **Francesco Proto** talks to Venturi and Scott Brown on their present thinking about iconography, transparency, spectacularisation, architectural pornography and the contemporary architectural avant-garde.

After 9/11, an electronic American flag went up on Times Square very quickly. The ability of today's architectural communication systems to respond quickly [...] involves a big difference for the designer: the messages are put there by someone else, not the architect.

Denise Scott Brown, 2008

In *Learning from Las Vegas* (1972),[1] the book that overturned classic understanding of symbolism in architecture, Robert Venturi, in close collaboration with his partner, the architect and planner Denise Scott Brown, and Steven Izenour, elevated the Las Vegas strip to a universal model for a new kind of architectural imagery. A result of this operation was the so-called 'decorated shed' – a billboard in front of a simple, undecorated building, reminiscent of Las Vegas casinos, where the facade is in effect detached from the building and overloaded with commercial signs. The scandal, at the time, was not so much this apparent oversimplification of the architectural organism, through which Venturi and Scott Brown opposed the elitist excesses of 1960s Modern architecture, but the very idea that decoration, previously rejected by Modernism, was an essential part of the architectural organism. This huge and flat facade in front of an ordinary shed thus became an internationally recognised prototype for the display of signs and symbols with which people could identify.

Many years have passed since the release of that eminently influential publication, and everywhere in the world architectural design has, one way or another, assimilated the ideas of Venturi and Scott Brown. Notoriously, the stress on a building's external surface has in fact assumed a strategic importance, to the degree that it has sometimes superseded the importance attributed to any other aspect of the building process. In the Vanna Venturi House (1964), for example, Venturi himself demonstrated a new way of thinking about external 'skin' in making it a complex exercise in architectural design. In this outstanding piece of contemporary architecture, he treated the building's facade as a superimposition of different layers, which soon became a kind of manifesto for *Complexity and Contradiction in Architecture* (1966),[2] his first theoretical work, which was to shock the academic world. However, while in the Vanna Venturi House the facade was not meant to stand alone, but to mirror the 'complexity and contradictions' haunting the

relationship between the building's plan and its elevation, more contemporary architecture seems to have renounced the richness of communication in favour of glass surfaces that dematerialise a building into an iconic urban sign, to the degree that over the last few decades we have witnessed an increasing diffusion of architecture's transparency. Working transparency according to several codes, in fact, has turned the former (transparency) into a purely aesthetic trend or, at best, into a metaphor for the dematerialised flux of communication in the so-called information society. This is at odds with the practice according to which transparency is an output derived from the intelligibility of communication rather than its disappearance. It comes, therefore, as no surprise that, to Venturi and Scott Brown: 'Transparency is not relevant; it is historical revival.' In fact, Scott Brown goes on to say:

'What is defined as "dematerialization" is, in effect, a Neomodernist return to transparency in architecture. This is done with glass cladding and with incandescence – with electric light, not electronic light such as video and LED. We feel the Neomodernist wave is suspect and will be forgotten. It's not part of a genuine culture. Now architects are again thinking of buildings as industrial products. And it is an old form of industry they talk about. The new form is electronic, but they still have the Industrial Revolution in their minds. That's why we feel the Neomodern return to transparency is suspect. So that is one answer to your question on transparency as metaphor. But a more interesting discussion concerns the imagery of the decorated shed. We're very involved with the imagery of LED. To change a message inscribed in stone is difficult, if not impossible. But to change an electronic image is easy. So after 9/11, an electronic American flag went up on Times Square very quickly. The ability of today's architectural communication systems to respond quickly is interesting, but it involves a big difference for the designer: the messages are put there by someone else, not the architect.'

'The idea of iconography as an essential element of architecture is interesting today,' insists Venturi, 'because we tend to forget that iconography has been important all through history. The idea of architecture as a medium of information in the pre-Information Age, is significant – while the idea of aesthetic abstraction is unique to the 20th century. And then the eclectic architects of the 19th century used symbolic reference derived from combining all sorts of historical styles. So the idea of architecture as essentially space is to us no longer relevant.'

The idea of architectural iconography in the electronic age has always been part of Venturi's and Scott Brown's DNA. In one of Venturi's latest publications, *Iconography and Electronics upon a Generic Architecture*, he in fact calls for an architecture that is not 'ideologically correct', rhetorically heroic, theoretically pretentious, boringly abstract, technologically obsolete,[3] and instead points to electronic surfaces as

Venturi, Scott Brown and Associates, Provincial Capitol Building, Département de la Haute-Garônne, Toulouse, 1999
At the entrance to the complex, stone-and-brick banding suggests a grand doorway in a simple brick wall. Before this gateway rise two-dimensional representations of ancient monumental columns once located beside the site.

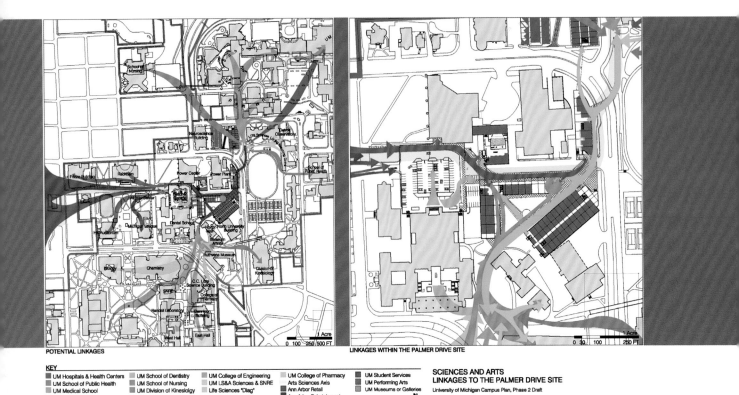

POTENTIAL LINKAGES

LINKAGES WITHIN THE PALMER DRIVE SITE

KEY
■ UM Hospitals & Health Centers ■ UM School of Dentistry ■ UM College of Engineering ■ UM College of Pharmacy ■ UM Student Services
■ UM School of Public Health ■ UM School of Nursing ■ UM LS&A Sciences & SNRE Arts Sciences Axis ■ UM Performing Arts
■ UM Medical School ■ UM Division of Kinesiolgy ■ Life Sciences "Diag" ■ Ann Arbor Retail ■ UM Museums or Galleries
■ Ann Arbor Entertainment

SCIENCES AND ARTS
LINKAGES TO THE PALMER DRIVE SITE
University of Michigan Campus Plan, Phase 2 Draft

Base Map: UM Facilities Planning & Design
Information Source: UM Office of Space Analysis, Hedberg
Maps, Inc.

Venturi, Scott Brown & Associates, Inc.   November 15, 1999

Venturi, Scott Brown and Associates, Campus Master Plan and Palmer Drive Development, University of Michigan, Ann Arbor, Michigan, 1997 and 2003
VSBA's campus plan identified the Palmer Drive site for the development of a sciences and commons complex that could connect the discrete Central and Medical Center campuses and help define an arts–science axis. The map shows the many linkages to and within the site.

a new form of functionalism in architecture, one where the building works as a source of light rather than a 'sculptural' form that reflects it. Buildings like the Centre Pompidou in Paris by Renzo Piano and Richard Rogers (1977) had already proved that the functional value of buildings lies more in the denotative display of flexibility than in flexibility itself (the latter, in fact, has never worked). It is therefore not surprising that, for Scott Brown, the Pompidou 'is a building with a certain rigidity of approach, as this is not the only way electronics can be used in architecture. From Times Square we see there are several levels of flexibility. First, the message is changeable, it can give constantly changing information. And it can change in an instant.'

This critique of the Pompidou is all the more appropriate since the building was meant, from the outset, to work as a giant billboard conveying light and electronic messages on its surface. On the other hand, it was intended to have movable floors and walls. Inspired by the Modernist principles of flexibility, everything in the Pompidou was to interact with the users, as they were assumed to be the only reason for the building's existence and, consequently, were meant to be in constant control of it too. 'Yes,' agrees Scott Brown, 'but that is expensive and often inappropriate. I had a great lecturer in

engineering at the AA in London, Felix Samuelly, who said there is "initial flexibility" and "subsequent flexibility". "Initial flexibility" is to plan the spacing of windows in such a way that you can insert partition walls on a module of perhaps two metres. The other kind is that everything can change all the time, where all partitions are movable. That is very expensive and most of the time it is not needed, because people's lives are not that movable. You have a wall and it can move. But if you put a table on one side of it and a desk on the other, and if you put 50 books on the table and 700 work files on the desk, then that wall will never move – not because *it* cannot, but because the people cannot. Therefore, that kind of flexibility is not really necessary much of the time.'

For Scott Brown, then, the growing interest that public buildings, of which the most spectacular examples are museums, arouse in people is only an effect of the sheer 'spectacularisation' of architecture and urbanism. 'Let's look at the "Bilbao effect",' she says. 'Frank Gehry said recently that he hated the Bilbao effect. The city of Bilbao decided that it needed more tourism, and sought something to bring people there. They succeeded, and many people came to see this museum. But let me highlight Bilbao's reasons for building it through a short story.

'There are primitive tribes in the Borneo jungle whose members watch planes flying overhead. To them, these are big birds, and the people know they bring untold riches to the cities beyond. They wish the birds would land where they are and bring them wealth. They know, too, that airports bring the birds to earth. So they make themselves an

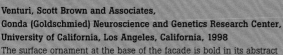

Venturi, Scott Brown and Associates,
Gonda (Goldschmied) Neuroscience and Genetics Research Center,
University of California, Los Angeles, California, 1998
The surface ornament at the base of the facade is bold in its abstract
reference to the historic north campus, and creates a strong edge for the
medical precinct against busy Westwood Boulevard. Small-scale
elements are also incorporated to be perceived by individuals walking by.

Venturi, Scott Brown and Associates,
Mielparque Nikko Kirifuri Hotel and Spa, The Ministry of Posts and
Telecommunications, Nikko National Park, Honshu, Japan, 1998
A Japanese 'village street' located within the hotel is decorated with symbolic signs and
banners representing commercial signs, mailboxes, pay phones, dispensing machines,
lamp posts, traditional lanterns and flowers. The ordinary is made extraordinary and
encourages guests to have fun.

airport. They scratch a landing strip in the ground and construct a spindly control tower of twigs and branches. This architectural supplication is intended to call the birds down. The belief system it serves is called a "cargo cult". The tribes believe the gods will descend to their airport.

'So the belief that extraordinary architecture will bring prosperity to a town in difficulty is a "cargo cult". And at Bilbao it worked – once, because the architecture was new. Build four more Bilbaos, and it won't work because it won't be new. People don't necessarily want to live with that structure; they want to see it. They want to say, "Oh, gee!"'

Seen from this particular standpoint, the iconisation of architecture is of course significant inasmuch as the spectacularisation of the urban context has highlighted an issue at the very heart of Postmodern architecture: the issue of the building's facade as a symbolic means for the 'democratisation' of the building itself.[4] In public architecture, for example, this has often addressed transparent facades as a means for visual appropriation, something that the fields of sociology and philosophy have both labelled 'architecture of consumption'. Interpreting the architecture of transparency as a result of the 'pornographic' display of over-exhibition has therefore turned the Postmodern facade into a metaphor for the

disappearance of certain values: stupefaction in place of surprise. But is it really so? Venturi pours water on the fire:

'Thinkers speak with too much alarm. Why must the tendency be towards pornography? Why must things need protection? Where is this big danger the doomsayers are seeing everywhere? This is the sociology of alarm. It is not scientific people who say these things. No one can prove these things. People who cry "The world is coming to an end! People are being oppressed by signs!" don't give human beings credit for the strength they have. There *is* much oppression in this world, but not that kind of oppression. People can fight back. Values are not being eroded. There have always been evil people. There has always been evil in people, and good, and I think the ratios are not changing too much.'

'It is therefore arrogance to say "I know better. I know better for everybody,"' Scott Brown continues. '"The poor little people. The little people are being oppressed by the things I do not like." In any case, the facade, minus pornography and other alarms, is conceptually interesting as the place between the outside and the inside. Aldo van Eyck talked about the in-between realm, about the facade as a taut skin, which stops the outside and stops the inside and represents both. Baroque architects designed rooms outside and rooms inside. Then between the two there is the wall itself which takes on the remaining shape – the *poché*. That *poché* is interesting: it has layers; it may itself contain small rooms or a stairway. The Sainsbury Wing of the National Gallery has two facades. Between the two is a space to shelter from the rain. That is an idea of facade that interests us.'

Venturi, Scott Brown and Associates, Provincial Capitol Building, Département de la Haute-Garônne, Toulouse, 1999
Administrative and legislative offices are arranged in two slender six-storey wings of flexible loft space linked by two glass-clad bridges. These linear buildings frame a pedestrian 'civic street' that cuts through the complex to join two surrounding districts.

'There is also the interesting characteristic ideal of mid-20th-century architecture where you design "from the inside out,"' Venturi concludes. 'But we say you design "from the inside out *and* from the outside in". And possible contradictions between inside and outside can produce aesthetic tension that is positive. There are interior functions *and* an exterior context to be accommodated – and this can be accomplished via layers, as in the Villa Savoye. So that can make for a lot of the dynamic of architecture, the fact that the inside requirements can be different from the outside requirements – and viva the resultant tension. The outside should not be just the result of the inside. And the outside requirements are especially significant in urban architecture. For these reasons we do not agree with the view of the facade as something that stops oppression or that is a part of oppression. Nor do we agree with the Modernists who said that the facade is something you should not be interested in. We view it as subject to change and permanence, to lightness and heaviness – and always as an in-between realm, as a place where the outside and the inside meet and both are affected. A facade is a fascinating thing. We feel we should be very interested in it, but we should also understand its anatomy.'

This study of a building's external surface, especially if seen in close relationship to its interior, has, of course, always paralleled Venturi's and Scott Brown's understanding of a building as a privileged place for the symbolic identification of its user. This brings to mind Marc Augè's notion of 'non-place' – places of transience that do not hold enough significance to be regarded as 'proper places' (motorways, hotel rooms, airports or supermarkets). However, contrary to Augè, Venturi and Scott Brown reject this viewpoint in favour of a much more positive understanding of the concept of individual and social identity.

'With regard to the concept of non-places,' says Scott Brown, 'we also heard about it from Melvin Webber, an American social scientist and planner. Webber is critical of architecture, but in a challenging way. He asks "Why do you talk about place?" You can have community without place. You can get community without propinquity. You can have "non-place realms". You do not need public space to have

Venturi, Scott Brown and Associates, Lehigh Valley Hospital (Muhlenberg), Lehigh Valley Hospital and Health Network, Bethlehem, Pennsylvania, 2005
A 14.6-metre (48-foot) blue 'H' in front of the hospital is at once a sign and an entry; the pedestrian pathway through the car park leads right through the base of the 'H' into the hospital.

Venturi, Scott Brown and Associates, Anlyan Center for Medical Research and Education, Yale School of Medicine, New Haven, Connecticut, 2003
The lobby is both an entrance to the medical complex and an urban pathway between the two buildings that make up the complex. The lobby is thus a place and a way that is both inside and outside.

society. But, and Webber agrees, it depends on the group. Some people are more place-based than others. Old people and mothers with small children are very place-based. Some classes are more place-based than others. "Street-corner society" is a place-based definition of a class of working men who lead their social life on street corners. And today we perhaps could define a "coffee shop society". All people are place-based in some way and at some stage in their lives. For this reason, I would not start by saying this is a difficult problem ... that people have no place, as we architects define it. I would ask myself, in our society and the way that it is set up, can I discover whether people have a place? It may not be where I think it should be, but let me look around and see where people are congregating.'

Indeed, throughout the ages, people have chosen different ways of socialising, whether through the piazza, the TV or the Internet. What is striking about Venturi and Scott Brown, however, is their pragmatic approach which emphasises faith in the present. This may seem at odds with a world obsessed by catastrophism, but it is born out

of their faith in peoples' innate tendency to adapt and react. In this respect, they reject the heroism and grandeur of contemporary architecture, especially when it tries, sometimes successfully, to convey technological clichés. Because, as Venturi says: '*L'avant-garde est devenue le pompier*'.[5] **ⅅ**

This interview originally took place in Rome in summer 2004, continued by email and concluded in early autumn 2008.

Notes
1. Robert Venturi, Denise Scott Brown and Steven Izenour, *Learning from Las Vegas*, MIT Press (Cambridge, MA), 1972.
2. Robert Venturi. *Complexity and Contradiction in Architecture*, The Museum of Modern Art (New York), 1966.
3. See Robert Venturi, 'A not so gentle manifesto', *Iconography and Electronics upon a Generic Architecture*, MIT Press (London), 1996, pp 11–38.
4. See Charles Jencks, *The Iconic Building: The Power of Enigma*, Frances Lincoln (London), 2005, where mega-logo buildings are interpreted as 'enigmatic signifiers' (p 21) whose eccentricity reminds the spectator of the highest possible number of images.
5. From *Iconography and Electronics*, op cit, p 304. 'Pompier' was the name the architects of the School of Beaux-Arts in Paris gave to the most rigidly traditional of its members.

The Center for Urban Pedagogy (CUP)

Mapping the Concourse, Bronx, New York, 2008
Prison City Comix, East Harlem, New York, 2007

A new generation of architects, urban designers and planners are rethinking the city. **Bill Menking** describes how the Center for Urban Pedagogy (CUP) has orchestrated a number of art-based collaborations in the New York boroughs that enable the community to participate in the reimagining of urban space.

Bill Menking

In 1932, at a symposium for the epic 'Modern Architecture: International Exhibition' at the Museum of Modern Art (MoMA) in New York, Lewis Mumford had a message for American architects who aspired to design housing schemes: 'You must plan them as though you were working for a Communist government!' This reference sat in stark opposition to the 'formalist' message of the MoMA exhibition that architecture is primarily form-making, not sociology. Mumford was probably trying to be controversial, to illustrate his message of the social nature of the profession, but nevertheless the quip highlights the ongoing divide in American architectural practice between those who believe it is simply a matter of form and those who believe it to be primarily a socially formed practice. Such division has long been encouraged at every level, in universities and in professional organisations such as the American Institute of Architects. The big loser in this historic split, however, is the American city, which has suffered from the creation of a larger collective urban identity and social space, and the continued marginalisation of the profession of architecture.

There have been many attempts to reorder architectural practice in the US to bring it closer to an urban reality: the efforts of the Regional Planning Association of America, the creation of the urban design academic programmes, the upheavals in architecture schools in the late 1960s – but all have failed. However, there are signs that a new generation of young architects,

urban designers and city planners are addressing and rethinking the relationship between the design professions and the city.

One such practice is the Center for Urban Pedagogy (CUP), a group of architects, urban designers and planners that works not as a traditional office, but more as an art-based collaborative practice that responds to local and specific problems and questions though its public lectures, gallery exhibitions, media projects and educational programmes. For example, in its Mapping the Concourse project (2008), CUP worked with students from a poor South Bronx community to organise an all-day charette that would produce a portrait of the neighbourhood around the Bronx Museum on the Grand Concourse, and also to come up with visions for its future. The charette eventually took place in the Bronx Museum, where the results were displayed as a magazine entitled *Archive City: A Grand Concourse Scrapbook*.

In the Prison City Comix project (2007), CUP worked with an English class in an East Harlem school to help the students understand the effects of the prison system on their community. Students were first taken to various correctional institutions to interview staff, prisoners and their families, and, using their design skills, CUP then helped the students to communicate their findings visually in the form of a comic book.

CUP's belief that the power of visual imagination is critical to the democratic process, and that to truly succeed it must realise the dreams and visions of citizens, is exactly what we should expect from our design professionals. Architects may yet come to believe that they must design with and for the citizens of the city and not just for themselves. ⚙

Text and images compiled by Anna Baldini

Text © 2009 John Wiley & Sons Ltd. Images: p 76 © Bill Menking; p 77(l) © CUP, digital images, layouts by teaching artist Kevin Pyle; p 77(tr) © CUP, photo Carol Sun; p 77(cr&br) © CUP, photos Rosten Woo

Prison City Comix
top left: The cover of the final comic book, which was distributed within Heritage High School and across East Harlem.
bottom left: The opening spread of the comic imagines a night in Prison City.

Mapping the Concourse
top right: Students begin their investigation with a visual census of the street, following up with interviews, mapping and conversations about what makes their neighbourhood good, what they would change, and what gives it character.
centre right: Students pin up their ideas for interventions on the Grand Concourse.
bottom right: A map of the South Bronx tagged with students' observations and what they learnt from the Mapping the Concourse project.

Spaces of Freedom

The predicaments of the current global climate bring a new poignancy and focus to architecture. **Emiliano Gandolfi,** the curator of the much lauded 'Experimental Architecture' exhibition in the Padiglione Italia at the 2008 Venice Biennale, outlines how an emerging group of designers are redefining architecture as they seek to provide solutions that identify people's needs and address the exigencies of global warning, the environmental crisis and migration.

Urban Think Tank, Metro Cable, Manguitos Station with San Agustin Music Theatre, San Agustin, Caracas, Venezuela, 2008
The aim of the Metro Cable system is to connect the *barrios* (informal settlements built on the hills of Caracas) to the rest of the city's public transport system. The system's stations also host community centres or sport facilities, or even, as shown here, a music theatre.

At a time of great urban emergency – it suffices here to think of the data collected by UN habitat, which show that by 2030 one person in three in the world will be living in a slum, and demonstrate the growing prevalence of social inequity – architects seem to be gradually losing their importance, squeezed as they are between the Star System of architecture as spectacle and the ever more imperious demands of a global capitalism that approaches urban growth exclusively on the basis of economic calculations. As is frequently the case, the crisis reveals itself as a most fertile and thrilling moment in which spaces of freedom are emerging, and a great opportunity to redefine the role of the architect, its priorities and its scopes.

In such a climate, an increasing number of architects are losing interest in the definition of exceedingly sophisticated new forms, in expressive qualities or biomorphic structures, and openly focusing on an observation of the current state of our cities and our world. Their work reveals a renewed social interest and aspiration to define new instruments for coping with the issues of our cities. They do not base their work on the plans of bureaucrats, authorities and market players. Instead, they listen to citizens' remarks, understand their problems and develop tools that stimulate people to think critically and actively about the built environment.

For these groups, architecture goes beyond just designing buildings. It has to identify the needs of people and possible forms of aggregation, while stimulating processes that will enable us to live better. Global warming, the explosive growth of cities, the environmental crisis and migration are the factors that ought to mould contemporary discourse. A new practice aims to define a different society that will be more equal and more permeable to different influences and cultures. If these objectives are to be attained, there is an urgent necessity for a redefinition of the architect's role, along with the formulation of strategies and instruments capable of comprehending the surrounding context, of acting on the complexities of the urban situation, and of imagining an alternative.

Groups like Team 10, and the movements of the 1970s, laid the bases of these practices but, unlike the past century, today every project becomes a sensitisation campaign that involves the community at the local level and stimulates collective processes, spontaneous creativity and activism in order to incite new political commitment for architecture. In opposition to architecture as formal design, the key is to be 'involved'. The architect leaves his office and becomes a seismographer who locates and identifies existing practices, interests and needs. The words of Aldo van Eyck resound like a distant echo, when he asked: 'Can

2012 Architecten, Espressobar *K, TU Delft, The Netherlands, 2008
Installed in the TU Delft architectural faculty, the *K bar is made completely from waste material, collected locally using a 'building materials harvester'.

architects meet society's plural demand? … In what are people to participate in fashioning their own immediate surroundings within a conceived overall framework? You see, when one says, "city" one implies the "people" in it, not just "population". This is the first problem confronting the architect-urbanist today.'[1]

But those same questions are today being given different answers. New tools have to be developed: buildings, zoning, land-use regulations and maps are ineffectual for the purposes of this change and simply become parts of a process in which the ultimate goal is always determined by the experience and the change in perspective of the people involved. The urgency lies in redefining the parameters of a language, broadening the discussion and identifying new tools for opening up the range of architecture's possibilities. Through investigations, temporary structures, urban interventions and visionary projects, a whole range of means is used to analyse, interpret and intervene in the complexity of urban reality. Architecture is no longer considered an autonomous discipline, and urban transformations are regarded in the first place as grand narrations, composed of material as well as immaterial elements, and of hybridisations between different disciplines and cultures. Within these general and shared assumptions, several different sensibilities and interests emerge.

Reuse: A New Urban Ecology
Sustainability is by necessity becoming one of the most relevant themes in architectural practice. Beyond the Hi-Tech, high-cost and low-consumption masterpieces, an emerging attitude is being developed around the notion of reuse. The work of the Dutch collective 2012 Architecten stands out here for its attempt to produce architecture in a continuous cycle, whereby each element is reutilised to reduce the consumption of energy. In their designs, construction materials are carefully selected on the basis of their proximity to the site and the ready-made qualities of individual elements. An adventure playground created out of recycled wind-turbine blades, a bar built from washing machines and a house constructed from reassembling cable reels are just some of their interventions. In each project, obvious environmental advantages became a symbolic manifesto on

the need to respect the environment. The momentum developed in terms of communication campaigns around their interventions, spreading a new sensibility for environmentally friendly design solutions. On a larger scale, the city can become a more habitable place in which a new balance with nature is re-established. The idea of designers who are shifting from landscape to architecture, such as the French Coloco and the Spanish [ecosistema urbano], is to treat urban reality as an ecosystem in which to intervene through processes that can shift urban environments into a greener and more sustainable balance. Their approach always starts out from an analysis of the potential for growth, from the exploitation of local qualities and an increase in biodiversity.

Rediscovering the Public Domain

With the now evident process of the loss of importance of public space in the face of the advancement of a commercial view of places for meeting (such as shopping malls), several architects are showing an increasing interest in projects aimed at reactivating spaces for exchange between cultures, ideas and customs. These projects, as in the case of a number of 'unsolicited' proposals, such as the work of Oslo-based architects Fantastic Norway, have the aim of bringing about a comparison, and if possible creating a consensus, that will promote the implementation of the proposals themselves. These are specific interventions that are always careful to safeguard and make the most of local characteristics and, on this basis, develop strategies and systems capable of triggering change. The use of public space and the vitality of urban culture take on greater significance than the actual form of buildings, and every project is an attempt to foster exchange and involvement. In the definition of a new public space, some designers and artists do not hesitate to get themselves directly involved in the organisation of cultural projects as means of urban action. For six weeks, Peter Fattinger, Veronika Orso and Michael Rieper, the conceivers of add on. 20 höhenmeter (add-on, 20 metres in height) turned Wallensteinplatz in Vienna into a centre of urban interaction through the construction of a multistorey structure composed of caravans, terraces, gardens, picnic tables and a hydro-massage tub. The bland square turned into a cluster of public spaces that permitted the creation of temporary meeting-places.

Empowerment

On a more international level there are groups that are trying to achieve worldwide attention on issues that are strongly related to architecture, but are mostly neglected by conventional practice. The Foundation for Achieving

Peter Fattinger, Veronika Orso and Michael Rieper with students from the TU Vienna, add on. 20 höhenmeter (add-on, 20 metres in height), Wallensteinplatz, Vienna, Austria, 2005
A stand-alone urban installation positioned in the middle of a city square becomes a place where local issues can be discussed in public.

Seamless Territory (FAST) is dedicated to exposing the global abuses of ideological planning, and aims to empower local populations through spatial planning. The foundation, with its headquarters in Amsterdam, intervenes in cases where governments, state architects or urban planners have created constraints on the local population through liberticide laws and oppressive spatial interventions. Its work is raising the awareness of inhabitants, and its aim is to think with them as to how to improve their living conditions and how to translate these ambitions into alternative plans. The study of specific conditions is accompanied by international campaigns of denunciation and projects aimed at enhancing the living conditions of local populations. Each FAST project seeks to promote alternative methods of urban planning in which an understanding of local issues is developed through the active involvement of the population, and adopts methods of negotiation or tactics embodying 'architectural survival techniques' that are capable of stimulating a sense of appropriation and creative responses.

Mediators

Collectives such as the Italian Stalker/Osservatorio Nomade, the Mexican-American Estudio Teddy Cruz or the American Centre for Urban Pedagogy (CUP) are questioning their local contexts and the people who inhabit them to understand the priorities they need to concentrate on. Their investigations are embodied in projects both in terms of construction and intangible actions – events aimed at affecting people's sensibility and taking the first steps towards change – where involvement with the local community and those who represent other disciplines is considered a resource in defining new connections and creating bridges. Projects may even take the form of simple educational programmes capable of stimulating a new sensibility to, and understanding of, urban dynamics, as in the work of CUP in New York City. To develop an understanding of our urban realm and to bridge the gap between the community and politicians, CUP proposes a wide

Estudio Teddy Cruz, A Housing Urbanism
Made of Waste, Tijuana, Mexico, 2008
A prefabricated frame acts as a hinge mechanism to mediate
across the multiplicity of recycled materials and systems
brought from San Diego and reassembled in Tijuana.

Santiago Cirugeda (Recetas Urbanas), Roof House, 2007
The architect is not building the houses, but instead he is providing materials, instructions
(resembling an Ikea flat-pack kit) and legal assistance in order to let people spontaneously
build temporary housing on roof terraces. A first house – a demonstration unit – was
assembled in Seville in Spain, but the Roof House can be built almost anywhere.

range of tactics and long-term strategies that include
educational programmes, panel discussions, walking tours
and media campaigns in many forms. Since 1997, CUP
has conducted educational projects about places and how
they change, bringing together art and design professionals
and community-based advocates and researchers.

Buildings become just one aspect of a more complex
work of mediation between the needs of citizens on the
one hand, and local politicians and builders on the other.
Teddy Cruz works between two such extremely close yet
different realities as San Diego and Tijuana. His approach
centres on a thorough study of local conditions, the
results of which he then uses to set up systems of self-
construction in Mexico and to promote public spaces on
the American side of the border. He proposes to export
local resources and qualities from one side to the other. In
the same way, Urban Think Tank starts out from a
meticulous study of local conditions in Caracas,
Venezuela, in order to develop projects aimed at the
regeneration of the *barrios* (informal settlements built on
the hills of Caracas). Each problem becomes the stimulus
for the development of new means: criminality is opposed
with sports facilities and social centres, and marginal
existence with cable railways capable of climbing steep
slopes. Local solutions stimulate progressive urban change.

Activism

In certain cases the architect is becoming more of a
strategist than just a designer of buildings. The work of
the groups mentioned above aims at developing long-term
strategies and intervention tactics to sensitise people and
push them to adopt new attitudes. In these kinds of
campaigns, the work of Santiago Cirugeda (Recetas
Urbanas) is particularly effective. Cirugeda's mission is to
'work from the citizen's point of view', and he is
developing subversive actions, via the media, to raise

awareness of the progressive reduction of the public sphere of our
cities, and the segregation of less wealthy people, who cannot afford to
live downtown in distant peripheral neighbourhoods. Each project,
whether housing or community spaces, is designed according to the
needs of its users and built by the users themselves. In fact, the
Seville-based architect is designing the instructions in an Ikea self-
assembly format, and providing cheap building materials and legal
assistance. His proposals consist of perpetually redefining systems in
terms of urban planning and legislation, looking for possible legal
loopholes and grey areas that allow the inhabitants freedom of action.
From the systematic occupation of unused public spaces to the
construction of prostheses in facades, patios, roofs and vacant plots,
Cirugeda negotiates legal and illegal zones. An interesting aspect is
that, as an artist, his projects benefit from a peculiar legal status and
as such are safeguarded by the same laws he is trying to swindle.

These are just some of the overall strategies and tools that are enabling
architects to obtain new scope while using the technologies of the
commercial world, the language of advertising and the laws of
marketing to overturn those same commercial messages and to open
our eyes to a world of different possibilities. Each project, each action,
each contribution defines a new intervention, a new way of practising
architecture and of imagining our future, to create a more equal society
that is more permeable to different influences and constantly shaped
by a more creative definition of the way we use the urban context.
Architecture is shifting from the image, the object, the building,
towards the definition of relational strategies in projects where the
process is more relevant than the result, and whose success lies in the
emancipation of the people involved, in the emergence of a new
awareness and the possibility of change. ⚿

Note
1. Aldo van Eyck, 'Team 10 Primer 1953–62', in Alison Smithson (ed), *Architectural Design*,
December 1962, p 564.

'To Go Beyond or Not to Be'
Unsolicited Architecture
An **Interview** with Ole Bouman

The complex dynamics of today's architecture require a deep intellectual freedom. This is something that Dutch architectural critic Ole Bouman espouses through his provocative writings and lectures and his advocacy of 'unsolicited architecture'. **Luca Guido** invited Bouman to reflect on what it means to be an architect today and how it might be possible to pursue critical practice beyond the conventional construction processes.

The phenomenon of 'theoretical meltdown' has created a varied and complex architectural landscape. In many cases architecture has moved away from the utopian impulse that characterised it in the past, and it seems that as a discipline it is no longer able to relate to the rapid changes in today's society or properly understand new urban paradigms.

Among those who are currently exploring and writing about the new dynamics of contemporary architecture, Ole Bouman is certainly one of the most interesting. One of his objectives is to make architects more aware of the frontiers of their profession. To him, 'to go beyond' – beyond form, beyond language, beyond disciplinary frontiers – is the new motto for architectural research. Indeed, 'Architecture must go beyond itself' was the key theme of the first issue of *Volume*, the now quarterly magazine Bouman edits, and which he founded with Rem Koolhaas and Mark Wigley.[1] And 'Out There: Architecture Beyond Building' was the title of the 11th International Exhibition of Architecture at the Venice Biennale (2008), directed by Aaron Betsky.

It is clear that over the last two or three decades the way of thinking about architecture has changed dramatically. Today brand, communication, and other instruments of the mass media circus that are subjected to the logic of capital and advertising, play a direct role in controlling the way we think. It is thus no coincidence that Bouman, in his articles and conferences, often deals with the concepts of intellectual freedom, agitation, power, destruction and so on. These are issues chosen by society, issues that are part of everyday reality and far from the classical contents of discipline. But how can we derive from this reality the stimulus to promote a new architecture? According to Bouman:

'In answering this question, I'd like to focus your attention on one of the phenomenal challenges of architecture: to design without a request. The questions you have posed seem rather instrumental to me, intended to solicit my opinion about something. However, the topics you raise are not about resolving something or expressing myself; rather, they represent fields of speculation and the exploration of opportunities for architecture today.

'My opinion doesn't really count. What interests me the most is an assessment of the cultural and historical dynamics in which architecture finds itself today. These dynamics, of a mind-boggling nature, affect everything that we consider architecture or architectural: its

'It's stunning how a discipline that we know to be so slow, expensive and respectable, today manifests itself as a swirl that doesn't stop anywhere. Buildings become "effects", interiors become "terminals", cities become instant skylines – everything at a pace that ridicules any reflexive attitude at the price of becoming completely irrelevant or obsolete.'

definition, its mandate, its output, its corpus of knowledge, its education, its inspiration, its legitimacy, its techniques and methods, its social status, its communication.

'It's stunning how a discipline that we know to be so slow, expensive and respectable, today manifests itself as a swirl that doesn't stop anywhere. Buildings become "effects", interiors become "terminals", cities become instant skylines – everything at a pace that ridicules any reflexive attitude at the price of becoming completely irrelevant or obsolete. The paradigm set by Shanghai or Dubai, and by Nazarbajev or King Abdullah, has nothing to do with heritage or history, classics or vernacular – not even with what we know as "city".

'Architecture as a discipline still has to come to terms with this. What does it mean if a new reality has to be created with brand-new money, on brand-new sites, by brand-new clients for brand new purposes that combine Dante and Disney? Or even without a purpose … Not all has changed. What keeps architecture for ever connected with its past is the way it articulates the encounter between space and human creativity. Perhaps it is extremely difficult to define a core for a profession that is at risk of being dissolved or realigned with new energies, but that doesn't mean there is no architecture. As long as we move around through virtual spaces, inside buildings, around buildings, between buildings, in streets, neighbourhoods, cities and landscapes, spatial creativity will have a rationale.

'The issue is that if you don't perceive the big-time changes, your creativity will never be as creative as it could be. To make sure it is, you have to go beyond. Moreover, it is a matter of "To Go Beyond or Not to Be," as *Volume* magazine puts it.[2]

'Going beyond the preconceptions, expectations and accomplished facts today is not just a matter of belonging to the avant-garde of architecture. It is now more than ever an existential necessity to continue as an interesting and appealing discipline that keeps attracting the brightest minds. Architecture has always been a very conservative discipline that stuck to its foundations: shape, construction, space and place. But if we consider the emergence of temporary shapes, moving constructions, interactive spaces, non-places, to name a few contemporary architectural

Milan, Italy, 2008
This view at night captures aspects of a part of this very traditional city. Buildings follow a regular logic, aligned to road axes and organised in similar-sized blocks.

Dubai City, Dubai, 2008
Skyscrapers and buildings under construction. Planning governed by complex
economic dynamics, money and entertainment, and the densification of
spaces and buildings, makes this city an urban and architectural
phenomenon hard to interpret with traditional disciplinary tools.

phenomena, even conservatism becomes transgressive. Never before has sheer disciplinary survival equalled such an interesting life.'

It is true that conceiving architecture as a discipline has its difficulties: if we try to understand contemporary phenomena using traditional instruments of interpretation, we will not see very far. Disciplinary autonomy has played a significant role in moving architecture further and further away from reality, but it is now evident that new architectural and urban paradigms cannot be interpreted through theories developed in libraries or university classrooms alone, or through the warnings of obsolete theories such as nihilism and neo-Heideggerism. However, despite this, many important values of the past are still deeply relevant to the challenges architects face today.

Space and time in architecture are still important, but in Issue 14 of *Volume*, Bouman introduced 'unsolicited architecture' – a new form of disciplinary autonomy for architecture, beyond building.[3] Such a concept, somewhere between manifesto and provocation, seems to be a challenge, an attempt to retrieve the utopian ideals that have been lost in favour of the logic of capital. However, if we look at the practices of many of today's great architects, we could say that they have escaped the social role and pioneering vision that characterised the work of the masters of the Modern Movement. Or perhaps, more likely, they simply play a neutral role as it becomes difficult to conceive of the new terms of architectural discipline as continuous mutations:

'Now, one particular way to go beyond is to give up on the eternal preconditions of architecture: client, programme, budget and site. Architects always reacted to at least one of these, and most of the time to all four of these pillars of their practice. And if you react, it is always difficult to go beyond. Thus there are a growing number of architects who do not wait until they can react: they just act. They make unsolicited architecture.'

According to Bouman, the time has come to design not as solicited by the client, site or available budget, but unsolicited – that is, by designing the architecture first, then finding the client, site and budget for it afterwards. However, though this idea is interesting, it is not without risks.

Traditionally, architecture's contact with other cultural arenas has been sporadic and, as mentioned earlier, disciplinary autonomy has been instrumental in widening the gap between the practice of building and architectural research. Could unsolicited research, or unsolicited architecture, become a marketing tool for those few architects who can also build it? In fact, the most prominent architectural themes and large-scale urban experiments are already the prerogative of just a few

There are many indications that architects must now act differently than they have done in the past in order to meet the challenges of a changing society. However, it is not clear where architecture is going, and whether it is still necessary as we know it.

architects who are part of the seemingly multinational corporation of the Star System. Indeed, there are nations and cities (especially those in the East) where important architectural firms are viewed as high-fashion shops. Such architects propose something that is a new brand of architecture, but at the same time a logo.

Architects' role in society is blurred and does not always allow for complete creativity. In addition, those who wish to be unconventional in their approach are rarely free from the compromises of the profession. So why should architects make unsolicited architecture?

'Why? Firstly because it keeps their architecture autonomous. The autonomy of architecture was once something about hermetic seclusion from reality; now we know that it is a matter of becoming inclusive beyond any client's expectation. Autonomy is in the drive, not in the territory. Secondly because as a service industry starts to resemble animal behaviour, only responding to a need, request or threat of a client, architecture as an art, a science, an innovation, an ideal, an adventure, an act of curiosity, an aid, a rescue, has its own agenda.

Thirdly because unsolicited architecture first of all relies on self-motivation, free thinking, curiosity, dignity, a sense of urgency and responsibility, and its antenna for opportunities.

And finally because by doing so it ultimately preserves architecture's long-term relevance and legitimacy. Unsolicited architecture is acquisition for the long term and finding new objects for the application of architectural intelligence.'

There are many indications that architects must now act differently than they have done in the past in order to meet the challenges of a changing society. However, it is not clear where architecture is going, and whether it is still necessary as we know it. It is likely that unsolicited architecture will not be the last of the theories; it is simply a part of the current general theoretical meltdown within art and architecture. ∆

This interview has been compiled from email correspondence between Luca Guido and Ole Bouman from May to August 2008.

Notes
1. *Volume*, No 1, *Beyond*, Archis Foundation (Amsterdam), 2005. The imprint for the magazine reads: 'Volume – independent quarterly for architecture to go beyond itself'.
2. This motto appears on the spine of each issue of *Volume* magazine.
3. Ole Bouman, 'Unsolicited, or: The new Autonomy of Architecture', in Arjen Oosterman (ed), *Volume*, No 14, '*Unsolicited Architecture*', February 2008, pp 26–8. Bouman first introduced the idea of unsolicited architecture in his article 'Unsolicited Architecture', in *Volume*, No 1, *Beyond*, 2005, pp 86–91.

MAD
Beijing 2050

Jiang Jun, Editor-in-Chief of *Urban China* magazine, marvels at the architectural phenomenon that is MAD. Riding on the crest of Chinese urban expansion, Ma Yansong has optimised on extraordinary architectural opportunities. His projects, such as Beijing 2050, display a savvy design approach that synthesises innovative forms with Chinese characteristics.

Jiang Jun

The phenomenal rise of Ma Yansong and his Beijing-based studio MAD is almost unprecedented in China or, indeed, the rest of the world. Having graduated with a Masters degree from Yale in 2002, Ma founded the practice in 2004, and is now designing and completing major projects across the world. These include: the Absolute Towers in Toronto; the 358-metre (1,174-foot) high Sino-steel International Plaza in Tianjin, China; Phoenix Island masterplanning; and large-scale public complexes and residential housing in Denmark, Hong Kong, Dubai, Singapore, Malaysia, Japan and Costa Rica.

Any attempt to explain the alacrity with which MAD has come to the fore must consider the industrial transformation upon which Ma's success is based. Large-scale change has been under way in China for many years, in terms of both international and domestic industrial structure. The shift, over the last two decades, of the international industrial centre to the coast in southeast China has been the cause of large-scale domestic migration with over 400 million people moving to seek work. It has also provided the catalyst for the 'hilarious' trend of urbanisation, which has produced more and more megalopolises with enormous construction demands. The process of globalisation has specifically benefited architects with bilateral access to the expanded market, giving significant priority to those with transnational architectural experience and fame, such as Ma who undertook postgraduate studies at Yale and also worked as a project designer with Zaha Hadid Architects in London and Eisenman Architects in New York.

In MAD's projects, the innovative design concept and the target marketing strategies assume equal importance. It is apparent in Beijing 2050, for instance, that on the one hand Ma is introducing innovative concepts into China, with an obvious connection to Zaha Hadid's work; and on the other is wisely applying Chinese characteristics, especially in the context of renovating more traditional architecture with typical leftist associations. This tactical design policy with diverse effects has various social aspirations, and contributes towards Ma's wider ambition to acknowledge different aspects in his work.

However, none of the above-mentioned elements are the essential feature of Ma's work that distinguishes him from his Chinese predecessors. It is his approach as a superior architect that marks him out. Ma is more resourceful in dealing with mass communication than previous generations. Through his conscious and unconscious cooperation with the fashion industry and media, he has effectively promoted his business, ensuring his position at home and abroad among the international 'stars' of architecture.

To sum up, it becomes apparent that MAD's astronomical rise must be attributed to much more than good fortune or good timing. In MAD, there is a crucial and harmonious integration of the avant-garde concept and personal ambition alongside an understanding of professional rationality and responsibility that are essential for the future development of Chinese architecture. ᴁ

Text and images compiled by Anna Baldini

MAD's futuristic interventions in detail: each block could provide private showers, childcare or other facilities that are not currently available to the neighbourhoods' existing residents.

top: MAD's proposal for a horizontally linked floating island above Beijing's Central Business District (CBD). An alternative to segregated and competing skyscrapers, the aim of the floating island is to emphasise connectivity and interdependence. As China begins to jump ahead of the West in terms of development, Beijing's CBD is an increasingly irrelevant copy of the Western model of modernisation.

above: Futuristic interventions complement Beijing's historic poor *hutong* neighbourhoods, which are increasingly being given over to tourism and gentrification. Rather than allowing such neighbourhoods to become fake historical playgrounds for the wealthy, MAD's super-modern interventions and structures provide for a mix of residents from all economic groups.

Cross the River by Touching the Stones

Chinese Architecture and Political Economy in the Reform Era: 1978-2008

China's Open Door Policy and economic development set in motion in 1978 can be regarded as the triumph of pragmatism over theory – specifically Chairman Mao's brand of Marxist theory. **Tao Zhu** traces the progress of reform over the last 30 years, and its impact on Chinese architectural culture.

Construction site of the new CCTV Headquarters in Beijing as of 2 January 2008.

Remains of Dongqi Middle School, Sichuan Province, after the earthquake, as of 22 May 2008.

May 12 2008 began as any other 'normal' day in China. The Central Government was concentrating on rousing the nation's zeal to embrace Beijing's Olympic Games. Beijing was eager to show the world its recently erected array of dazzling buildings, such as the Bird's Nest National Stadium, the Water Cube National Aquatics Centre and the new China Central Television (CCTV) Headquarters. The government was convinced that the world would be in awe of China, a giant superpower about to stage the most spectacular Olympic Games, enshrined in an architectural triumph it believed no other country could possibly achieve.

At 2:28 pm, an 8-magnitude earthquake struck the rural area of Sichuan Province, southwest of Beijing – a catastrophe that revealed a far different aspect of the country.

Amid the calamity and misery of the earthquake, one factor stood out: in the rural quake zone there were about 10,000 schools that had collapsed, killing more than 10,000 children. This disproportionate destruction and extraordinary number of deaths quickly ignited public anger, which immediately focused on the shoddy construction of rural schools, a dire problem that had been ignored for decades due to the government's meagre spending on rural education.

China has failed to achieve its goal, set in 2000, to spend the equivalent of at least 4 per cent of national GDP on education, a figure internationally accepted as the threshold for basic funding.[1] Moreover, since the late 1980s China's rural education has gathered a $7.3 billion debt, most of which comprises construction fees owed to school-building contractors and salaries owed to teachers.

In contrast, government officials annually spend nearly $120 billion on dining, entertaining, the use of vehicles, and domestic and overseas tours.[2] At the last count, the government spent $40 billion on Olympics-related projects.

Not only in Beijing, but in all of China's large cities, numerous iconic buildings are being erected with the full consent of the government, demonstrating excessive spending; in rural quake zones, flimsy schools collapse like houses of cards. These contrasting images dramatically illustrate China's current extreme social conditions and exemplify as well the present state of Chinese architecture, which has been on a 30-year journey along with the country's uneven political and economic development.

1978: The Theory of 'Touching'
'Cross the river by touching the stones; take one step and then watch for the next one.' This is a classic phrase coined by China's central leaders to depict the country's economic reform, officially launched during the Third Plenum of the Eleventh Chinese Communist Party (CCP) Congress held in December 1978.

The major outcome of this meeting was a shift in the CCP's focus from class struggle to economic development. Between 1949 and 1976, due to the party's enactment of Mao Zedong's orthodox version of Marxism–Leninism centred on class struggle, millions of people died. With respect to economic development, the party displayed another dismal record, of which the 'Great Leap Forward' is the most wretched example.

The Great Leap Forward (1958–60) was an economic and social plan formulated by Mao Zedong for the radical collectivisation of the country in an attempt to mobilise mass labour to rapidly industrialise China. This movement quickly led to major political, economic and environmental disasters, and to what is believed to have been the greatest famine in human history: during a brief span of time from 1959 to 1961 it resulted in the horrific death toll of an estimated 35 million to 50 million people.[3] Significantly, it was during the same period that the CCP decided to build 'Ten Great Buildings' in Beijing to commemorate the 10-year anniversary of the People's Republic of China. The 10 grand projects, which consumed enormous resources and labour, were completed in 10 to 12 months, meeting the government's deadline of 1 October 1959. The massive array of monumental buildings, which had radically transformed Beijing, was celebrated as the 'ground-breaking of Chinese architectural history' at the moment when China was experiencing one of its most serious socioeconomic crises.

'Ten Great Buildings' in Beijing, 1959

In 1976, a year marked by Mao's death and the dissolution of the 'Great Cultural Revolution', China's socioeconomic system was on the verge of total collapse. By the end of 1978, the party realised that without any proven experience to fall back on, or guiding theory to follow, it could only wade across the river of reform by 'touching the stones' step by step.

Today, this trial-and-error approach is often described as anti-theoretical pragmatism with 'Chinese characteristics'. However, a historical awakening that preceded this project should not be overlooked: it was precisely through an intensive theoretical discussion that Chinese politicians and intellectuals finally arrived at their 'anti-theory' position in 1978.

Early in 1977, Hua Guofeng, Mao's chosen successor, launched his notorious principle of 'Two Whatevers' in order to secure his newly gained position: 'Whatever decisions Chairman Mao has made, we shall support, and whatever instructions Chairman Mao has given, we will all follow.'

During this period, there was enormous bottom-up pressure as a result of both the demands of intellectuals for democratisation and spontaneous land-contracting experiments being carried out by local peasants. Acknowledging this duress, and as a way to counter Hua's dogmatism, late in 1977 Deng Xiaoping set out to mobilise a nationwide theoretical debate dealing with the question: 'What is the Judgment of Truth?' A great many intellectuals and party members, at the risk of their own lives, participated in this debate. In mid-1978, a conclusion was crystallised into one slogan: 'Practice is the sole arbiter of truth.' Deng, who replaced Hua and became China's central leader, officially endorsed this new ideological consensus during the Party Congress in December 1978.

The 'practice/truth debate' was known as the 'First Wave of Emancipation of Thinking'. After ideological dogmas had finally run their course, and through an adventurous theoretical investigation, the 'anti-theoretical' pragmatism centred on 'practice' finally prevailed.

1978–2008: Crossing the River
Between 1979 and the mid-1980s, the CCP set out on a 'river-crossing' journey by steadily stepping on to a series of large stones. It launched agricultural reform, established township and village enterprises, opened international trade through coastal cities and special economic zones (SEZs), and implemented fiscal decentralisation to encourage the development of local governments.

The period between 1984 and 1988 saw the first 'high wave' of reform, consisting of a series of attempts to boost the market economy through a dual-track pricing system, improve state-owned enterprises, encourage the growth of non-state-owned enterprises and initiate financial reform.

The overall programme was successful. However, serious problems began to emerge in the mid-1980s. The neo-liberalisation of the economy without a rule of law quickly led to a surge of corruption, inflation and social inequality.

The negative outcome of reform triggered the Tiananmen Square Movement in 1989. Students, intellectuals and workers in all major Chinese cities protested, and appealed to the party for freedom in the media as well as legal independence and political liberalisation. In response, on 4 June 1989, the CCP cracked down violently on the movement during the Tiananmen Incident, and chose to go along with economic development only at the expense of genuine political reform.

Early in 1992, after a short economic depression and political uncertainty, Deng Xiaoping made his Southern Tour to the SEZs. Recapturing regional support, Deng was able to tip the political balance within the Central Government and once again set China on a journey of economic reform instead of political restructuring: 'Speedy development is the only hard truth.' Realising that its economic system was still a halfway house between a planned and market economy, the Central Government established another set of ambitious goals to fulfil a thorough transition towards a market system.

This measure lays bare a fundamental paradox: in order to achieve this objective, Chinese policy-makers would have to draw a clear boundary between the government and the party, establish a rigorous rule of law, and create a multicentred network of independent processes to scrutinise the market operation and ensure its accountability. These prerequisites would entail a far-reaching political reform, a subject that the CCP had always been reluctant to confront.

In short, the economic reform of China is one of the great success stories at the turn of the century. The key factor contributing to this success was the CCP's decision to transfer a high level of economic authority to provincial and local officials to encourage their reliance on the market and private sector as a way to energise agricultural production and urban development. By shifting from a state-directed command economy to a market-based one, the party's economic reform not only produced a great economic boom, but also transformed China into an economic global powerhouse.

However, this same economic dynamic has also wreaked havoc on both the social structure and natural environment of the country, especially since the 1990s. The neo-liberalisation of the economy, unaccompanied by a stream of institutional progress for human, civil and democratic rights, did not foster an equitable system. Instead, through a close integration of party members and business elites, it created a hybrid type of economy with 'Chinese characteristics' that was blended with the features of both 'crony capitalism' and 'crony socialism'. While rapidly reconstituting a 'crony class' power, the market force of this type of economy has led to endless corruption as well as ruthless exploitation of the country's natural resources and brutal demolition of the social welfare system.

'Practice is the sole arbiter of truth.' If this principle, established 30 years ago, is still to be followed, it must be examined in greater depth. If the subjects of 'practice' are plural, then *whose* practice should be considered the *arbiter* of truth? If the consequences of a practice are many-sided, *which side* should be chosen? Most importantly, *who* should serve as the 'judge' in these matters?

It appears that after 30 years of 'crossing the river by touching the stones', China has finally reached the middle of the river where the water is unfathomably deep. It flows by rapidly. There is no clear destination or direction to follow, not even any readily accessible stones to step on. The essential questions that China now faces are: *what* river, *how* to cross it, *which* stones to touch, and above all, *where* to go?

Architecture's Will to Power

The development of contemporary Chinese architecture has experienced an immense 'time–space compression' emanating from the drastic transformation of China's society over a short span of time. Following the uneven 30-year journey of 'river crossing', Chinese architects have not only been compelled to fulfil an enormous demand for production due to the imperative of development; they have also been obliged to project various cultural images imposed by their powerful clientele. A period of great haste and confusion has led to a typical mindset among Chinese architects: total indifference, a state of oblivion to the requirement for critical reflection on the political implications of Chinese architecture, whether related to its production processes or cultural expression.

Production

China's building industry started to boom in the 1980s when it was considered to be one of the main pillars of the economy. Through its production processes, architecture has served as a major component in linking political and economic structures; yet the attitude of the major participants in this process, the Chinese architects, has remained extremely passive while the social and physical consequences of their products have been significant.

While the state's role in strategic planning has been greatly diminished during the economic reform process, most local officials have been preoccupied with the Great Leap Forward mentality that envisions a society capable of 'jumping ahead' overnight. When establishing close ties with short-term, profit-driven investments, this attitude has tended to result not only in corruption, but also in arbitrary, uncoordinated and often wasteful projects that have beset China's urban/suburban development efforts, especially over the last two decades.

While being involved in this process, Chinese architects could have assumed a greater proactive political role by collaborating with local officials and clients to achieve more socially responsible results. However, the concept of social consciousness is a new one for China – 'star' architects pander to a *nouveau riche* clientele, devoting themselves only to an exclusive range of elite projects. Moreover, when 'normal' architects produce massive housing projects or city planning schemes almost on a weekly basis, they have little concern for the general public as a client, almost no interest in considering housing as a social programme, and often no time to explore more balanced urban development options. They are unable to grasp the social and physical consequences of their own products, nor do they still share the Modernist belief in the redemptive social power of architectural production. Either by choice or, more likely, through default, the application of their professional skills is absorbed into the new Great Leap Forward development process, which often leads to dire results.

Rem Koolhaas once remarked that Chinese architects are a thousand times more efficient than their Western counterparts. Is it not a troubling irony that the new Great Leap Forward, in fact, constitutes the hyper-productivity of Chinese architects?

Even more ironically, many scholars have wasted no time in paying lip service to China, asserting that it has stepped into a 'post-critical'

Cai Peiyi's International Exhibition Center, Beijing, 1985

Dai Nianci's Queli Hotel, Qufu, Shandong, 1985

stage in which the ideological struggle has been transcended by market forces in the globalised world. This clearly is not the case. In the 1980s, the early stages of the market economy made a strong contribution to the creation of a relatively more liberal political and cultural atmosphere, especially when it was working in confluence with the massive political-cultural New Enlightenment Movement. The CCP put a violent end to the movement, as mentioned earlier, in 1989, prioritising economic development over political reform. The market forces in China have not transcended the ideology, but have instead been utilised by the authoritarian regime as a major force to suppress, or bypass, the intense ideological struggle in the country. This basic factor is omitted from many enthusiastic accounts of contemporary Chinese architecture and urbanism, including Koolhaas' report on the Pearl River Delta, entitled *Great Leap Forward*.[4]

Expression
Between the 1950s and the late 1970s there had been only two 'master narrative' languages for Chinese architects to apply: Modernism, identified as the International Style or Structuralism, and the 'National Form', which often combined Beaux-Arts composition with Chinese classical elements and the Socialist Realism promulgated by the Soviet Union. Apprehensive about China's unpredictable politics and disillusioned by the gradual realisation that the link between formal expression and political content could be arbitrary, Chinese architects developed an eclectic attitude towards architectural form: they chose one or combined the two, depending only on the particular political-economic circumstances of the moment. One can clearly recognise this approach in the Ten Great Buildings of 1959.

This formal eclecticism hardened into a reductivist notion of form between the 1980s and 1990s, when China started its economic reform and the nation eagerly embraced modernisation. Often, in the 'progressive' architectural debates, the undecorated Modernist form was attributed to open, forward-looking, democratic and, above all, uncompromising modernity; conversely, the National Form was identified as authoritarian, conservative and burdened by tradition.

However, since the mid-1990s the opposition between the two languages and overall monotonous architectural culture that had been determined by only two 'master narrative' languages, quickly dissipated under the impact of four major forces.

First, the accelerating culture of consumption tended to explode all of the stabilised language 'systems' into floating, value-free fragments.

Wei Dazhong's Guanghua Changan Building, Beijing, 1996

Liu Jiakun's Luyeyuan Museum of Stone Sculpture, Chengdu, Sichuan, 2001

Second, government officials began to promote the practice of juxtaposing sleek Modernism with National Form, or whatever fashionable cultural kitsch, on their building facades.

Third, a group of young, emerging 'experimental' architects not only struggled to gain practice independence from the design-institute system, but also aimed to develop an 'autonomous' architectural language that was detached from any ideological connotation. From the mid-1990s, in order to construct a new architectural discourse, they borrowed a series of theoretical subjects – pure form, abstract space, conceptual design, tectonics, critical regionalism and other

The Shanghai Pudong skyline, as of February 2008

concepts. Regrettably, as a dragonfly skims across the surface of the water, none of the theoretical investigations delved into China's sociocultural reality deep enough to define a solid stepping stone for Chinese architects.

Fourth, foreign architects started to flock to China, often treating the country, as Zaha Hadid put it, 'like an incredible empty canvas for innovation'. It is this group of architects that has produced the most dazzling architectural icons throughout China's major cities. Surfing on the top waves of the Chinese *Zeitgeist*, foreign architects, whether as carpetbaggers or cultural radicals, have been seamlessly co-opted by a regime determined to demonstrate its super-power. The glitzy icons they have produced, whether well designed as ad hoc objects or poorly designed as isolated incidents, have too easily been turned into spectacular objects of propaganda.

Despite the fact that the commercial, official, 'experimental' and international groups departed from different places and followed different directions, in a surprising way they all reached the same place in the middle of the river, where there is neither a clear social vision ahead nor any formal or cultural continuity behind. Also missing is a rigorous discourse that constitutes the core of Chinese architectural discipline. In this situation, Chinese architectural culture appears no longer able to evolve, step by step, but rather to float around, while passively being pushed by external random forces: nothing alternative can be done and, therefore, anything goes.

The rubble of the collapsed schools in the rural countryside lies in sharp contrast to the iconic buildings found in large cities – when the images are juxtaposed, they constitute a striking iconography that signifies the deep-rooted contradictions in contemporary China. It is certainly the most damning indictment of the government's unchecked economic development, one that has been made at a huge cost to social equity and justice. It can also serve as a reminder to Chinese architects: the blind submission to power, the ahistorical, apolitical and value-free attitude towards architectural practice without consideration of its social responsibility and consequences, which are so pervasive in the contemporary Chinese architectural community, all urgently require a critical re-examination. ∆

Notes
1. Quoted from an official report by China.org.cn on 16 January 2007: http://www.10thnpc.org.cn/english/education/196208.htm (accessed on 11 July 2008).
2. Wang Xiangwei, 'Glitzy Icons Contrast with Fallen Schools', *South China Morning Post*, 26 May 2008.
3. Judith Shapiro, *Mao's War Against Nature: Politics and the Environment in Revolutionary China*, Cambridge University Press (Cambridge), 2001, pp 82–3.
4. In the book *Great Leap Forward* (Taschen, 2002), the Tiananmen Square Movement/Incident of 1989 was conspicuously missing from both the 'Chronology' section and the one on 'Ideology'. In fact, throughout this huge book it was only briefly mentioned in a single reference in the section on 'Policy/Politics' in connection with China's 'temporary economic recession'.

Exit Ltd

5 Codes_Space of Conflict (The Temple of Janus Revisited), Washington DC, 2009

For London-based editor, author and curator **Shumon Basar**, The Temple of Janus Revisited by Exit Ltd is an effective critique of post-9/11 politics and culture. A virtual re-enactment of the Roman Temple of Janus in Washington DC, it evokes the imminent collapse of the American Empire.

Shumon Basar

Soon after the Twin Towers fell in 2001, the US government launched its War on Terror. Invoking political scientist Samuel P Huntingdon's rousing notion of 'the clash of civilizations', as well as philosopher and political economist Francis Fukuyama's 'end of history', the neocons had given birth to a new ideological war for the 21st century. An extraordinary glut of vivid titles emanated from the Republican propaganda machine, including the now memorable 'axis of evil' as well as the aborted moniker of America's military response: Operation Infinite Justice (quickly renamed Operation Enduring Freedom after certain Muslim lobbyists argued that 'infinite justice' could only be carried out by Allah).

For many, the 21st century truly began on 9/11, in the way that the 20th century ended in 1989 with the fall of the Berlin Wall and the end of the Soviet Union. You could say that words do not mean as much as actions do. But in the War on Terror, specific words are used to invoke a future that is decidedly archaic in its Manichean worldview of good versus evil, democracy versus tyranny. It is in this recapitulation towards the very roots of Western freedom – as well as architectural truth – that I would like to introduce Exit Ltd's Temple of Janus project.

One finds the project, with its nocturnal Photoshop renderings and computer-game topography, published at the end of Stephan Trüby's treatise *Exit Architecture: Design Between War and Peace* (Springer Wien, New York, 2008). Trüby considers the history of one of the lesser concerns in architectural virtuosity: that of the way out. Grand entrances steeped with ritual steps and colonnades litter great buildings over the course of human achievement. But their exits are often somewhat less dramatic, figured as functional solutions to quantitative problems. Put another way, the mouth is an aesthetic organ denoting orality, pleasure and eroticism. The anus, less so (unless in more esoteric, less family-oriented circles).

I read the desire to re-enact the Temple of Janus in Washington DC as a massive 'exit strategy' for both the new political hegemony of our times and architecture's own endgame. Pitched somewhere between a Postmodern sampling of Neoclassical styles and a theme park dedicated to our era of ambient fear, the Temple of Janus looks backwards and forwards into history past and history to come. It is strident and weak, urgent and fatally redundant: a mock-classical confection that mirrors the potentially imminent collapse of the American Empire, much as the ruins of the Roman Empire today are our tangible link to a time of greatness that also came to a bitter end. ⚙

Text and images compiled by Anna Baldini

top left: Detail of the ceiling – an upside-down landscape of UV-lit 'Exit' signs.

top right: Two tilted mirror walls give the impression of an endless 'equator space'.

centre left: View of the 'Electromagnetic Janus', a technical unit that records and transmits debates around the table.

above: View of the interior with displays for commodity artefacts. Green display cabinets show 'peace products', red display cabinets show 'war products'.

left: Exit Ltd logo – a Janus-faced 'Exit' sign.

bottom left: The Temple of Janus of antiquity, on a coin from Nero's reign.

Some Conclusions

Liberating Ourselves from the

Guest-editor **Luigi Prestinenza Puglisi** closes the issue with a positive reflection on the impact of theoretical meltdown. He recognises in the featured architects in this volume a 'shared attitude, notwithstanding diversity' that represents a liberation from the last decade's over-concern with form and super-creativity and a rediscovery of the political dimension of architecture.

What effects will 'theoretical meltdown' have on the future of architectural production? The answer to this question, as highlighted in the contributions to this issue of *AD*, is not a simple one. What is certain, however, is that in the recent past theoretical meltdown has produced at least four results.

The first is an extraordinary perception of freedom. The protagonists of contemporary architecture have demonstrated that when designing buildings it is possible to successfully employ any idea, any form and any technology.

The second has to do with an awareness of the relational value of architecture. In fact, we have developed a new sensibility towards context and the natural environment. Buildings, even those with an overpowering iconic component, have become the signs of a new landscape to be exalted, completed, re-created or invented *ex novo*.

The third element is popularity. Never before has architecture, once of interest to only a select few, been the object of such interest by the media. This attention has been obtained by experimenting with seductive forms and a highly metaphorical content capable of involving the senses and stimulating the imagination of the general public.

The fourth element is the *koiné* of the Star System: the diffusion of a language that is recognisable anywhere, and equally successful in such distant places as New York and Moscow, London and Beijing, or Amsterdam and Dubai.

The super-creativity triggered by theoretical meltdown has been favourably accepted not only by the man on the street, but also by large corporations who quickly understood the positive force, in terms of publicity and promotion, of such an effective manifestation of creativity. The result is that architects have been transformed into the captains of a new, innovative and optimistic capitalism that operates at the global scale. Foster, Gehry, Hadid, Koolhaas, Foster, Nouvel, Piano and Rogers, whatever their intentions and political ideologies, have, in fact, become the voice of an economic system that, however, is certainly not suited to the ambitious objectives it aimed to pursue: as demonstrated by the tragic events of 11 September 2001, the war in Iran, the collapse of the stock market, the sub-prime loan crisis, an increase in the cost of primary goods and the oil crisis.

This is the reason why designers, mainly from the younger generation, even while they feel at home working within the plural universe stimulated by theoretical meltdown, feel that they are progressively further and further away from the proposals made by the Star System. What bothers them most is the bulimic excess of technologies, of materials and signs; an excess that a few years earlier was the indication of a turning point with respect to the monotonous repetition and fetishism of Postmodernism.

Towards Freedom

All of this has generated new strategies that no longer consist of recapturing the freedom of the sign, but are concerned with the more subtle liberation from the sign itself. If everything really is architecture, it is not clear why it must not lose its alterity, disappearing into the everything to which it belongs. In this way the game becomes more interesting, even in aesthetic terms.

Observed from this point of view, the projects selected by the 11 critics scattered throughout the pages of this issue of *AD* demonstrate a shared attitude, notwithstanding the diversity of the individual choices. This shared attitude consists of the need to free ourselves of the tyranny of architecture, of form and super-creativity.

In particular, I believe that the featured projects define four possible approaches to research.

Tyranny of Architecture

The first tends towards ultra-Minimalism. Chaos and formal exuberance are opposed by an aesthetic of order that is aseptic, abstract, immaterial, non-hierarchical, monochrome and inflexible, a trend that is spearheaded by the Japanese duo Kazuyo Sejima and Ryue Nishizawa. The work of one of their former employees, Junya Ishigami, is presented here among the featured projects. Ishigami is clearly one of the most rigorous interpreters of this approach. Deprived of signs of life, the building becomes pure space, a platonic grid that is the result of a pure and simultaneously sophisticated conceptual operation.

In order to maintain its ideal aspects, an architecture of this type is obviously unable to tolerate the concrete realities of daily life, such as disorder, dirt and the passage of time. Perhaps its success is precisely to be found in the abstraction of the materiality of the body and a laic asceticism that refutes the values of a consumer-based society even if, at the same time, it pursues them through the search for an extreme level of refinement.

The second approach focuses on simplicity, clarity, logic and economy. Of the members of this group, those represented here include muf, Nàbito, Mateo, Kempe Thill, Supersudaca and [ecosistema urbano]. In particular, the project by Kempe Thill demonstrates that it is possible to return to Functionalism, a dimension of the Modernist Movement that met with little success with respect to the formalism of the schools of Le Corbusier or Mies van der Rohe. The projects by [ecosistema urbano] propose a simple and unexpected way of introducing, without passing through the rhetoric of metaphor, the themes of nature and ecological awareness. If we wish to be attentive to the environment, they seem to suggest there is no need to design buildings in the form of a tree or fish, to dabble in morphogenesis, challenge technologies or create sculptural objects inspired by fractals or Boolean geometries.

The third direction of research places its bet on people and the relationships they develop with the spaces that surround them, more than on the works of architecture themselves, or what is intended by them. It renounces the invention of new spaces in order to stimulate users to inhabit those that already exist in new ways. It leads to the creation of workshops for adolescents or prisoners. It involves the alienated, nomads and those with no fixed address. This is the line of research pursued in Italy by Stalker, and in the US by CUP. In contrast to the world of gleaming architecture, they rediscover political involvement and the attitudes adopted by the Situationist avant-garde. In opposition to the specialisation of the discipline of architecture, they offer the expectations and desires that emerge from the process of participation.

The fourth dimension of research focuses on the symbolic universe. This is the approach pursued by MAD and Exit Ltd. However, the difference here is that, with respect to the Star System, these groups do not raise the issue of rendering their work commercially viable by building easy-to-consume iconic buildings.

For each of the four directions of research identified above it is not difficult to find precedents, in particular in the research of the avant-garde in the 1970s. Together they share the desire to rediscover the political dimension of architecture, and the need to escape from an excessive formalism. However, there is a difference with respect to this period, identifiable in the disenchantment resulting from the awareness that if there is to be a revolution it will certainly not be political, but structural. This new revolution will affect the primary structural system that many of the protagonists of the 1970s perhaps underevaluated, but which at the theoretical level in a society founded on theoretical meltdown demands more consideration. ∆

Translated from the Italian version into English by Paul David Blackmore

A Not So Well-Reasoned Bibliography

Anthony Vidler, *Architecture Between Spectacle and Use*, Yale University Press (New Haven, CT), 2008
'As Sigfried Giedion realized, the demand for "monumentality" did not go away with the massification of society; indeed it is intensified as a desire for that very spectacle apparently eschewed by rationalist modernists [...] [W]hile rejecting the "pseudomonumentality" of nighteenth-century eclecticism, [Giedion nevertheless] called for a new attention to be given by architects to the representation of the "social, ceremonial, and community life" desired by the people "who want these buildings to be more than functional fulfilment. They seek the expression of their aspirations in a monumentality, for joy and excitement." [...] Paradoxically, of course, it was also against the implied vulgarization of architecture as advertising or historicist repetition that architects like Gehry originally forged their aesthetic of assemblage, a process that eventually resulted in the production of another kind of monumental spectacle in Bilbao. Thus we are presented with the dilemma of monument conceived against the perceived pseudomonuments of postmodernism and with a conviction that an aesthetic might be developed organically out of formal experiment and material innovation.' (p xi)

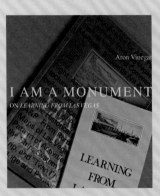

Aron Vinegar, *I AM A MONUMENT: On Learning from Las Vegas*, MIT Press (Cambridge, MA), 2008
'Venturi and Scott Brown's "recommendation for a monument" is a Decorated Shed with a blinking sign on top that reads, "I AM A MONUMENT." At first glance, this image seems to be an exemplary expression of *Learning from Las Vegas*'s brand of postmodern irony, its fundamental concern with architecture as representation or spectacle, its initiation of a text based approach to architecture, and its seamless equation of signs, signification and meaning. It has certainly been taken in these ways. I try to demonstrate that the "I am a Monument" proposal puts into question all of these characterizations. It is more about evidencing the force of imaging; showing the *work* of representation; suggesting ways that text, matter, and image touch on each other without claiming that any one subtends or veils the other; and opening up the possibility of meaning beyond signification, with an emphasis on the phatic rather than the semantic. In this way, it fosters the conditions for encounter and community. Simply put, the "I am a Monument" proposal explores how one might "make sense" in architecture that links its aesthetic and material possibilities with its social and political dimensions.' (pp 8–9)

Gert Wingårdh and Rasmus Wærn (eds), *Crucial Words: Conditions for Contemporary Architecture*, Birkhäuser (Basel), 2008
'Architecture requires constant explanation. Vagueness causes problems, both in the creation of architecture and the understanding of it. ... In his work, the architect uses more words than pictures. Although many of the words have a decisive bearing on the genesis of architecture, their meaning is often unclear. There is nothing to be gained from such vagueness. To understand the preconditions of architecture – our own as well as other people's – the key concepts must be brought out for scrutiny.' (p 3)

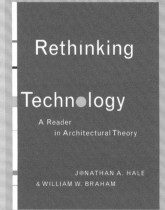

William W Braham and Jonathan A Hale (eds), *Rethinking Technology: A Reader in Architectural Theory*, Routledge (Abingdon), 2007
'... sometime during the 1980s the technological society which began in the fourteenth century came to an end. Now I recognize that dating epochs involves interpretation and perhaps some fuzziness in assigning beginnings and endings; but, nevertheless, it appears to me that the age of tools has now given way to the age of systems, exemplified in the conception of the earth as an ecosystem, and the human being as an immune system.' (p XII)

Mark Linder, *Nothing Less Than Literal: Architecture After Minimalism*, MIT Press (London), 2007
'What if Le Va's artwork is neither expressive nor an enactment of a desire to escape the gallery, but rather a plea for artists to engage architecture? If this is the case, then accepting the relationship between art and architecture does not mean, as Radcliff implies, that literalism condemns artists to bang their heads against the wall. Rather, Le Va demonstrates the necessity of architecture, and the absurdity and paradox in the promise that it would feel so good if they'd stop.' (p 230)

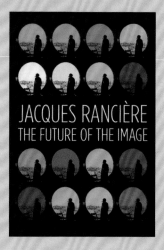

Jacques Rancière, *The Future of the Image*, Verso (London), 2007
'Under what conditions can it be said that certain events cannot be represented? Under what conditions can an unrepresentable phenomenon […] be given a conceptual shape? […] The issue then becomes how, and under what conditions, it is possible to construct such a concept, which proposes to cover all spheres of experience univocally.' (p 109)

Paul Virilio, *The Original Accident*, Polity Press (Cambridge), 2007
'Indeed, since cinema is time exposing itself as the sequence scrolls past, with television, it is clearly the pace of its "cross-border" ubiquity that shatters the history that is in the making of our eyes. […] And so, General History has been hit by a new type of accident in its perception as visibly present – a cinematic and shortly "digital" perception that changes its direction, its customary rhythm, […] the pace of the long time-span, promoting instead the ultra short time-span of this televisual instantaneity that is revolutionizing our vision of the world.' (p 25)

Bernd Evers and Christoph Thoenes, *Architectural Theory*, Taschen (London), 2006
'[In] the "Generic City" […] Koolhaas summarizes his observations about urbanism in the age of globalization and global urbanization. A central question posed in this work is that of which form of urbanism and urban identity to choose in the light of factors like worldwide analogous phenomena in late capitalist land use, architectural corporate identity by global players, global tourism as well as the loss of historical identity. Koolhaas […] rejects dogmatic affirmations concerning historical urban structures, saying that they are too restrictive and ultimately ahistorical. The city without characteristics is, by contrast, the result of liberation by historical patterns of identity; it is without limitations but at the same time available and open.' (p 559)

Gevork Hartoonian, *Crisis of the Object*, Routledge (London), 2006
'The accommodation of architecture to the nihilism of technology has opened a new chapter in the book of the crisis of architecture written since the Renaissance. However, the current rush to absorb technology into every facet of culture does not allow for the ideology of postmodernism, which has to sell architecture its architectural vision as an indicator of progress. The question to ask is whether the present esteem for technology has learned its lessons from the modernists' understanding of the *Zeitgeist*. It is equally important to ask whether modernists' theorization, aiming at uniform response to the spirit of the time, did not eliminate the possibility of linguistic difference. Paradoxically, present architectural praxis is over-determined by the very infusion of the *Zeitgeist* with linguistic multiplicity. Any attempt to answer these questions necessitates, in the first place, an investigation into the historicity of the crisis of the object.' (p 6)

Neil Leach, *Camouflage*, MIT Press (London), 2006
'Camouflage can be taken as a term to encapsulate various visual strategies that have been developed in recent years in response to an image driven culture. These strategies have evolved as a knowing manipulation of the use of images, whose early antecedents include the work of the photographer Cindy Sherman, but whose more recent articulations can be found through popular culture, and especially the realm of design [...] Far from being a distraction from the actual business of leaving, the domain of camouflage now delineates the horizon of much of contemporary existence.' (p 241)

Sunil Manghani, Arthur Piper and Jon Simons, *Images: A Reader*, Sage (London), 2006
'Considering ambiguous figures [...], Wittgenstein remarks that it is one thing to say "I see this ..." and another to say "I see this as ..."; and he adds: "seeing it as ..." is "having *this* image". The link between "seeing as" and imagining appears more clearly when we go to the imperative mood where, for example, one may say, "Imagine this", "Now see the figure as this." Will this be regarded as a question of interpretation? No, says Wittgenstein, because to interpret is to form a hypothesis which one can verify. There is no hypothesis here, nor any verification [...] The "seeing as", therefore, is half thought and half experience. And this is not the same sort of mixture that the iconicity of meaning presents.' (p 176)

Francesco Proto, *Mass, Identity, Architecture: Architectural Writings of Jean Baudrillard*, John Wiley & Sons Ltd (Chichester), 2006
'Is there nothing more to architecture than its reality – its references, procedures, functions, techniques? Or does it exceed all these things and ultimately involve something quite different, which might be its own end or something which would allow it to pass beyond its own reality, beyond its truth, in a kind of radicality, a sort of challenge to space (and not simply management of space), challenge to this society (and not simply a respect for constraint and a mirroring of its institutions), challenge to architecture creation itself, and challenge to creative architects or the illusion of their mastery?' (p 159)

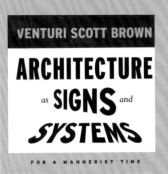

Robert Venturi and Denise Scott Brown, *Architecture as Signs and Systems*, Harvard University Press (London), 2004
'Here is Architecture as Sign, rather than architecture as Space. Here is architecture for an Information Age, rather than architecture for an Industrial Age. Here is architecture engaging: Explicit Communication, rather than Artistic Expression ... Electronic Technology, rather than Electrical Games; Digital Splendour, rather than Gloomy Glow ... Evolutionary Pragmatism, rather than Revolutionary Ideology.' (p 12)

Yves Michaud, *L'Art à l'état gazeux. Essai sur le triomphe de l'esthetique*, Editions Stock (Paris), 2003
'[N]ous ne sommes plus face à des mai istallès dans l'experience esthétique comme dans les vapours d'un hamman – pas concetrés sur des objects ni assujettis à un programme [...] On pourra regrettir que le temps n'ait plus assez de forme, lus assez de style, plus assez de project, plus assez de *Gestalt*, aurait dit Hegel, pour se saisir de manière solide et sculptèe dans des œuvres d'art plus pérennes que l'airain. De quoi se plaindrait-on pourtant quand on voit que cette situation fluide et gazeuse est seulement la contropartie du trionphe de l'esthetique? De quoi pourrait-on se plaindre quand le monde est devenu tout entier si beau? Il n'y a plus d'œuvres mais la bautè est illimitée et notre bonheur en elle s'illimite telle une fumée ...' (pp 118–204)

Compiled by Francesco Proto

Contributors

Anna Baldini is an expert in contemporary architectural history and architectural criticism. She promotes an awareness of new forms of architecture and art for preS/Tmagazine, of which she is a director. She is also the editor of a number of online architectural magazines and collaborates on specialised technical publications.

Shumon Basar is a co-founder of sexymachinery magazine, co-editor of Tank and a contributing editor at Bidoun. He has also written as a columnist and journalist for a number of art and design magazines. He is Director of Curatorial Practices and Cultural Projects at the Architectural Association (AA) in London, and has taught at the Royal College and London Consortium. He is also a member of the Research Architecture doctoral programme at Goldsmiths College, directed by Eyal Weizman. He is co-author of a number of books including Did Someone Say Participate (MIT Press, 2006), Cities from Zero (AA Publications, 2007), With/Without (Bidoun/Moutamarat, 2007) and The World of Madelon Vriesendorp (AA Publications, 2008), which accompanied a touring exhibition of the same name.

Ole Bouman has been a director of the Netherlands Architecture Institute (NAi) since April 2007. He was previously editor-in-chief of the periodical Volume, a collaborative venture between Stichting Archis, AMO (the research bureau of OMA/Rem Koolhaas) and the Graduate School of Architecture, Planning and Preservation at Columbia University. He has curated a series of public events on the reconstruction of the public domain in cities that have been hit by disasters, such as Ramallah, Mexico City, Beirut and Prishtina. He has been a lecturer in design at the MIT and regularly lectures at internationally acclaimed universities and cultural institutions. He is a co-author of The Invisible in Architecture (Academy Editions, 1994) and Al Manakh (OMA, Archis and Moutamarat, 2007), as well as the manifestos RealSpace in QuickTimes (NAi Publishers, 1996) and De Strijd om Tijd (2003). He has also curated exhibitions for the Milan Triennale, Manifesta 3 and Boijmans Van Beuningen Museum.

Hsueh, Cheng Luen is an architect and lecturer at the Department of Architecture, National Cheng Kung University in Taiwan. He received his Master of Science in Architecture and Urban Design from Columbia University in 1997. He lived and worked in New York until 2006. Since then he has been teaching in Tainan, Taiwan.

Paul CHU Hoi Shan is an architect and convener of the Hong Kong Urban Design Alliance, and Head and Associate Professor in the Department of Architecture at Chu Hai College, as well as an adjunct assistant professor at the University of Hong Kong. He was awarded the Hong Kong Young Architect Award and also received a grant from the Asian Cultural Council.

Michele Costanzo graduated from 'La Sapienza' University of Rome in 1968, and lives and works in Rome. He currently teaches theories of contemporary design at the University of

Architecture 'Valle Giulia' in Rome, and is an architectural critic, writing for several Italian magazines. Publications include Bernard Tschumi. L'architettura della disgiunzione (Testo e Immagine, 2002), Claus en Kaan. L'architettura dell'attenzione (Edilstampa, 2005), MVRDV. Opere e progetti 1991–2006 (Skira, 2006) and Museo fuori dal museo (Francoangeli, 2007).

Emiliano Gandolfi is an architect and independent curator with specific interests in art and architecture. He was the curator of the experimental architecture section of the Italian Pavilion at the 2008 Venice Biennale, and several travelling exhibitions including 'Newer Orleans', 'A Better World', 'Spectacular City' and 'Happening', projects initiated at the Netherlands Architecture Institute (NAi) in Rotterdam. He edited Spectacular City (NAi Publishers, 2006) and has written for a number of other books including Al Manakh (OMA, Archis and Moutamarat, 2007), and Douala in Translation (Episode Publishers, 2007), and the journals Volume, Artforum and L'espresso.

Joseph Grima is a New York-based architect, writer and critic. He is the current executive director of Storefront for Art and Architecture, a seminal gallery and events space in New York City devoted to the advancement of innovative positions in architecture, art, design and spatial practice. He has previously worked as an editor and international correspondent for Domus magazine. He is the author of Instant Asia (Skira, 2007), a critical overview of the recent work of young and emerging architecture practices across the Asian continent, co-editor of Shift (Lars Müller, 2008), and has contributed to numerous books and publications. He is a special correspondent for the Italian architecture magazine Abitare and a contributor to a wide range of international magazines including AD, Abitare, Domus, Tank, Volume and Urban China.

Luca Guido is an architect and architectural critic. He is an assistant professor at the Faculty of Architecture in Venice (IUAV), and speaks at conferences and lectures on contemporary architecture. His studies and research examine the theories and problems faced by avant-garde architecture of the 20th century and architects on the sidelines of the Modern Movement.

Christopher Hight is an assistant professor at the Rice School of Architecture where he is pursuing design research on the nexus of landscape, ecology and emerging forms of urbanisation. He has been a Fulbright Scholar, and obtained a masters degree in histories and theories of architecture from the Architectural Association (AA) and a PhD from the London Consortium at the University of London. He has taught in the AA's Design Research Laboratory (DRL) and has worked for the Renzo Piano Building Workshop. He was joint guest-editor of AD Collective Intelligence in Design (2006), and is co-author of the forthcoming Wiley title Heterogeneous Space. He has recently published a book on cybernetics, post-humanism, formalism and post-Second World War architectural design entitled Architectural Principles in the Age of Cybernetics (Routledge, 2008).

Hans Ibelings is an architectural historian and critic. He is the editor and publisher of A10 – new European architecture, and author of several books including Supermodernism: Architecture in the Age of Globalization (NAi Publishers, 1998).

Krunoslav Ivanisin graduated from the Faculty of Architecture, University of Zagreb, where he was teaching assistant from 2002 to 2005. He has been editor-in-chief of Arhitektura and Covjek i prostor (Man and Space) magazines, and is the co-founder of the Dubrovnik Festival of Architecture. Since 2007 he has been a teaching assistant at the ETH Zurich Department of Architecture. He has previously worked for the Urban Planning Institute of Croatia and in his own practice in Dubrovnik. He now shares the practice Ivanisin. Kabashi. Arhitekti in Zagreb with Lulzim Kabashi. The practice is research oriented, focusing on the fields of architectural design and urban and territorial planning.

Jiang Jun is a designer, editor and critic whose work focuses on urban research and experimental study, exploring the interrelationship between design phenomenon and urban dynamic. He founded Underline Office in late 2003, and has been the Editor-in-Chief of Urban China magazine since the end of 2004, while also working on his book Hi-China. His work has been presented at exhibitions such as 'Get It Louder' (2005/2007), the Guangdong Triennale (2005), the Shenzhen Biennale (2005/2007), 'China Contemporary' in Rotterdam (2006), and 'Kassel Documenta' (2007). Born in Hubei in 1974, he received his bachelor's degree from Tongji University in Shanghai and his master's degree from Tsinghua University in Beijing. He currently teaches at the Guangzhou Academy of Fine Arts.

Olympia Kazi, a writer and curator of architecture, is the executive director of the Institute for Urban Design in New York. She trained as an architect at the University of Florence, and served as Junior Curator at the Milan Triennale before moving to the US. In 2006/07 she was Fellow of Architecture and Urban Studies at the Whitney Museum of American Art, and since 2007 has been a member of the Exhibitions Committee of the Architecture League of New York. She has written for The Architect's Newspaper, AD and Wound Magazine, and was the US radio correspondent for the 2008 UIA World Congress of Architecture.

Derrick de Kerckhove is a leading expert in communication technologies. Heir to Marshall McLuhan, he relaunched his predecessor's ideas in the era of digital culture. He directs the McLuhan Program in Culture and Technology at the University of Toronto, in addition to teaching sociology of digital cultures at the 'Federico II' University of Naples. Of his many publications, translated into more than 10 languages, are Brainframes (Bosch&Keuning-BSO, 1991), La civilisation vidéo-chrétienne (Retz, 1990), Connected intelligence (Somerville, 1997) and L'architettura dell'intelligenza (Testo & Immagine, 2001).

Peter Lang holds a Bachelor in Architecture from Syracuse University (1980) and a PhD in history and urbanism from NYU (2000). A Fulbright Fellow, he is currently an assistant professor at the Department of Architecture, Texas A&M University at the Santa Chiara Study Center in Castiglion Fiorentino, Italy. He writes on the history of environmental design and postwar Italian architecture, and is an active member of Stalker/ON, the urban arts research group based in Rome.

Neil Leach is Professor of Architectural Theory at the University of Brighton, and has also taught at the Architectural Association (AA), Columbia Graduate School of Architecture, Planning and Preservation, Cornell University, the Dessau Institute of Architecture and SCI-Arc. He is the author, editor and translator of many books, including *Rethinking Architecture*, *The Anaesthetics of Architecture*, *Designing for a Digital World*, *Digital Tectonics* and *Camouflage*, and was the co-curator of the '(Im)material Processes: New Digital Techniques for Architecture' exhibition at the Beijing Biennial in 2008. He is also guest-editor of the forthcoming issue of *AD* entitled *Digital Cities* (July/August 2009).

Brian McGrath is an architect and Associate Professor of Urban Design at Parsons The New School for Design. He is the founder of urban-interface (www.urban-interface.com), a design studio that works at the intersection of new media, urban design and ecology. He is the co-author of *Cinemetrics: Architectural Drawing Today* (John Wiley & Sons, 2007) and *AD Sensing the 21st-Century City: Close up and Remote* (Nov/Dec 2005), and author of *Digital Modelling for Urban Design* (John Wiley & Sons, 2008). He received his masters of architecture from Princeton University and served as a Fulbright Senior Scholar in Thailand. He recently completed a two-year fellowship at the New School's India China Institute and currently serves as an external adviser for the Chu Hai College Department of Architecture in Hong Kong and the International Design and Architecture Program at Chulalongkorn University in Bangkok.

Victoria Marshall is a practising landscape architect and urban designer. In addition she is Assistant Professor of Urban Design at Parsons The New School for Design in New York where she teaches urban design with a focus on the North East Megalopolis – translating urban ecology frameworks as urban design models. She is the founder of TILL (2002).

Bill Menking is the founder and editor of *The Architect's Newspaper* (www.archpaper.com). He has organised and curated exhibitions on architecture and urbanism for venues in the US, UK and Europe and was commissioner and curator of the US Pavilion at the 2008 Venice Biennale. The title of the exhibition 'Into the Open:

Positioning Practice' proposes that social, cultural and spatial boundaries be understood as a new kind of centre that can and should act as a definer of architectural problems. He has degrees in architecture, city and regional planning and the history of modern architecture. His writing has been published widely, including in *The Architect's Newspaper*, *Monocle*, *AJ* and *Time Out*.

Luigi Prestinenza Puglisi is an architectural writer and critic. He teaches contemporary architectural history at 'La Sapienza' University of Rome. He writes for *Domus*, *The Plan*, *L'Arca*, *Abitare* and *AD*, is the Italian correspondent for *A10* (The Netherlands), *Monument* (Australia) and *The Architects' Newspaper* (US), and an editor at *Le Carré Bleu*. He is the director of the weekly presS/Tletter (www.presstletter.com) and curator of numerous exhibitions and events. His many books include *HyperArchitecture* (Testo&Immagine & Birkhäuser, 1998), *Antonio Citterio* (Edilstampa, 2005), *Dieci Anni di architettura: 1996–2006* (Prospettive edizioni, 2006) and *New Directions in Contemporary Architecture* (John Wiley, 1988). He was also guest-editor of *AD Italy: A New Architectural Landscape* (2007).

Francesco Proto is a practising architect and a theorist. He researches in the fields of visual culture, critical theory, architectural design and cultural studies. He currently teaches design strategies and history of contemporary architecture at the DeMontfort University in Leicester. His forthcoming release is a study on Western subjectivity as mirrored by art and architecture.

Roman Rutkowski and **Lukasz Wojciechowski** are architecture fans and critics working in tandem under the brand ReWritable (www.rewritable.pl). Based in Wroclaw, Poland, both are university design tutors, researching in the field of architecture and writing for various magazines, in particular *A10 – new European architecture*. They are also practising architects running their own offices: Roman Rutkowski Architects and VROA.

Carlos Sant'Ana graduated from the Faculdade de Arquitectura da Faculdade Técnica de Lisbon in 1998 and received his MArch from the Universidad Politécnica da Catalunya in 2000. He is director of S'A arquitectos, and spends his time developing his expertise in the field of large-scale work, environmental issues and the new tools of architectural design. Like the ACTAR Arquitectura team he worked with in Barcelona, he thinks of himself as an 'actor of architecture', a producer of projects, books and exhibitions. Concerned with 're-democratising' architecture by linking it with and making it responsive to the local–global flow, he readily explores themes of flexibility, mobility and ecology. He has been widely published on the subject of contemporary architecture, and is a regular contributor to magazines such as *A10 – new European architecture* and *Domus*.

Claes Sörstedt is a Swedish architect and critic based in Stockholm. He studied the history of art in Stockholm and Norwich, and architecture in Lund and Oslo. He currently divides his time between teaching architecture at KTH (Royal Institute of Technology), as an editor of *Arkitektur* and running his own practice.

Antonio Tursi investigates the impact of new media on art and politics. A pupil of Alberto Abruzzese and Derrick de Kerckhove, he studied at 'La Sapienza' University of Rome, the University of Sussex at Brighton, and Toronto and Macerata universities, where he completed his research doctorate in communication theory. He is the co-author, with Derrick de Kerckhove, of *Dopo la democrazia?* (Apogeo, 2006) and, with Mario Pireddu, of *Post-umano* (Guerini, 2006), and author of *Internet e il Barocco* (Cooper, 2004) and *Estetica dei nuovi media* (Costa&Nolan, 2007). He is currently completing a forthcoming book on the public sphere.

Josè De Jesús Zamora ia an assistant professor at Parsons The New School for Design in New York. He is a practising sculptor, and earned an MFA from the Graduate School at the New York Academy of Art. He has exhibited in the Dominican Republic, at La Galeria of the Altos de Chavon in Puerto Rico, and in New York.

Tao Zhu is an assistant professor in the Department of Architecture at the University of Hong Kong, and a PhD candidate in architecture history and theory at Columbia University. He is also a practising architect and a co-founder of the design firm ZL Architecture. He received his Bachelor of Engineering in Architecture from Chongqing Architecture and Engineering Institute, China, in 1990, and his Master of Architecture from the Graduate School of Architecture, Planning and Preservation at Columbia University in 2001. While practising in China, he writes extensively on contemporary Chinese architecture and urbanism.

C O N T E N T S

104+
Interior Eye
WORK Architecture Company's
Diane von Furstenberg Studio,
New York
Jayne Merkel

108+
Building Profile
Vassall Road Housing and
Healthcare Centre,
Brixton, London
David Littlefield

112+
Practice Profile
51% Studios
Howard Watson

118+
Spiller's Bits
What Are You Looking At?
Neil Spiller

120+
Unit Factor
Algorithmic Design
Maria Bessa

124+
Yeang's Eco-Files
Nanoenergy
Ken Yeang

126+
McLean's Nuggets
Will McLean

128+
Userscape
Investigating Culture
Through the Senses
Valentina Croci

132+
Site Lines
Baroque Parameters
Andrew Saunders

WORK Architecture Company's Diane von Furstenberg Studio, New York

In what was once the goriest part of Manhattan – the Meatpacking District on the far west side – WORKac has created a glittery collection of showrooms, studios and offices spread over four floors, sandwiched between a rooftop dwelling and a street-level flagship store within a pair of 19th-century warehouses. **Jayne Merkel** explains how sunlight from an angular jewel-like skylight fills the interior, which is intersected by a bejewelled, precast-concrete grand staircase, with refracted, reflected, constantly changing and relatively natural-looking light.

'WORK' may seem a strange name for a glamorous young firm whose partners met working for Rem Koolhaas in Rotterdam and helped launch his New York office and design his Prada stores. Although when they started in 2003 their five-year plan was to 'say yes to everything' and their first project was a dog house (for Puppies Behind Bars – an organisation that helps prisoners train guide dogs for the blind), they were soon offered luxurious apartments, an art gallery, a temporary Isaac Mizrahi boutique for Target at Rockefeller Center (six weeks in design, six weeks in construction, eight weeks in operation), and offices for Creative Time Inc. Still, the husband and wife team of Dan Wood and Amale Andraos leads one of the most hard-working firms in New York. Their research is extensive and impeccable. They just go back to the drawing boards (or

model shop) when a winning competition scheme, such as the Creative Time Information Hub in Times Square, turns out to be too expensive.

They look glamorous, but they are far from prima donnas. Last summer they won the prestigious annual competition for the courtyard of the P.S.1 Contemporary Art Center in Long Island City, Queens – an affiliate of the Museum of Modern Art (MoMA) in Manhattan. In the past, the winning schemes were pavilions for dancing and outdoor 'urban beach' parties. But here WORK built an Urban Farm – complete with live chickens and plants that were harvested throughout the summer – which was also a structural *tour de force*.

The farm was composed of recyclable cardboard drums filled with dirt, bolted together, and stacked diagonally to create a shelter with a butterfly roof. Other drums were distributed throughout the large, open, irregular fenced space. Wood, who grew up on a real farm in Rhode Island, says the couple are interested in the Slow Food and Locally Grown Food movements, but they had no idea how complicated

WORK Architecture Company, Diane von Furstenberg Studio, Washington and 14th Streets, Meatpacking District, New York, 2007
Under the jewel-like skylight, the precast-concrete 'stairdelier', which spans from floor to floor, slices through the five-storey space, widening as it descends and filling the interior with refracted and reflected light. The staircase is framed by a guardrail of stainless-steel cables braced by tubular Swarovski crystal beads. A moving rooftop heliostat mirror tracks the sun throughout the day, focusing light on the crystals and spreading it across the ceilings of each floor, giving the light inside the ever-changing quality of sunlight.

Showrooms and studios are distributed throughout the interiors. These spaces, which can be rearranged for events, are both divided and connected by the dramatic translucent staircase and energised by its presence. The designer's art collection and her own creations also give each area a character of its own.

building vegetable gardens in the air would be when they prepared the winning scheme. They eventually figured it out, with the help of a bevy of consultants: they just kept asking people and solving problems as they encountered them until the farm grew up and grew produce.

Andraos and Wood took the same carefully researched approach to the more spectacular Diane von Furstenberg Studio in New York's Meatpacking District. Nothing was easy there either. They felt very lucky when a friend ran into the fashion designer on a yacht in San Tropez and recommended them for the job. They had met her once before while they were working for Koolhaas who was doing a house for a friend of hers in the Bahamas, but she did not recall them at the time. Still, when she returned to New York she asked them for sketches of ideas for her space. Andraos and Wood developed three separate concepts in the light-blue Styrofoam models they had learnt to use at OMA, thinking they were the only architects being considered.

But when they went to von Furstenberg's former studio in Greenwich Village, the place was littered with schemes – models, sketches, presentation boards, wooden boxes with 'DvF' pink ribbons – probably from a dozen other architects or more. Happily she fell for one of theirs – with a big shaft of light in the middle.

In the eventual design, aspects of WORK's other two schemes crept in. One had a series of courtyards and voids, the other a large theatre in the middle. (The conference room ended up in the rooftop 'diamond'.) But none of their early schemes had the enormous staircase which contains the shaft of light that constitutes a kind of theatre and fills a series of voids. That emerged from an intense collaboration with von Furstenberg, who has an extensive collection of modern art and furniture.

The gritty brick facades of two adjacent warehouses were preserved since the studio is in the Gansevoort Market Historic District, and had to be approved by the New York City Landmarks Commission. The two most visible facades, on 14th and Washington streets – where brick was repointed, a copper cornice was sealed, rust spots were repaired, and cast-iron columns were repainted – still have a 19th-century feel.

The flagship store occupies the ground floor of the historic warehouses where the designer's company is located. New plate-glass windows inserted between Classical columns are shaded by translucent, corrugated-wired-glass canopies. The shop itself, which has a wall wrapping around its centre, is a horizontal version of the staircase that unwraps through the interior.

The studio was inserted in a pair of 19th-century warehouses where the flagship store occupies the ground floor. Showrooms, studios and offices are located on the first, second, third and a recessed glass-walled fourth floor. The fashion designer lives above these in a rectangular glass-walled pavilion that has a green (living) roof; the diamond-shaped structure next to it contains her studio and meeting rooms.

At night, LED screens in the windows come down so that the DvF Studio glows from within as the Meatpacking District comes alive with a hopping club-and-restaurant scene. Its diamond-studded crown provides a beacon for the neighbourhood.

The architects even found deep, translucent, corrugated-wired-glass canopies from the Philadelphia Navy Yard to replace the old rusty corrugated-metal ones over the sidewalk. But the bold new structure of steel I-beam columns, metal and concrete decking, and poured-resin floors is visible through new plate-glass windows as, of course, is the base of the dramatic five-storey crystal-lined, skylighted staircase that Wood calls a 'stairdelier'.

To meet building codes, the staircase was built in two parts and connected at a gigantic second-floor mezzanine. It widens as it descends, and passes through a series of double-height spaces, including the dramatic 464.5-square-metre (5,000-square-foot) showroom. Studio and office space for 120 employees is distributed over four floors. There are dressing rooms, a silk-screening workshop, and storage rooms in the basement. Many mechanical services are housed in a building that the designer owns next door.

What the public cannot see, except in a glimpse from a few perspectives below and from a high-rise perch above, is the designer's personal studio in the faceted gem, or her glass-walled, grass-roofed residence on the top of the building. The progression from public space on the street to private space in the air is dramatic, as is almost everything else about the project. The block on which it is located, where commercial butchers once worked, is now lined with boutiques, clubs, restaurants and art galleries. It is only a few blocks south of the Chelsea gallery district and north of the chic historic West Village (Greenwich Village). The Meatpacking District is an area now abuzz with life, night and day, so this building fits right in here.

As the studio design neared completion, WORK went to work on what they call a 'DvF Worldwide Rollout' – 18 stores in 14 countries in nine months. All involved a 'wrap' concept after the designer's famous 'wrap' dress, which is conveniently back in fashion as her empire expands. All have white plaster walls, low-iron glass fixture walls, and Diane von Furstenberg's signature mirrored ceilings. The architectural 'wraps' swell to create habitable spaces and shrink to provide niches for the display of special gowns and her H Stern jewellery, which is embedded in the walls. There are stores on Bruton Street in Mayfair, rue François 1er in Paris and the Ginza in Tokyo, as well as in numerous other locations in the US, Europe and Asia.

In 2007, WORK also designed clever stores for the innovative Philadelphia-based retail chain Anthropologie. But now the partners are more interested in doing institutional projects, such as galleries for the Clark Institute (a museum in Williamstown, Massachusetts), at the nearby Mass MoCA (the Massachusetts Museum of Contemporary Art in an old factory space), a Children's Art Museum in Manhattan's Tribeca, a library in Kew Garden, Queens, New York, and a warehouse for the city's Department of Environmental Protection. Their practice is starting to sound a little more like its name. Δ+

Vassall Road Housing
and Healthcare Centre,
Brixton, London

Tony Fretton's latest project is a demonstration of what can be achieved on a tight budget. **David Littlefield** describes how the practice has managed to create a thoughtful and yet highly practical health and residential centre on a rather typical south London street.

Tony Fretton Architects, Housing and Healthcare Centre, Vassall Road, Brixton, London, 2008
The first-floor walkway at the rear of the building provides access to private little courtyards which function as the maisonettes' front gardens. The bay windows contain translucent glass to prevent overlooking (and being overlooked by) an adjacent block; the slender side windows in each bay are, however, transparent.

Large steel balconies are cantilevered from the front of the building. Big enough to accommodate a small table and chairs, these projections act as extensions to the main living spaces.

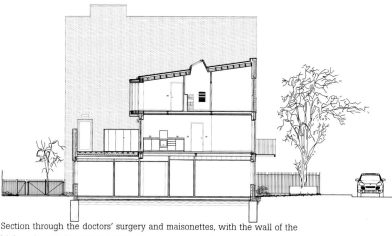

Section through the doctors' surgery and maisonettes, with the wall of the higher element (containing apartments and the circulation core) behind.

Site plan. The building occupies a corner plot in an area comprising Victorian villas and 1960s social housing.

This modest private housing and healthcare development, designed by Tony Fretton Architects, adds a dose of long-lost refinement to this corner of south London. It is built on a tight budget, and Fretton and his team have combined their architectural sensitivity with an intelligent use of suppliers to deliver an artfully composed building with the quality you would expect in a chic new suburb of Amsterdam or Copenhagen. In fact, the practice designs far more buildings across the English Channel than it does in the UK, including the Fuglsang Kunstmuseum in Denmark.

Fretton speaks a broadly Continental architectural language of highly researched, exacting details; of space planning that is derived from anticipated use rather than from minimum standards; of dispensing with applied ornamentation in favour of allowing the building to ornament itself. Little wonder, then, that the practice was selected to design the new British Embassy in Warsaw, which opens next year, while Fretton's expertise in housing is also being celebrated in this year's Venice Biennale.

He is also rather good at texture. As the Vassall Road building comes into view it appears (rather arrestingly) as a carved block of variegated purples, a stippled counterpoint to the crispness of its form. Despite the summer rain, a good deal of our inspection of this building was conducted outside, peering closely at the

brickwork. It sounds impossibly geekish, but the brickwork really is worth getting wet for. What gives the building its distinctive hue is a single coat of black mineral paint which mixes with the redness of the brick to effect something of the colour of a storm cloud by JMW Turner. The practice says the colour was decided upon by trying to simulate the patinas, films of soot and general weathering of nearby 18th-century villas. It is a plausible explanation, but one that sounds more like an argument prepared for local-authority planners rather than an architectural truth.

The mineral paint unifies into a single rippling surface the handmade bricks (all rejects from the Kent company that made them) and the entire building is transformed into a monolithic whole, as if fashioned by giants from a whopping piece of slate. It may well be that the colour of this building softens it and makes it slightly more contextual than it would otherwise have been, but the presentation of the new development needs no excuse. It is part of a considered enquiry into the nature of texture and surface, and confidently outclasses the recently disfigured 1960s social housing, now sporting pitched roofs and uPVC windows, that flanks it.

The building is a hybrid, comprising a ground-level doctors' surgery and 10 dwellings (three apartments and seven maisonettes) above. In form, it is remarkably simple. A slightly higher corner element contains the apartments and the circulation core; the lower central element is pulled back at the rear, reducing the mass of the building and boosting the amount of daylight available to the neighbours, while providing

The ground floor of this development provides accommodation for a general practitioners' surgery. Housing sits above: the apartments are stacked in a taller element to the right of the picture, while the maisonettes recede into the distance.

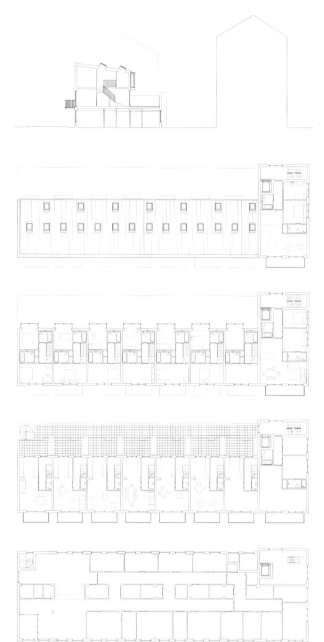

Plans and section through the site, with the pre-existing social housing block illustrated in outline on the right. Each maisonette is fitted with three Velux skylights, adding daylight to the stairwell and both bedrooms.

first-floor access to the maisonettes. This cutaway is sufficient to provide each of the seven larger units with its own private 'yard', separated by steel lockers that are large enough to hide unsightly wheelie bins. Better than that, though, are the generous balconies that cantilever out from the front of the building.

The entire assembly, commissioned by an alliance of private firm Baylight Properties and the Servite Housing Association, was built for a trifling £2.4 million and it could so easily have become an exercise in cheapness. Instead, we have a demonstration to all builders and housing agencies of the value that a bona fide intelligent architect can add to any project: entrances to dwellings

are generous enough to greet small parties of visitors; the ventilation system is such that bathrooms do not whirr into irritating life when the light goes on; windows are generous; a careful use of voids means the building is not disfigured by soil vent pipes and other extraneous details; and money has been spent carefully enough to allow items of reasonable quality to be specified. 'You don't want to touch a door and find that it's hollow … You understand, as an architect, what it is to look out of a window,' said Fretton, who is just as happy talking about the psychology of space as he is about the virtues of specific fixtures and fittings. 'Having worked in Denmark, we've discovered quite a lot of rather beautiful, standard products that are well-designed, functional and of moderately high quality.'

Actually, the approach to specification in this project has been one of the trade-offs. Money was saved in buying reject bricks (each wonderfully unique in form and texture), but invested in designing a bespoke terrazzo tile for the common areas, incorporating shells in the aggregate; similarly, low-budget Norwegian radiators contrast with the cost of super-insulating the development to standards found in the new draft of Part L. Project Associate David Owen recalled that Baylight Properties chief Crispin Kelly had declared: 'Everything you design, I have to sell.' Nothing, therefore, could be extraneous, and everything had to have a virtue.

In contrast, Fretton seems slightly embarrassed about the fit-out of the doctors' surgery below, which was designed by another practice with a better track record in the health sector. Many of the colour schemes and much of the furniture was approved, or even selected by, the doctors themselves, and the interior is distinctly NHS. Owen regrets that he had to hand this space over to a third party. He is also disappointed that the local authority, which insisted that its own staff tackle the pavement rather than leave it to the building contractor, has made such a hash of it. It is, indeed, a shame, not least because there is a general attitude of 'make do' rather than 'make well' in the UK's housing sector.

This low-key neighbourhood, a 10-minute walk from Oval tube station, should be thankful that Fretton was commissioned at all, and this building needs to be looked after as a distinctive yet polite demonstration project. Running through the analysis of the building is a simple question: why don't we see more of Fretton's work in the UK? The answer is that clients elsewhere in Europe understand that they have to pay for quality, or at least give architects the time to search for it. 'As an architect, you have to take a businesslike approach. You have to be concerned with financial success and profit,' says Fretton. 'There is much greater scope to do this in Holland, for example. We're European architects, and we go where the work is.' Their gain is our loss. ⚙+

David Littlefield is an architectural writer. He has written and edited a number of books, including *Architectural Voices: Listening to Old Buildings*, published by John Wiley & Sons (October 2007). He was also the curator of the exhibition 'Unseen Hands: 100 Years of Structural Engineering', which ran at the Victoria & Albert Museum in 2008. He has taught at Chelsea College of Art & Design and the University of Bath.

51% Studios

Peter Thomas and
Catherine du Toit

Howard Watson profiles a London-based studio whose practice results from the interplay of a wide range of influences spanning contemporary culture, history, nature, landscape and the ephemeral. Working at a variety of scales from the domestic to the urban, partners Peter Thomas and Catherine du Toit demonstrate a natural bent for the arts-related in undertaking collaborations with artists and exhibition installations.

Vicco's Tower, London, 2007
The steel, stiletto-shaped extension to the back of a Georgian house in London is clad in heat-treated larch, which is guaranteed to last for 30 years without further treatment. The use of timber and the sympathetic pitch of the glazed roof helped to ease the concerns of building a contemporary extension within a conservation area, while also creating a union between the original building and the garden. Thomas says: 'We used an architectural lens to frame the relationship of the site to nature, to the perpendicular of the tree.' The extension projects slightly from the side of the house so that it 'looks around the corner', offering viewers from the road an inviting perpendicular strip of glazing and slice of larch. Within, the designers recycled floorboards from the original building, kept the old sink and used plywood wall-covering to continue the theme of a graceful union between the existing building, the extension and the garden. The design won a RIBA Regional Award in 2008.

'State of balance is at constant play in what we do – the stability of things that have only just come to rest. The arrangement is only just fixed,' says Peter Thomas of 51% Studios, which has gained huge plaudits for its domestic architecture, but is equally at home contemplating urban planning, art-led or educational projects. The statement lies at the heart of this small London practice, led by Thomas and Catherine du Toit, as it suggests an obsession with the portrayal of movement through the traditionally fixed form while also underlining the practice's fluid nature as it constantly absorbs new thoughts and influences, and integrates them into a hugely diverse range of projects.

51% Studios officially came into being in 1995 with a commission for the Cornwall Centre for the Arts and Environment, but its genesis began a decade earlier at the Architectural Association (AA) in London. Students Thomas, du Toit and Peter Sabara exchanged ideas and became collaborators, continuing to work together while moving on to teach at the AA. Sadly, Sabara, who has been recognised as a great lost talent to the world of design, died in 1993, and it was left to Thomas and du Toit to take their shared enthusiasms forward into formal practice. At the AA they were influenced by Nigel Coates, but not so much by the emergence of NATO (Narrative Architecture Today) as by his approach to landscape and by his desire to fuse design and ephemera together. Both Thomas and du Toit went on to work on projects for Branson Coates, Nigel Coates'

design practice, before setting up 51% Studios. Another influential association that began in the world of academia was with the artist Richard Wentworth. In the mid- to late 1990s their collaborations with the sculptor included designs for the Will Adams Environment Centre competition, winning third prize, and the 'Swing' Financial Times Millennium Bridge competition.

During the early years of the practice, Thomas and du Toit developed a language whereby design ideas are not constrained by architectural form or typologies, but result from the interplay of wide-ranging influences, be they from contemporary culture, history, nature and landscape, or the utterly ephemeral. The practice, which now has an architectural staff of six, is collectively driven by an investigation of the possible, by new adventures, combinations and collaborations. Although ephemera play an important part in the design process, the practice soon created a robust, whimsy-free working method that would suit all scales of projects: 'The first thing to understand is the use [of a building], in parallel with understanding where it is going. We don't actually look for repetition, but subtler things, perhaps unwittingly, do get carried through. We do have a library of things, materials, but the composition is always varied.' They explain that: 'The physical model is always the first thing that we do. There's nothing like it to really check the effect of an idea. We model throughout the process to get a more visceral realisation.' Du Toit also believes that it is often best to show clients models rather than drawings as 'the angle of vision of a drawing, and its foreshortening, can be distracting'.

The Cornwall Centre for the Arts and Environment in Bodmin proved to be ill-fated. It was one of the first National Lottery applications to be given the green light. As a result, there was a political interest in making a statement about the value of lottery funding which forced the original concept to mushroom among overblown hopes and the project never came to fruition. However, the design itself – an environmentally sustainable building imbued with flair and veracity – was a graceful, intelligent response to the brief and the topography. Du Toit does not look back at the project with any bitterness: 'It was influential, showing us how to work with a nonstandard client in a staggering landscape.' It revealed that 51% Studios has a natural propensity to absorb and evolve influences and to adapt to the particularities of a site, while also pronouncing the quality of the human experience.

As the Bodmin arts centre project suggests, 51% Studios' ideas are not cowed by scale. Large plans, such as for the 2005 Dover Sketch Idea Competition and the ongoing 18.6-hectare (46-acre) Mineral County Agricultural Fairgrounds development in Colorado, carry

through a similar approach to the arts centre design, revealing that the practice is always able to emphasise the benefits of the existing landscape through a combination of strong, broad concepts and the detail required to enhance personal experience.

Working on arts-related projects has continued to be a notable strand for the practice.

Their exhibition designs include 'Enthusiasm' for Neil Cummings and Marysia Lewandowska at the Whitechapel Art Gallery, London, in 2005, and they collaborated further with the same artists for 'Social Cinema', which formed part of the 2006 London Architecture Biennale. Films about London and its architecture were projected in temporary cinemas which used the fabric of London buildings themselves, including the Millennium Bridge. Thomas and du Toit are currently involved in a huge urban collaboration with the artist Hannah Collins in Barcelona. Funded by the local authorities, Drawing on the City is a multilayered community project which merges art and

Bridging the Playground, London, 2006
above left: A paper bridge built as part of a yearly educational project that 51% Studios conducted with pupils from Dallington School in Clerkenwell, London.

Greenhouse, London, 1999
above right: While converting a dilapidated Georgian cottage into a modern family home, 51% Studios realigned the building and introduced a skyroom, with a glazed ceiling incorporating glass rafters.

Dover Sketch Idea Competition, 2005
right: 51% Studios proposed redefining aspects of Dover to reconnect the town to both its sea frontage and surrounding countryside by redirecting the passage of traffic away from the centre and introducing a car-free, landscaped public space and improved pedestrian orientation.

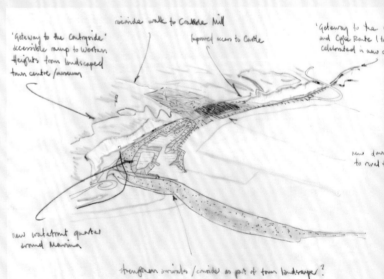

Drawing on the City, Barcelona, 2007–

Peter Thomas and Catherine du Toit are collaborating with artist Hannah Collins on a multidimensional project backed by the Barcelona Town Hall. Originally inspired by Collins' film work with gypsies in La Mina district, the project links seven sites in an architectural and sculptural walk through the changing city. At each site, a structure evokes the sense of place through both past and present, sometimes resurfacing forgotten or secret histories. For instance, one site is the Place of Horses where a panelled sculpture of hooves and footprints evokes the recent past of La Mina, where gypsy horses roamed everywhere and were central to everyday life and trade. Another structure is the living, nature-inspired Wall of Dreams, while at a third site a house made entirely of doors floats on the sea, symbolising the portal for the city's migrants. The project has been successfully exhibited and the sites will be completed over the course of the next couple of years.

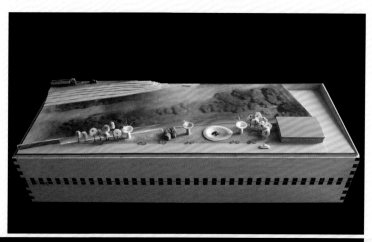

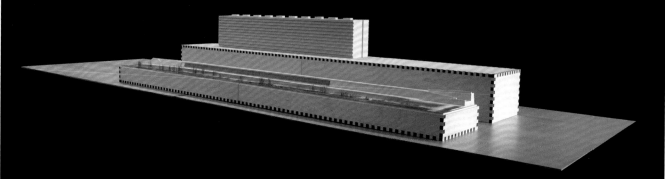

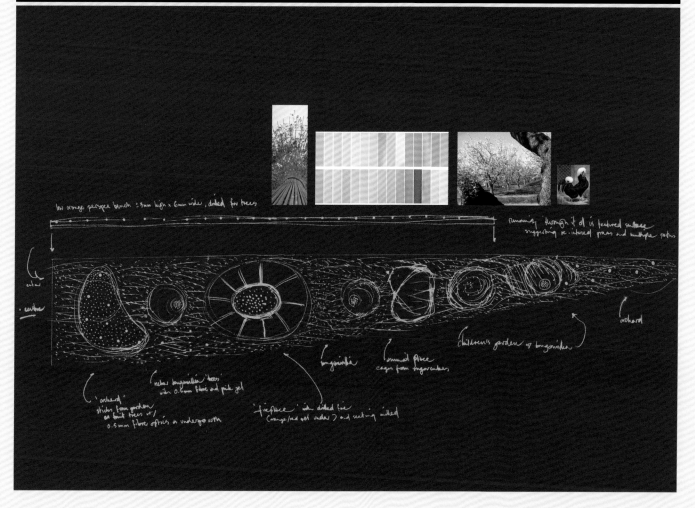

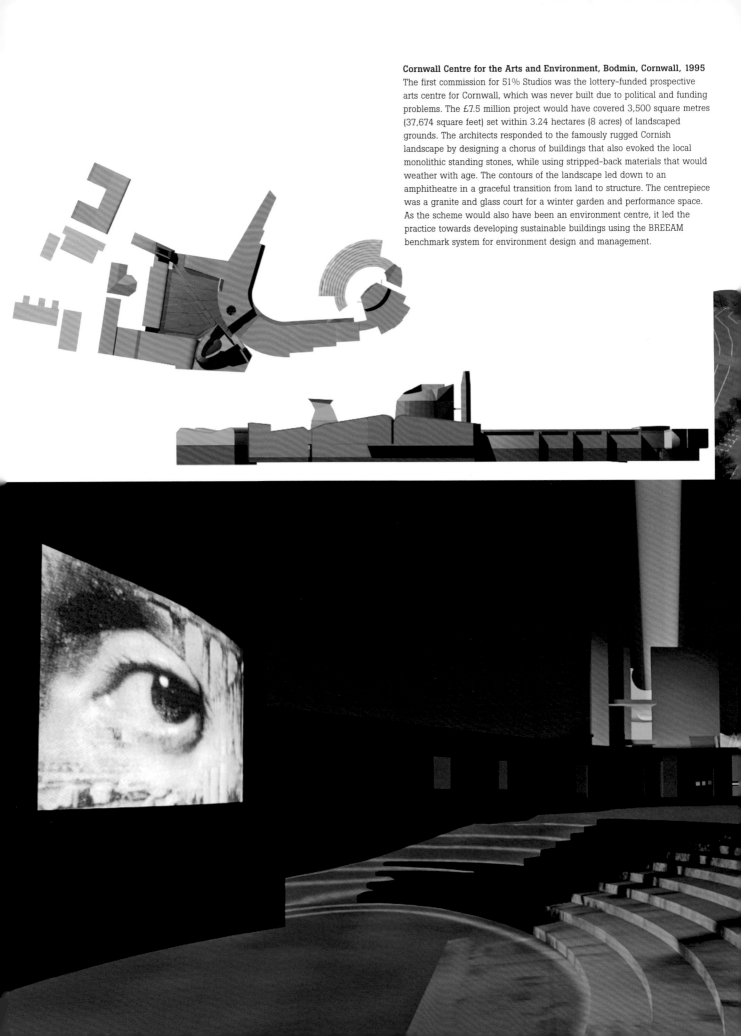

Cornwall Centre for the Arts and Environment, Bodmin, Cornwall, 1995
The first commission for 51% Studios was the lottery-funded prospective arts centre for Cornwall, which was never built due to political and funding problems. The £7.5 million project would have covered 3,500 square metres (37,674 square feet) set within 3.24 hectares (8 acres) of landscaped grounds. The architects responded to the famously rugged Cornish landscape by designing a chorus of buildings that also evoked the local monolithic standing stones, while using stripped-back materials that would weather with age. The contours of the landscape led down to an amphitheatre in a graceful transition from land to structure. The centrepiece was a granite and glass court for a winter garden and performance space. As the scheme would also have been an environment centre, it led the practice towards developing sustainable buildings using the BREEAM benchmark system for environment design and management.

architecture to play on aspects of the city's memories, secret histories and places, allowing Thomas and du Toit to give full reign to their love of ephemera and cross-association. Thomas' remark about trying to evoke the state of things that have only just come to rest is particularly relevant to this project as it captures the transience of urban life at a point when histories are still relevant even if momentum is about to shift the sense of place onwards.

The relationship with artists has also crossed into the domestic arena. 51% Studios has become well known for its innovate approach to housing, not least because of *Grand Design* magazine's belated front-cover exposure of their 1999 Greenhouse design, involving a glazed-ceiling conversion of a dilapidated Georgian cottage. However, it is their more recent Vicco's Tower, designed for the artist Anne Katrine Dolven, that shows the practice's ability to conclude a topographic response with elegance, sustainability and innovation. The glass and timber extension to a Georgian house in London manages to be both utterly contemporary and sympathetic to its surroundings and consequently won a RIBA Regional Award in 2008. No two of 51% Studios' house designs are alike. Thomas says that they are aided by the type of client they attract: 'The ones who choose us recognise that in no sense will they inherit what they have already seen of our work.' Two newbuilds are now under way in London and promise to further illustrate the practice's unfettered delight in new adventures.

Although Thomas and du Toit no longer teach at the AA, they have kept an interest in education, particularly through their 'Bridging the Playground' series of exercises conducted with young pupils at a local school in London, building humpback, floating, wobbly and paper bridges since 2003. Whether dealing with architecture graduates or schoolchildren, their educational purpose is the same, says Thomas: 'We do not wish to stifle. We want students to question the aesthetic, to dynamically think across disciplines. The most important thing is to try to teach an integrity to aesthetics – sustainability, community, etc; to understand the interplay between things.'

The architects cite Frederick Kiesler and Carlo Mollino as influences but, in truth, they are most influenced by what is immediately before them: 'We continue to do things that quicken the heart. We have a tremendous interest in things, how they are.' The nobility of this practice is such that the architects talk with the same high level of enthusiasm whether discussing a large-scale urban plan or getting children to build a bridge. They bring to every project a combination of aesthetic integrity and delight, and seem continually thrilled by the tumult of histories, possible futures, influences and associations that has led to each standing object – the still, permanent marker of the restless commotion. *Δ+*

Howard Watson is an author, journalist and editor based in London. He is co-author, with Eleanor Curtis, of the new 2nd edition of *Fashion Retail* (Wiley-Academy, 2007), £34.99. See www.wiley.com. Previous books include *The Design Mix: Bars, Cocktails and Style* (2006) and *Hotel Revolution: 21st-Century Hotel Design* (2005), both also published by Wiley-Academy.

What Are You Looking At?

There is a rebirth of interest in anamorphic perspective – that erudite artistic trick that allows one to represent different points of view in a single plane or view. Neil Spiller sees a new future for this arcane spatial practice that enables objects to dissolve their muteness.

Recently there seems to have been a renaissance in the architectural appreciation of perspective and particularly anamorphic perspective. Anamorphic perspective was most famously used by the artist Holbein in his painting *The Ambassadors* (1533) where an anamorphic skull is painted seemingly at odds with the rest of the picture and viewed by positioning oneself in a wholly different position to that taken when viewing the rest of the picture. Another example is during the English Civil War when publicans sympathetic to the king inscribed anamorphic portraits of him, that could only be read in the reflection of a glass of ale, on bar tables.

Salvador Dalí saw the potential of anamorphosis and harnessed it to the Surrealist cause. Dawn Ades, in *Dalí's Optical Illusions*, describes Dalí's point of view, as it were:

'Dalí recognised that the sixteenth and seventeenth century theories of perspective were wrestling with the problem of marrying empirical observation of the natural world with the belief in a world beyond it. Reality, in other words, was a contestable issue, and such interventions as anamorphic perspective … posited a "hidden reality" which was to suggest analogies with the unknowable of the unconscious.'[1]

Contemporary architectural concern is not so much with the unconscious as with the virtual. Many architects are coming to the conclusion that the architecture of the 21st century is implicitly

Melissa Clinch, Anamorphic Stations, St Ignatius of Loyola Church, Rome, 2005–06
Clinch uses ideas of architectural anamorphosis to create a series of spaces and semiotics that inhabit that great exposition of anamorphic painting, the St Ignatius of Loyola Church in Rome. The church has an extraordinary painted anamorphic dome. From certain positions in the nave it looks perfectly real, and from others it is revealed as what it is: a distorted painted form on the ceiling. Clinch positions three-dimensional forms within the church to form tableux that illustrate the stations of the Cross, each set piece opening up dependent on the position of the observer.

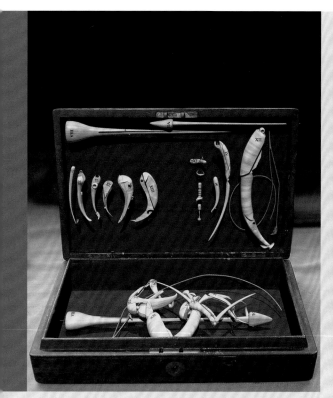

Oliver Moen, Anamorphic Rhino Space, London, 2006
Moen created these new architectural setting-out measures from the Fibonacci series and the rhinoceros horn so beloved by Dalí. The pieces can be used as new standards of measurement akin to Duchamp's *Stoppages*.

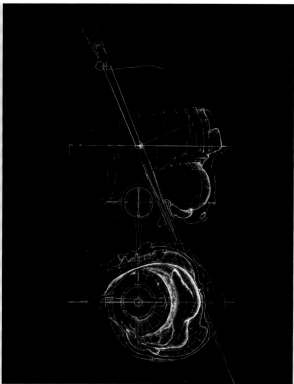

Tim Norman, Cosmic Haus, London, 2008
This drawing explores the anamorphic distortion of a miniature planet Venus orbiting through Velazquez's canvas *The Rokeby Venus* (c 1648–51) in the National Gallery, and its effect on the painted flesh.

related to divergent realities, differing points of view and the notion that objects have different guises in differing spacescapes. The anamorphic object changes form when observed from certain viewpoints, in different spatial fields or in distorted mirrors. The new technologically augmented objects will have formal qualities that are determined by the virtual or physical terrain in which they are viewed or manipulated. Anamorphosis is merely another aspect of recent architectural preoccupations that dissolve traditional architectural space into networks and fields of interconnected potential.

I would like to illustrate the potential of anamorphosis to the contemporary architect by describing briefly three recent projects that use the technique. Melissa Clinch uses it to act as an orderer of circulation and augmenter of ritual. Oliver Moen uses it as an optical machine/setting-out device, and Tim Norman uses it as a method to record a collapsed solar system compressed to the size of London. 'Listen!: The Solar System has come unstuck in Time, Venus reclines nonchalantly in the National Gallery, people *gawk* at her everyday, Saturn is a grapefruit, its pips orbit its citrusian satellites, Jupiter parades through Buckingham Palace ... the Thames like all great rivers of the world is a Milky Way.'[2]

Objects are losing their muteness. Objects have for too long floated in a sea of objectivity. Our technologies have developed a series of interlinked spatial fields, each with differing qualities and with blurred boundaries. The objects that inhabit those fields are capable of being seen in a myriad of ways. One of the tasks of the cyber- or bio-tect will be to design ecologies of what I shall call 'object fields', and not just to define the definite object that operates in a uniform spatial field. An object will have many selves, many simultaneous forms. Technology is forcing the object to become a subject, partial and anamorphic. In my opinion it is often within the arcane spatial practices that contemporary architecture likes to deny that methodologies for a new future for architecture reside. Makes you think doesn't it? *Δ+*

Neil Spiller is Professor of Architecture and Digital Theory and Vice Dean at the Bartlett, University College London.

Notes
1. Dawn Ades (ed), *Dali's Optical Illusions*, Yale University Press (New Haven and London), 2000, p 17.
2. Tim Norman, 'The Cosmic Haus', unpublished thesis, Bartlett, UCL, 2008.

Algorithmic Design

Maria Bessa provides a masterclass in algorithmic design, tracing the roots of the algorithm back to Aristotle and 9th-century Persia. She explores innovative contemporary examples of the application of the algorithm and highlights its potential for architects working intuitively in a way that will enable them to achieve a level of performance that was once only attainable at a post-design stage.

Kohn Pedersen Fox, The Pinnacle, London, 2006
Aerial rendering of the Pinnacle in context.

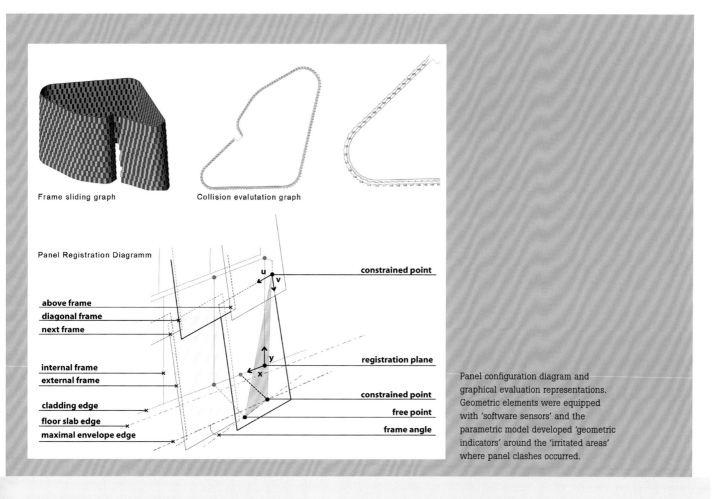

Frame sliding graph

Collision evalutation graph

Panel Registration Diagramm

constrained point

above frame
diagonal frame
next frame

internal frame
external frame

registration plane

constrained point

cladding edge

free point

floor slab edge
maximal envelope edge

frame angle

Panel configuration diagram and
graphical evaluation representations.
Geometric elements were equipped
with 'software sensors' and the
parametric model developed 'geometric
indicators' around the 'irritated areas'
where panel clashes occurred.

The organisation of logic was introduced by the ancient
Greek philosopher Aristotle, who systematised it as a
series of categorical statements known as 'syllogisms':
arguments in which a conclusion follows from a major and
a minor premise. Such a process of logical organisation is
apparent in Vitruvius' *De Architectura*, which outlined the
principles of classical architecture for 1st-century BC
Rome; Vitruvius asserted that architecture must refer to
the unquestionable perfection of the laws of symmetry
and ideal proportions found in nature. In this way, the
overall architectural object was regarded as the product of
a specific design process driven by the geometrical
interrelations between its parts. However, it was not until
the 9th-century Persian mathematician al-Khwarizm
managed to solve linear and quadratic equations
systematically and logically that algebra was conceived
and algebraic solutions gained ground in mathematics
over geometrical problem-solving.

In recent times this branch of mathematics has been
coupled with the development of the computer as a design
tool, stimulating rational and systematic design processes.
Algorithmic processes have become the contemporary
means of seeking design solutions. An algorithm, as
defined by American author and mathematician David
Berlinski, is a finite procedure, written in a fixed
vocabulary, governed by precise instructions, moving in
discrete steps and that sooner or later comes to an end.[1] Architects
and engineers use algorithms for the conceptual design and form-
generation of buildings, and the organisation of material components
over a predefined form. They are more widely used by all the
associated industries as problem-solvers at every stage of the design,
production and realisation of buildings.

Mathematics is used to create an exchange between schematic
design and production. The transition involves the rationalisation of
complex forms by fundamental geometries since cost is always a
crucial limitation. The design of a double-curved, 'snake skin' facade
for the Pinnacle using a single, yet flexible module type in order to
avoid wastage in fabrication is an example of how a rather common
problem was solved. The designers, Kohn Pedersen Fox, developed a
novel approach by embedding analytical algorithms within the design
process. This enabled them to integrate optimisation routines for
constructability and cost efficiency. 'Unlike geometric modelling where
the process is typically suffocated by the tight relationship between the
form/product and the rules/process, our method draws a clear line
between them,' says Stylianos Dritsas.[2] The heuristic process that
guides the search towards the tightest packing orientation of the
panels relies on intuitive decisions made during the design process.

The optimisation method develops the concept of intuitive
computation as a process executed by a person who is physically
engaged in the three-dimensional on-site assembly of the facade.
There is just one fixed-in-space point and two degrees of freedom for
every module. The 'divide and conquer' algorithm works recursively by

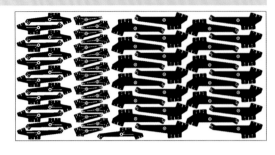

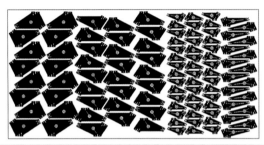

**Marc Fornes, Skylar Tibbits and Jared Laucks,
Aperiodic Vertebrae v2.0, 2008**
Built prototype using polyethylene panels, acrylic
connections and a zip tie fastener. Two people
assembled 360 panels and 320 nodes in 24 hours.

Marc Fornes, Aperiodic Vertebrae v2.0, 2008
Description of the form by planar elements and
nesting of identical components for laser-cutting.

breaking down the problem of optimisation into a number of simpler problems that can to be solved directly. Construction details were expressed as physical dimensions and tolerances, and assembly considerations were thus encapsulated in clearances. Environmental performance criteria were also 'captured' by the gap dimensions for ventilation, and aesthetic desires expressed as criteria for geometric continuity. Other functional requirements were allowed for in zones set out for maintenance, and more traditional ratios of cost efficiency were continuously measured by building area. This analytical problem-solving approach was incorporated into the design process, rather than being a process of validation applied to a finished design.

The application of algorithms for the organisation of proliferated material components over a predefined form is increasingly used in the design of structural skins. In

this way of working, the most critical factor to be incorporated in the design process is structural stability. Algorithms have been developed that inform the design in a feedback loop as the design is developed. The prime objective of the Serpentine Pavilion of Toyo Ito and Cecil Balmond was the integration of a structural system as an integral function of the skin. Since the form of the structure was given as a simple rectangular box, it was necessary to find a technique for subdividing the skin in order to create a structure. Fractals are chosen as the process for subdivision since they enable the design of a structural system based on a square shape that could be propagated to infinity. The output of the algorithm was a two-dimensional pattern, and the thickness of each beam was defined according to the distribution of stresses along the surface.

The algorithm developed by Chris Bosse for the design of the National Aquatics Centre in Beijing, the Watercube, moves the algorithmic process one step further. In this design a single material system produces structure and at the same time defines space. Structural stability is *a priori* assured by the design choice itself – the formation of a stable configuration of the geometry of bubble packing that also occurs spontaneously in many natural systems.

There are few known examples of architectural forms that are completely generated from scratch by algorithms. Marc Fornes' research interests lie in the generation of built prototypes that are originated entirely from a set of codes. Fornes is seeking to evolve new algorithms for a more exploratory 'non-deterministic' generative process. His Aperiodic Vertebrae explores complex and aperiodic stacking by successively subdividing four primitives over many generations. The description of form by the primitives provides flexibility when it comes to manufacturing. Depending on fabrication requirements, the primitives can be described by planes or even double-curved components. This process also looks

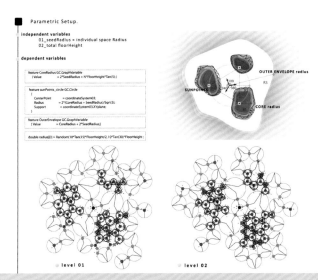

Parametric Setup.

independent variables
01_seedRadius = individual space Radius
02_total floorHeight

dependent variables

feature CoreRadius GC.GraphVariable
{ Value   = 2*SeedRadius + N*FloorHeight*Tan(5); }

feature sunPoints_circle GC.Circle
{
  CenterPoint   = coordinateSystem03;
  Radius   = 2*(CoreRadius + SeedRadius)/Sqrt(3);
  Support   = coordinateSystem03.XYplane;
}

feature OuterEnvelope GC.GraphVariable
{ Value   = CoreRadius + 2*SeedRadius; }

double radius[i][i] = Random(10*Tan(15)*FloorHeight/2, 10*Tan(30)*FloorHeight);

OUTER ENVELOPE radius
SUNPOINTS
R3
CORE radius

level 01   level 02

Maria Bessa, Phototropic Response informing housing distribution, MArch Dissertation project, EmTech, 2008
Parametric set-up of the conditions of adaptive growth using Generative Components software. Phototropic response results in aggregation of branches around the areas of sunlight densities. Evaluation allowed geometric constraints for structural stability and maximisation of sunlight penetration to be incorporated in the generation process.

Light cores varying in width are formed around the areas of sunlight densities to allow for differentiated light conditions. An increase in the width towards the top maximises sunlight penetration.

for efficiency in assembly and in manufacturing cost, and a nested three-dimensional array of identical pieces was the optimum solution.

A wide range of other parameters can also be incorporated within the algorithmic process. For example, evolutionary biologists analyse the developmental processes of plants as the execution of highly parameterised 'programs' or developmental algorithms. L-systems are the most widely used algorithms for capturing the dynamics of developmental processes in plants. Their main advantage lies in the fact that they can easily describe self-similar structures by starting from a simple initial object and by successively applying a set of rewriting rules. They can also incorporate competition for space between segments, and competition for light. The directional curvature of plant branches or stems in response to lateral differences in light intensity represents one of the most rapid responses of plants to changing light conditions. Phototropism, or growth in the direction of light, is produced by differential rates of growth.

My research, developed as part of the Emergent Technologies and Design course at the AA School of Architecture, explores the potential for using these codes in design processes. Positive phototropic responses informed the generative process for the distribution of housing units, and L-systems' formal grammars were used to incorporate responses to environmental stimuli and structural performance. Design tools were developed in the Generative Components parametric software for distributing the housing units and for the organisation of

internal space within each housing unit, and geometric constraints of structural stability, criteria for maximising sunlight penetration and space area requirements were also incorporated. A range of different-sized units enabled the optimal packing of units and ensured a range of occupation types. The 'designs' emerge from what seem to be conflicting constraints – the composite algorithm is able to resolve multiple parameters, and generated appropriate variants for differing structural, environmental and social conditions.

The algorithmic design approach can deal with a large number of competing constraints simultaneously, and can be used to explore numerous differently weighted design solutions within time frames that are just not economically feasible by more traditional methods. Though algorithms are becoming widespread in many design and fabrication industries, perhaps their best use is in architectural design, where they can enable designers to work in intuitive and non-deterministic ways. Thus new and innovative designs can be produced that achieve structural and environmental performances that were once considered to be post-design optimisation processes. Δ+

Maria Bessa is an architect registered in Greece. She studied at the Technical University of Athens and earned her MArch degree in the Emergent Technologies and Design programme of the Architectural Association in 2006/08. She is currently working as a computational designer at AEDAS Architects in London. Her interests focus on the application of algorithms in architecture and she has participated in workshops on computational design.

'Unit Factor' is edited by Michael Weinstock, who is Academic Head and Master of Technical Studies at the Architectural Association School of Architecture in London. He is co-guest-editor with Michael Hensel and Achim Menges of the *Emergence: Morphogenetic Design Strategies* (May 2004) and *Techniques and Technologies in Morphogenetic Design* (March 2006) issues of *Architectural Design*. He is currently writing a book on the architecture of emergence for John Wiley & Sons Ltd.

Notes
1. David Berlinski, 'Introduction', *The Advent of the Algorithm*, Harcourt (New York), 2000, p IX.
2. Conversation with the author, 21 July 2008.

Nanoenergy

The development of a clean, plentiful and low-cost alternative energy source is the holy grail of the 21st century. Ken Yeang looks into his crystal ball and asks whether the future could lie in nanoenergy and the proliferation of numerous personal nanogenerators – attached to buildings, individuals or under bridges.

If the future of our civilisation hinges on one defining issue, it is energy. Without readily available, cheap and abundant energy to fuel our transportation, healthcare, businesses, communications and manufacturing, there will be devastating changes to our existing social stability – and this will happen long before the world runs out of oil.

It is vital that we find an alternative energy source – one that is clean, plentiful, and available at low cost throughout the world for its 6 billion people today and for the more than 10 billion people expected by the middle of the century. Could nanotechnology (the manipulation of individual atoms and molecules to produce new substances) provide the solution? Current research indicates that, if further developed, nanoenergy could potentially replace fossil fuels as the energy source of the future. However, the nanogenerator systems currently being developed require considerable advancements before they could ever become practical or commercially viable.

The technology showing the most promise is the piezoelectric nanogenerator, which takes advantage of the unique coupling of the piezoelectric and semi-conducting properties of zinc oxide nanostructures that produce small electrical charges when mechanically flexed. The nanostructures are tiny nanowires composed of layers of zinc oxide (which are grown on a substrate to collect the current) that stand on end on top of an electrode. In the fabrication process, silicone 'zigzag' electrodes containing thousands of nanometre-scale tips (made conductive by a platinum coating) are lowered over the nanowires, which are vertically aligned approximately half a micron apart on gallium arsenide, sapphire or a flexible polymer substrate, leaving just enough space for them to flex within the gaps created by the electrodes.

Mechanical movement (such as vibration) of the whole set-up causes the nanowires to periodically brush over the electrode tips, transferring their electrical charges and sending a stream of electricity to the nanogenerator.

Currently, each thread (nanowire) produces only pico-amps (one million millionths of an ampere) of current, but this is predicted to eventually increase to 20 to 80 milliwatts per square metre of 'fabric'. Though this is not yet sufficient to power even a single light bulb (today's LED light bulbs require about 1 watt), with simultaneous output from many nanowires greater power is possible. There is thus a need to better control the growth, density and uniformity of these tiny wires in order to make as many as millions or even billions of them produce current simultaneously to allow optimal operation of the nanogenerator. This could produce as much as 4 watts of energy per cubic centimetre of nanowire, which would be enough to power nanometre-scale applications such as a micro-surgical implant.

What is required now is the technology to enable the thin nanowires to bend more without breaking, making it possible to apply more strain and so generate more electricity. In addition, optimal operation of the nanogenerator is dependent on all of the wires being connected to the circuit simultaneously. However, while it is currently possible to grow nanowires that are approximately the same length (about 1 micron), there are some variations: wires that are too short cannot reach the electrodes, while those that are too long cannot flex to produce electrical charge. This said, there is potential in the fact that the chemical process by which the nanowires can be grown is inexpensive; thus with further development it should eventually become practical to produce large arrays capable of providing enough power for consumer electronics and personal appliances.

Scientists are already looking at a variety of applications in buildings: for example, nanogenerators that make use of the constant sway of tall buildings to produce energy, placing them underneath passageways to generate energy from people walking above, the manufacture of fabrics for personal wearable nanogenerators, piezoelectric treadmills and so on. Thus the future may not lie in centralised energy sources, but in individual personal energy nanogenerators, where each of us generates our own energy as and when we need it: living and working off the grid, so to speak, and experiencing the true meaning of freedom. ⌂+

Ken Yeang is a director of Llewelyn Davies Yeang in London and TR Hamzah & Yeang, its sister company, in Kuala Lumpur, Malaysia. He is the author of many articles and books on sustainable design, including *Ecodesign: A Manual for Ecological Design* (Wiley-Academy, 2006).

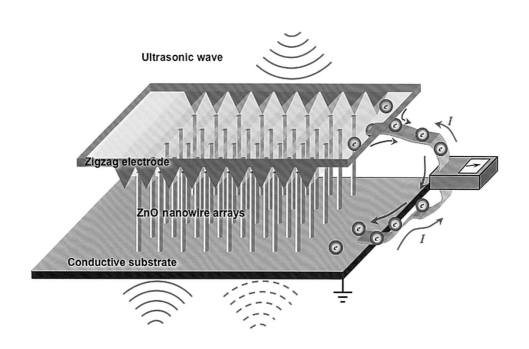

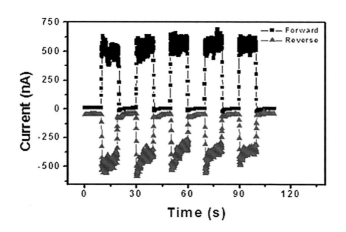

Schematic (top) showing a direct-current nanogenerator built using aligned zinc oxide nanowire arrays with a zigzag top electrode. The nanogenerator is driven by an external ultrasonic wave or mechanical vibration, and the current output is continuous. The graph below shows the output from a nanogenerator when the ultrasonic wave was on and off.

MCLEAN'S NUGGETS

All Mine?

A recent issue of *The Engineer* featured an extraordinary cover image of the iron-ore fields of Pilbara, Western Australia. In an article entitled 'The New Iron Age',[1] features editor Jon Excell describes the technological developments of a physically massive mining industry, with single sites like Rio Tinto's Pilbara the size of the UK. The massive scale and remoteness of the site has led to increased automation with fleets of driverless trucks and trains and a pilot project led by roboticists at Sydney University, which will see remote monitoring and control of the mine 1,600 kilometres (994 miles) away in Perth. Excell quotes John McGagh, Rio Tinto's head of innovation, who describes the rise in demand for their steel ingredient as 'unbelievable' and adds 'We've been digging the stuff up since the 1700s, we've supported about 20% of the planet and now the other 80% is moving through to an industrialisation phase'. In physical demand terms Excell explains that in the UK each person accounts for the use of about 400 kilograms (882 pounds) of steel a year, while in China it is more like 200 kilograms (441 pounds), with this figure projected to rapidly rise beyond 400 kilograms in a case of living standards 'catch-up'. China and India's appetite for steel and other base metals such as copper has seen the price of these commodities rise rapidly in the last few years, which has incentivised more rapid recycling in a way any number of initiatives fail to do, and despite the recent increase in the theft of lead from church roofs this seems like progress. Buckminster Fuller examined the systematic 'up' and 're'-cycling of metals in 1963 in his *Inventory of World Resources, Human Trends and Needs*.[2]

He seriously questioned the need to continually mine for finite raw materials when 'above-surface mines of refined materials' (products) already existed. He clearly illustrated this when he claimed that the US at that time had the largest inventory of available tin in the world, in a country with 'little tin ore of workable quality'. In Fuller's astonishing (part-retrospective) final publication *Critical Path*,[3] he states 'that (with few rare exceptions) humanity need do very little further mining. The metals already scrapped from obsolete machinery and structures, which recirculate on a sum-total-of-all-metals-average every twenty-two years, are now able to do so much more work with ever less weight per each given function with each recirculation as to make the present scrap resources of almost all metals adequate to take care of all humanity's forward needs'. So through the process of what Fuller called 'ephemeralisation' (doing more with less) and an unblocking of the metals re-circulatory mechanism there may well be enough to go around without the expanding robotic excavations of the earth's surface. One potential new area for the industrial excavation business is landfill mining. In a recent Reuters report in the *International Herald Tribune*, Kate Kelland details how increasing oil prices are pushing up the value of dumped (oil-based) plastics, creating the potential for a whole new recovery industry.[4] With an estimated 200 million tons (181 million tonnes) of old plastic in UK sites alone valued at £60 billion for recycling or conversion to fuel, companies like New Earth Solutions are keen to exploit this dormant commodity. Avoiding any burying and excavation though is Closed Loop London (www.closedlooprecycling.co.uk), a newly opened plant in Dagenham which is the UK's first food-grade plastics recycler and processes 38.5 million tons (35,000 tonnes) of mixed plastic bottle waste per year.

(Two) penny loafers. A pre-1982 US cent, which weighs 3.11 grams (0.11 ounces), is composed of .950 grams (.034 ounces) of copper and .050 grams (0.002 ounces) of tin and zinc, which at current prices on the London Metals Exchange makes it worth more than 2 cents in scrap.

Expositions

Universal Expositions (Expos) are held every five years, they last six months on a city site with no specific area limitations and a general theme. International Expositions are held every couple of years, over three months on a limited site and address a specific theme, such as that of 'Water and Sustainable Development' at Zaragoza 2008. Cities bid for this kind of architecture and technological Olympiad for the same reasons as they bid for the Olympics or any other international sporting and cultural event – to precipitate economic development, attract investment and hope that the 'legacy' of such events will be the beginning rather than the end of a particular socioeconomic story. Whatever the intention, the Expo always seems to deliver at least one interesting architectural artefact that might not be bad value. The first such event was the Great Exhibition of 1851, whose Crystal Palace remains an as yet unsurpassed exercise in biomimetic prefabrication. Brussels 1958 gave us the Atomium, a 165-billion-to-one scale model of an iron crystal, and the less permanent but hugely intriguing Phillips Pavilion,[5] an audiovisual collaboration between Le Corbusier, Iannis Xenakis and the composer Edgard Varèse. Montréal 1967 gave us Buckminster Fuller's Taj Mahal of geodesic domes, Moshe Safdie's modular Habitat housing and Frei Otto's tensile experiments. More recently Otto collaborated with Shigeru Ban to create a huge gridshell caterpillar of cardboard tubes at Hanover 2000, and in Switzerland (2002), Diller + Scofidio's tensegrity 'Blur' Building reintroduced the 'fog nozzle', which was subsequently sprinkled on to a generation of student projects. What the sun-scorched environs of Zaragoza 2008 have given us is still up for debate, while we await Expo Shanghai 2010.

View from inside Buckminster Fuller's USA Pavilion – a legacy of Expo Montréal 1967 – looking towards the city.

All the Right Components

Recent advertisements in the trade magazine *What's New in Industry*[6] for Ford Component Sales[7] have been promoting the use of their automotive spares for uses outside the moving vehicle business. With 100,000 parts to choose from this will hopefully encourage the house builder or designer to employ a whole host of human comfort delivery systems that are currently packed into increasingly sophisticated and highly tuned environment vehicles (cars). The gradual productification of kitchens and bathrooms could be extended into (super-responsive) general living areas of the home with controllable compact heating/ventilation systems, opening windows of more sophisticated deploy, never mind the craft conceits of a well-placed wood veneer panel. It is certainly time for some more technology transfer. 𝐃+

'McLean's Nuggets' is an ongoing technical series inspired by Will McLean and Samantha Hardingham's enthusiasm for back issues of *AD*, as explicitly explored in Hardingham's *AD* issue *The 1970s is Here and Now* (March/April 2005).

Will McLean is joint coordinator of technical studies (with Pete Silver) in the Department of Architecture at the University of Westminster. He recently co-authored, also with Pete Silver, *Introduction to Architectural Technology* (Laurence King, 2008).

Notes
1. Jon Excell, 'The New Iron Age', *The Engineer*, 14–27 July 2008, pp 22–5.
2. RB Fuller and J McHale, *Phase 1 (1963), Document One: Inventory of World Resources, Human Trends and Needs*, World Resources Inventory, Southern Illinois University (Carbondale, IL), 1963. http://challenge.bfi.org/reference/
3. RB Fuller and Kiyoshi Kuromiya, *Critical Path*, St Martin's Press (New York), 1981.
4. Kate Kelland, 'Oil Prices Inspire Landfill Mining', *International Herald Tribune*, 27 August 2008.
5. Mark Treib, *Space Calculated in Seconds*, Princeton University Press (Princeton, NJ), 1996. This book documents the remarkable fabrication and collaboration of the Phillips Pavilion, Brussels, 1958.
6. www.wnii.co.uk.
7. www.fordcomponentsales.com.

Investigating Culture Through the Senses

Preserved for many centuries by volcanic rubble, the Roman sites of Pompeii and Herculaneum, in Southern Italy, most effectively evoke how the ancients lived. **Valentina Croci** reveals how MAV, the world's first virtual archaeology museum in Herculaneum, now enriches the visitor's experience and understanding of archaeological culture.

Gaetano Capasso, MAV (Museo Archeologico Virtuale), Naples, Italy, 2008
The CAVE, a cubic room covered entirely with full-scale three-dimensional projected images, represents one of the most immersive moments of the MAV experience. Here, visitors can physically perceive the colours and dimensions of the domestic environments of ancient civilisation.

A screen reproduces the large paintings and mosaics found in the archaeological area of Naples. With a simple movement of the hand, visitors can 'wipe away' the dust and dirt.

The Baths area reproduces the smells of perfumes and unguents used in the ancient past. An interactive device produces a cloud of smoke that covers a screen; this surface can be cleaned with a simple swipe of the visitor's arm, creating a multisensorial experience at the limits of voyeurism.

After three years of development, Herculaneum (Naples) is now home to the MAV, the world's first virtual archaeology museum, built at a cost of €10 million. A former school building was transformed into a highly original 1,500-square-metre (16,146-square-foot) space, with 70 interactive installations that recount life in the Roman cities of Pompei, Herculaneum and Stabia prior to the eruption of Mount Vesuvius in AD 79. The project was designed by Gaetano Capasso, an electronics engineer and expert in virtual reality in the field of cultural heritage. Capasso, one of the members of the virtual reality production company Capware, was assisted by Valter Ferrara, the Director of Cultural Policies for the Naples Provincial Government, now director of the MAV.

The museum is the first example of an immersive structure: the experience is based on virtual reality and interactive electronic installations activated by tactile digital interfaces or motion sensors, similar examples of which can only be found in theme parks. The MAV, the result of an attentive study of historical sources and archaeological reconstructions, is also proposed as a didactic instrument to be used in parallel to a visit to a more traditional type of museum. One of the limits posed by the latter has to do with the difficulty in understanding faced by the general public. Virtual reality, on the other

hand, allows for a re-creation of what has been lost, bringing the visitor closer to the world of archaeological culture by directly involving the visitor's senses, an application that may lead to new synergies between traditional museums and multimedia research. In fact, there is already a growing demand and numerous experiments are under way: Capasso has produced a virtual installation focused on the discovery and excavations in Trajan's Market in Rome, and the Museum of the History of Science in Florence has tested simulations of the machines designed by Leonardo da Vinci.

The experience of visiting the MAV results from the juxtaposition between real architecture and virtual simulation. The museum's first room is dedicated to the concept of 'Connective Intelligence' developed by Derrick de Kerckhove. It underlines the creative and multiplicative power of human networks: the importance of connections between intelligence, assisted by new digital technologies. It is not a virtual archaeological installation, but is rather focused on investigating the dematerialisation of the physical body and understanding the alternative dimensions into which the visitor is projected while inside the museum.

Visitors continue among the sounds, voices and faces of the ancient inhabitants of Herculaneum, and once inside the Soundgallery, the computer system recognises the badge worn by each individual and, based on his or her identity (Italian, foreigner, adult or child) and the length of time he or she remains in the room, produces spatially oriented sounds. The visitor is thus immersed in a crowded street of women shopping in the market, street pedlars and soldiers, experiencing sound simulations that expand into the room, in points far from their origin (the software was developed by the US army to confuse enemy troops).

In the Baths area, home to the Room of Perfumes, a sophisticated machine produces the smells of the spices, unguents and balsams used at the time. Visitors then move on through the reconstruction of the Bourbon tunnels – the subterranean archaeological excavations in the area of Herculaneum, Pompei and Naples supported by the Bourbon dynasty, beginning in 1783. The experience allows them to relive the discovery and marvels of the re-emergence of a buried past. Within this theatrical backdrop, the physical construction increases the sense of immersion, as the multimedia installations progressively unfold, heightening the sense of wonder. Upon leaving the tunnels, a thin sheet of atomised water simulates a pyroclastic cloud (the lapillus of a volcanic eruption) as visitors arrive in a virtual reconstruction of the panoramas and interiors of the houses in Pompei, Stabia and Herculaneum. The walls of the spaces here are treated with encaustic Roman finishes, increasing the integration between physical space and the virtual installations. This area also features a CAVE, a cubic room inside which special software projects three-dimensional full-scale images that cover all the surfaces. This system was experimented with by the CUNCE in Pisa, a university research centre investigating multimedia software.

The visit ends in the Lupanare, the Room of Delights, with its erotic paintings. However, the visitors' badges allow the system to recognise the presence of small children, and when necessary replace the erotic images with those of landscapes. Finally, a light indicates the end of the visit and illuminates the way back to reality.

The challenge faced by the museum was that of rendering technology transparent: mouse, mechanical pointers and computer screens have all been eliminated, and instead it is the body of the visitor that becomes the 'trigger' that activates the electronic and digital devices. For example, motion detectors activate the installations based on the presence of visitors, visitors can consult a virtual book by turning its pages, or 'wipe away' the dust from a mosaic by passing their hand over a screen. The mechanisms of interaction respond to natural gestures and require no specialised knowledge of computers. During the opening days, more than 6,000 visitors, many elderly, moved easily through the museum.

The amount of written information is reduced to a minimum. Interaction is thus efficient, even in the presence of a non-homogeneous public, and the installations function in the most intuitive manner possible. At present, the visit is organised for groups of

The installation dedicated to 'Connective Intelligence' inaugurates a visit to the MAV, and is focused on transmitting the nature of the virtual experience. The concept of connective intelligence was developed by Derrick de Kerckhove and symbolises the dematerialisation of the body and the languages of new media. New technologies allow for an integration and connection between individual knowledge, creating a new digital humanism.

The Bourbon tunnels, excavated by slaves and prisoners using pickaxes and found in the archaeological areas of Naples, were begun during the Bourbon reign in 1783. Inside the MAV, fibreglass reproductions of the tunnels contribute to increasing the visitor's sense of immersion as he or she discovers the installations that are part of the visit, almost reproducing the original archaeological discovery. Views out are offered from the tunnels, for example towards the Villa dei Papiri.

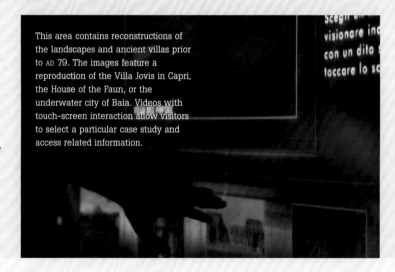

This area contains reconstructions of the landscapes and ancient villas prior to AD 79. The images feature a reproduction of the Villa Jovis in Capri, the House of the Faun, or the underwater city of Baia. Videos with touch-screen interaction allow visitors to select a particular case study and access related information.

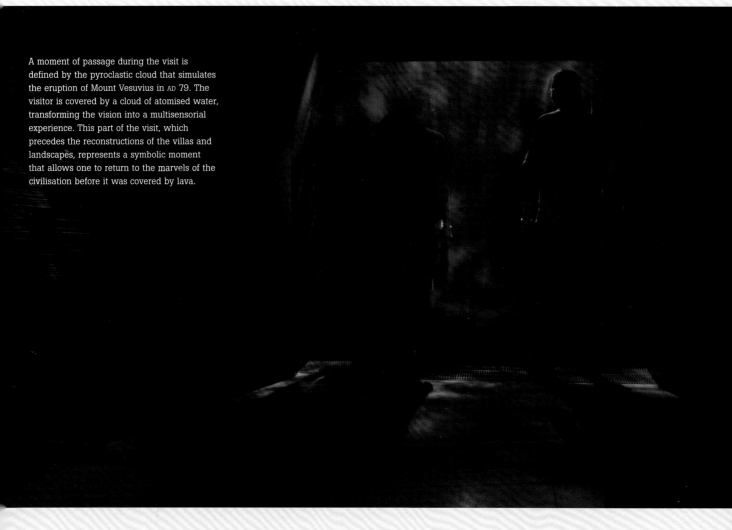

A moment of passage during the visit is defined by the pyroclastic cloud that simulates the eruption of Mount Vesuvius in AD 79. The visitor is covered by a cloud of atomised water, transforming the vision into a multisensorial experience. This part of the visit, which precedes the reconstructions of the villas and landscapes, represents a symbolic moment that allows one to return to the marvels of the civilisation before it was covered by lava.

50 people at a time. This meant renouncing more advanced systems of interaction, similar to the CAVE, with motion tracking devices that can be used by a maximum of three people at once. However, these technologies can be integrated in the future.

The MAV aims to be a centre of technological innovation and a home to digital culture. In fact, there are also spaces for temporary exhibitions and for experimenting with new virtual applications in the field of cultural heritage. Valter Ferrara has brought together an interdisciplinary group of experts who act as consultants for these types of project. Participants include the Fondazione CIVES (Integrated Centre for the Valorisation of Herculaneum and its Excavations) and a range of university professors, including the communications sociologist Alberto Abruzzese, the semiotician Omar Calabrese, Robert Scopigno from the Department of Information and Computer Sciences at the University of Pisa, Derrick de Kerckhove from the McLuhan Program at the University of Toronto, who also teaches in Naples, and Robert Perpignani from the Centro Sperimentale di Cinematografia in Rome. These and other international figures guarantee an approach to research that is both practical and theoretical. For instance, in interaction design the main focus is on the sensorial involvement of the visitor, thus the design of digital technologies requires an accurate analysis not only of the user's physiological perception, but also of the way senses are used – which depends on the cultural background of people. Concerning the latter there is still much to be done.

The objective of the MAV and its team of experts is that of transmitting the technical and cultural richness of the archaeological patrimony through alternatives to traditional museology. However, this does not depend as much on technological applications – the 'how' – as it does on the study of 'what' is represented. What is therefore required is a shift in focus away from the function of the project to the methods with which we approach these technologies. Δ+

Translated from the Italian version into English by Paul David Blackmore

Valentina Croci is a freelance journalist of industrial design and architecture. She graduated from Venice University of Architecture (IUAV), and attained an MSc in architectural history from the Bartlett School of Architecture, London. She achieved a PhD in industrial design sciences at the IUAV with a theoretical thesis on wearable digital technologies.

Baroque Parameters

Andrew Saunders describes how students on Rensselaer School of Architecture's Rome programme were encouraged to explore the geometry and mathematics that underlie the architecture of the Baroque through parametric design.

Re-Interpreting the Baroque, Rensselaer School of Architecture Rome Program (studio coordinators Andrew Saunders and Cinzia Abbate in collaboration with Jess Maertterer), Rome, 2007
Sinusoidal landscape designed by Andrew Saunders and fabricated by Rensselaer students Michael Visovsky, Erica Voss, Andrew Chardain, Michelle Schrank, David Holbrook, Chelsea Anderson and Patty Clayton.

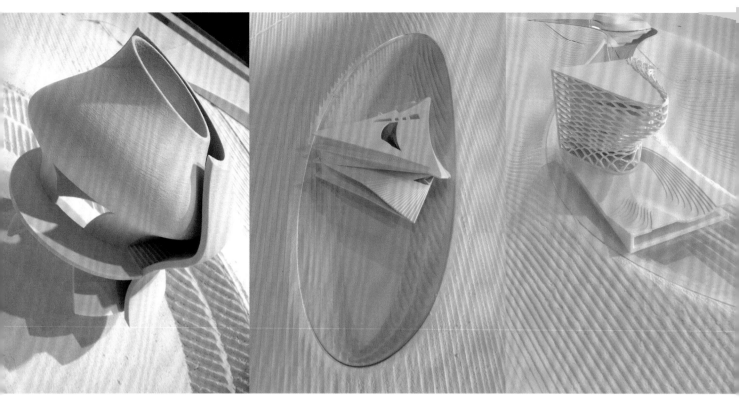

Rapid prototype model of a parametric variation of Baroque geometry by (from left to right) Rensselaer students Andrew Diehl and Jenna Lettenberger, Stephanie Mendelson and Morgan Wahl, and Andy Zheng and Christine Eromenok.

Though few modern scholars make use of the fact, or even seem to realize it, Baroque architecture was above all mathematical.
 – George L Hersey, *Architecture and Geometry in the Age of the Baroque*, 2001, p 4.[1]

Scripting: The Return of Mathematical Intuition

One of the most promising aspects of parametric design is that it promotes a distinct and disciplined bottom-up process of modelling geometry. A scripting-based approach to parametric modelling utilises features of programming within a native modelling environment. Geometry can then be generated by flow control (skipping and repeating lines) and variable control (logical and mathematical operations – data storage).[2] The ability to model with mathematical operations allows unprecedented accessibility to the generative possibilities and comprehension of equation-based geometry.

An Instrument for Analysis

The Rensselaer School of Architecture Rome Program studio entitled 'Re-Interpreting the Baroque' (2007) explored scripting as an instrument for analysing how geometry operates in Baroque architecture. Geometry and mathematics were integral to 17th-century science, philosophy, art, architecture and religion. They are what

link Baroque architects Francesco Borromini and Guarino Guarini to other great thinkers of the period including Descartes, Galileo, Kepler, Desargues and Newton.[3] Plasticity and dynamism are explicit signatures of Baroque architecture; less obvious are the disciplined mathematical principles that generate these effects.

Trigonometry Through the Arc and the Chord

Borromini is often portrayed with traditional drawing tools of the 17th century: the compass to draw an arc, and the ruler to draw a straight line or chord. In order to construct a square, architects of his time would first compose a governing circle and segment it with chords to constitute the four sides.[4] Geometry derived from this process is related by its association with a governing circle. As a result, triangles, circles or any equal-sided polygons can be understood as parametric variations of each other. To script these relationships, trigonometric functions are used to plot geometry by polar coordinates.[5] Trigonometry originated from chords (Ptolemy's Table of Chords was the most famous trigonometric table), and calculations used for these chord lengths are equivalent to the modern sine function.[6] Through the exploitation of these ingrained trigonometric parameters, Baroque architects produced astonishing effects, performance and continuity.

In his Sant'Ivo alla Sapienza church in Rome (1642–60), Borromini capitalises on the verticality by transitioning parametrically from the most basic of polygons (two overlapping triangles) at the base of the chapel to the infinite-sided polygon – the perfect circle crowning the cupola. One can trace the movement downwards from the chastity of

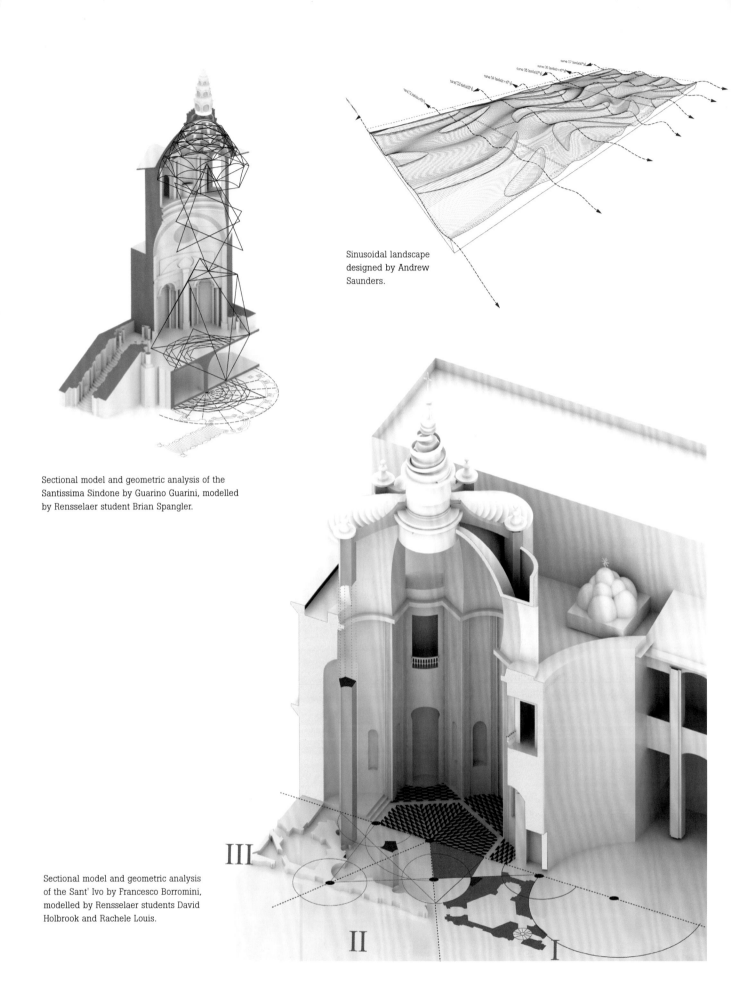

Sinusoidal landscape designed by Andrew Saunders.

Sectional model and geometric analysis of the Santissima Sindone by Guarino Guarini, modelled by Rensselaer student Brian Spangler.

Sectional model and geometric analysis of the Sant' Ivo by Francesco Borromini, modelled by Rensselaer students David Holbrook and Rachele Louis.

III

II

I

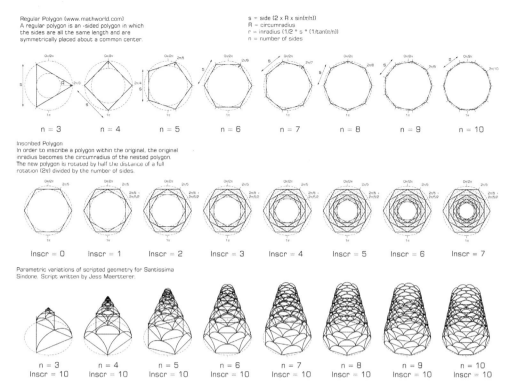

Regular Polygon (www.mathworld.com)
A regular polygon is an -sided polygon in which the sides are all the same length and are symmetrically placed about a common center.

s = side (2 x R x sin(π/n))
R = circumradius
r = inradius (1/2 * s * (1/tan(π/n))
n = number of sides

| n = 3 | n = 4 | n = 5 | n = 6 | n = 7 | n = 8 | n = 9 | n = 10 |

Inscribed Polygon
In order to inscribe a polygon within the original, the original inradius becomes the circumradius of the nested polygon. The new polygon is rotated by half the distance of a full rotation (2π) divided by the number of sides.

| Inscr = 0 | Inscr = 1 | Inscr = 2 | Inscr = 3 | Inscr = 4 | Inscr = 5 | Inscr = 6 | Inscr = 7 |

Parametric variations of scripted geometry for Santissima Sindone. Script written by Jess Maertterer.

| n = 3 | n = 4 | n = 5 | n = 6 | n = 7 | n = 8 | n = 9 | n = 10 |
| Inscr = 10 | Inscr = 10 | Inscr = 10 | Inscr = 10 | Inscr = 10 | Inscr = 10 | Inscr = 10 | Inscr = 10 |

Polar-coordinate regular polygon geometry diagrams by Andrew Saunders and Jess Maertterer.

forms in the heavenly zone to the increasing complexity of the earthly zone.[7] This continuous morphology from crude to smooth in turn initiates a novel structural performance. Because it cannot be reduced to a static element, the cupola of Sant' Ivo avoids technical classification as a dome and is its own unique structure.[8]

In the Santissima Sindone chapel in Turin, Guarini uses a similar strategy to progress from a triangular base geometry, and culminates in a kaleidoscope of hexagons. The staggering hexagons on the interior create an effect of perceptual psychology, fostering an illusion of extreme depth through telescoping vertical space.[9] The porosity of the nested geometry results in a relatively lightweight structural solution of an openwork dome and allows for maximum light to penetrate the chasm below. A parametric model reveals that Guarini integrates both structural performance and spatial effect through equation-based scalar and rotational operations.

Re-Interpreting the Baroque

The geometry of Baroque architecture gains a renewed relevance when understood parametrically. By merging the capabilities of programming within the digital modelling environment, scripting, unlike traditional two-dimensional or static projected analyses, reveals the flexible and generative aspects of the equation-based geometry of the Baroque. More importantly, it exposes how these geometric principles were intuitively deployed in order to integrate a wide range of effects and performance. Δ+

The analysis of Baroque geometry was the starting point for the 2007 Rensselaer School of Architecture Rome Program that took as its premise 'Re-Interpreting the Baroque'. The studio went on to problematise the original parametric principles of the 17th century with contemporary design parameters of performance and effect in the design of a Counter Reformation Art and Architecture Museum located in the historic centre of Rome. Research from the 'Re-Interpreting the Baroque' studio was exhibited at the Italian Cultural Institute in New York City from 1 to 9 October 2008.

Andrew Saunders is an assistant professor of architecture at Rensselaer Polytechnic Institute in New York. He received his Masters in Architecture from the Harvard Graduate School of Design. He has significant professional experience as a lead project designer for Eisenman Architects, Leeser Architecture and Preston Scott Cohen, Inc, and has taught and guest-lectured at a variety of institutions including Cooper Union and the Cranbrook Academy of Art. He is currently working on a book on the use of parametric modelling as an analysis tool for 17th-century Italian Baroque architecture (see www.rpi.edu/~saunda2/ICIRPI/).

Notes
1. George L Hersey, *Architecture and Geometry in the Age of the Baroque*, University of Chicago Press, (Chicago, IL), 2001, p 4.
2. David Rutten, *Rhinoscript101*, Robert McNeel & Associates, 2007, p 4. See http://en.wiki.mcneel.com/default.aspx/McNeel/RhinoScript101
3. John Beldon Scott, *Architecture for the Shroud: Relic and Ritual in Turin*, University of Chicago Press (Chicago, IL), 2003, p 157.
4. Antonino Saggio, 'Give me a cord and I will Build … Construction, Ethics, Geometry and Information Technology', in Maria Voyatzaki (ed), *AAVV: (Re)searching and Redefining the Content and Methods of Construction Teaching in the New Digital Era*, Eaae-Enhsa (Athens), 2005, pp 13–34.
5. Jess Maertterer, *Script to Create Nested Regular Polygons*, Rhino 3DE Online Education, 2007. http://www.rhino3.de/educate/
6. Morris Kline, *Mathematical Thought from Ancient to Modern Times*, Oxford University Press (New York), 1972, pp 119–20.
7. Rudolf Wittkower, *Art and Architecture in Italy 1600 to 1750*, Penguin Books (Baltimore, MD), 1958, p 138.
8. Federico Bellini, *Le cupole di Borromini. La 'scientia' costruttiva in età barocca*, Documenti di Architettura (Milan), 2004.
9. HA Meek, *Guarino Guarini and His Architecture*, Yale University Press (New Haven, CT), 1988, p 75.

Architectural Design **Neoplasmatic Design** November/December 2008

What is Architectural Design?

Launched in 1930, *Architectural Design* is an influential and prestigious architectural publication. With an almost unrivalled reputation worldwide, it is consistently at the forefront of cultural thought and design.

Architectural Design is published bimonthly. Features include:

Main section
The main section of every issue functions as a book and is guest-edited by a leading international expert in the field.

𝝙+
The 𝝙+ magazine section at the back of every issue includes ongoing series and regular columns.

Truly international in terms of the subjects covered and its contributors, *Architectural Design*:

- focuses on cutting-edge design
- combines the currency and topicality of a newsstand journal with the rigour and production qualities of a book
- is provocative and inspirational, inspiring theoretical, creative and technological advances
- questions the outcomes of technical innovations as well as the far-reaching social, cultural and environmental challenges that present themselves today

How to Subscribe

With 6 issues a year, you can subscribe to 𝝙 (either print or online), or buy titles individually.

Subscribe today to receive 6 issues delivered direct to your door!

£198 / US$369	institutional subscription (combined print and online)
£180 / US$335	institutional subscription (print or online)
£110 / US$170	personal rate subscription (print only)
£70 / US$110	student rate subscription (print only)
To subscribe:	Tel: +44 (0) 843 828
	Email: cs-journals@wiley.com

To purchase individual titles go to:
www.wiley.com

Congratulations to Michael Weinstock, AD Editorial Board Member and Contributing Editor

Michael Weinstock is recipient of the 2008 ACADIA Award for Innovative Academic Program. This award is conferred to academic leadership work that advances the discipline of architecture through the use of digital media. Inaugurated in 1998, the ACADIA Award of Excellence is the highest award that can be achieved in the field of architectural computing.

The award is recognition of Weinstock's 'innovative and pioneering leadership' in developing the academic programme at the Architectural Association (AA) in London and his contribution to the development of its Emergent Technologies and Design programme.